Something's Wrong With Us

NATSUMI ANDO

STORY

As a child, Nao met Tsubaki at Kogetsuan, the historic *wagashi* shop where her mother worked as a live-in confectioner. One fateful day, her mother was arrested on murder charges and Nao was forced to leave.

15 years later, when Tsubaki and Nao met once more, Tsubaki asked for her hand in marriage without knowing she was his childhood friend. Although Nao was unsure of Tsubaki's intentions, her desire to know her mother's true story compelled her to accept the proposal. She then began living at Kogetsuan.

With the old master accusing her of being a phony bride, and the proprietress suspicious of her identity, Nao is constantly surrounded by enemies at Kogetsuan. However, during one steamy night with Tsubaki, Nao discovered that his first love was none other than her childhood self—the girl he once called "Sakura."

In the background, the proprietress continued to pry into Nao's life, prompting Tsubaki to lock Nao away in an attempt to protect his fiancée. But Nao escaped, unaware of his intentions. Then, Tsubaki was injured in an attack meant for her.

As an important tea ceremony approaches, Tsubaki confessed to Nao that he was beginning to fall for her.

CONTENTS

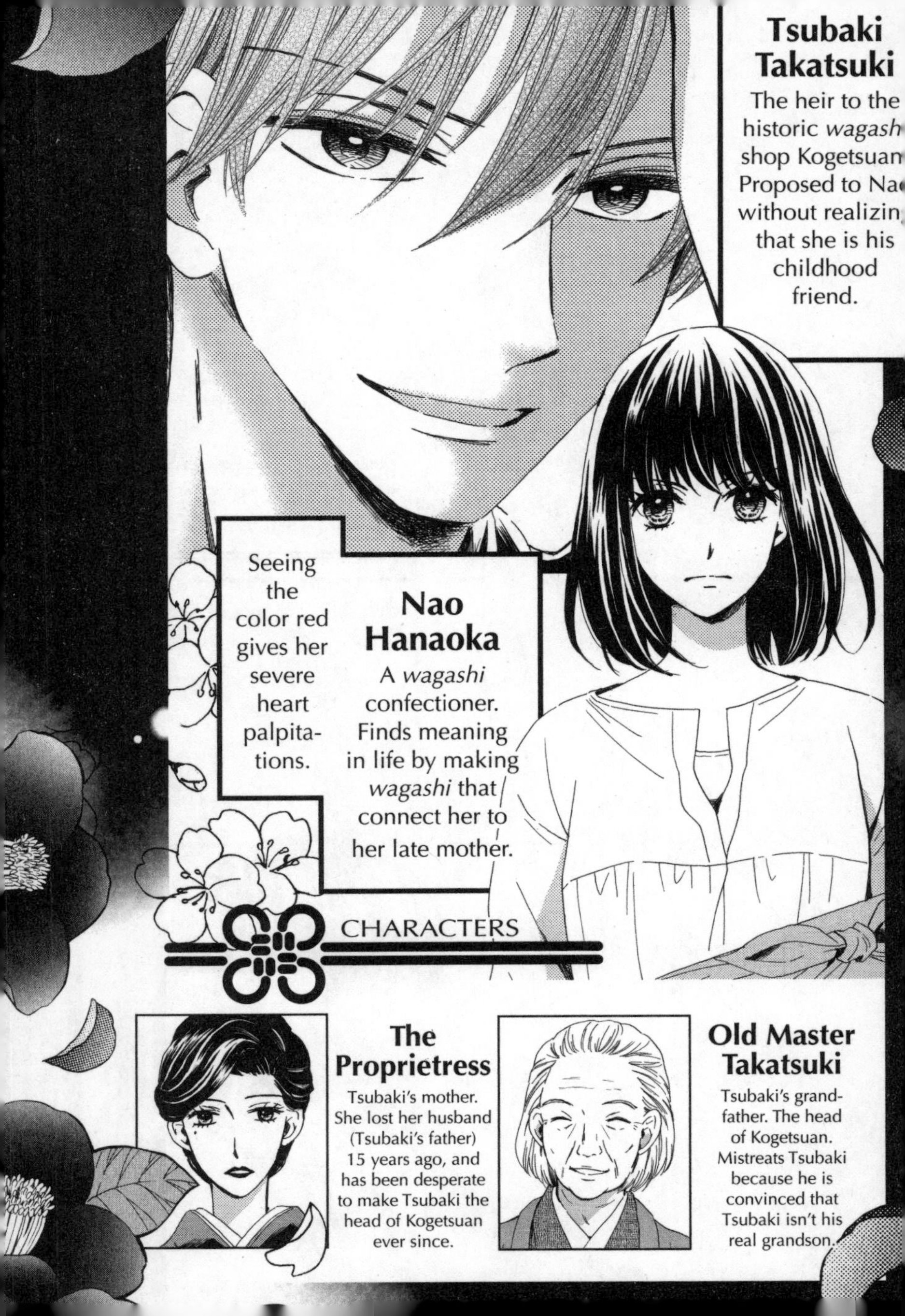
Tsubaki Takatsuki
The heir to the historic wagash shop Kogetsuan Proposed to Na without realizin that she is his childhood friend.
Nao Hanaoka
A wagashi confectioner. Finds meaning in life by making wagashi that connect her to her late mother.
Seeing the color red gives her severe heart palpitations.
CHARACTERS
Old Master Takatsuki
Tsubaki's grandfather. The head of Kogetsuan. Mistreats Tsubaki because he is convinced that Tsubaki isn't his real grandson.
The Proprietress
Tsubaki's mother. She lost her husband (Tsubaki's father) 15 years ago, and has been desperate to make Tsubaki the head of Kogetsuan ever since.

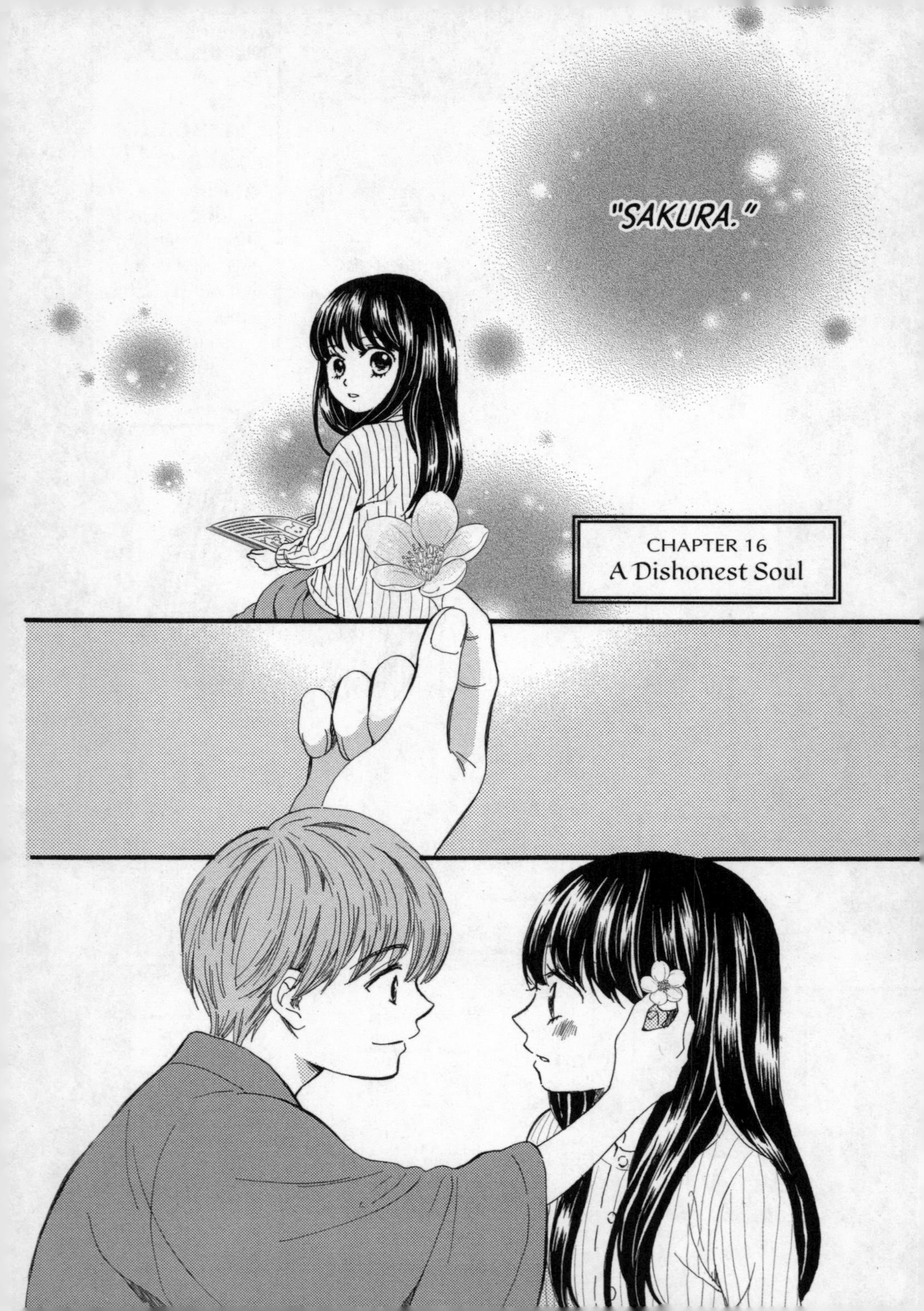
"SAKURA."
CHAPTER 16
A Dishonest Soul

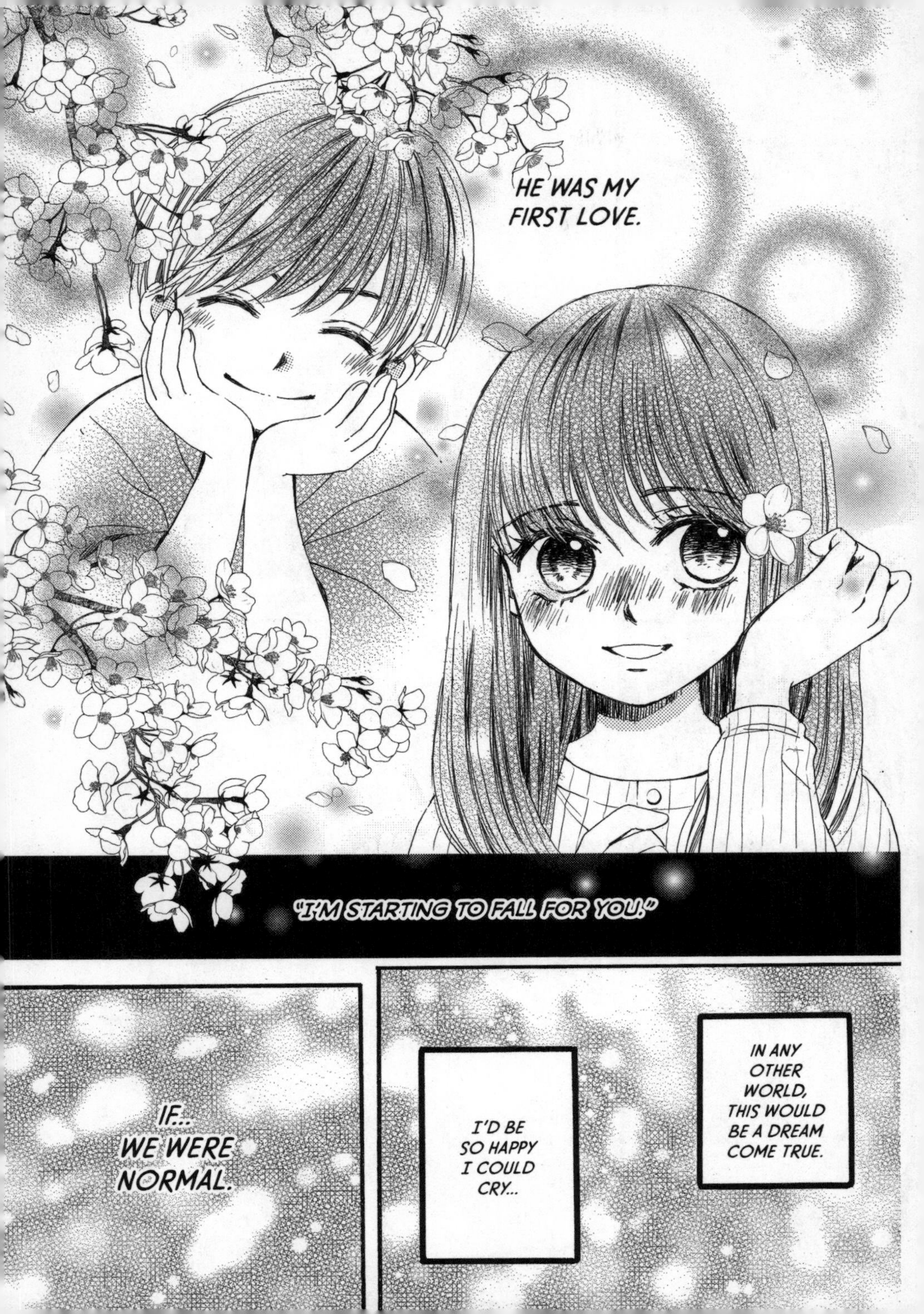
HE WAS MY FIRST LOVE.
"I'M STARTING TO FALL FOR YOU."
IN ANY OTHER WORLD, THIS WOULD BE A DREAM COME TRUE.
I'D BE SO HAPPY I COULD CRY...
IF... WE WERE NORMAL.

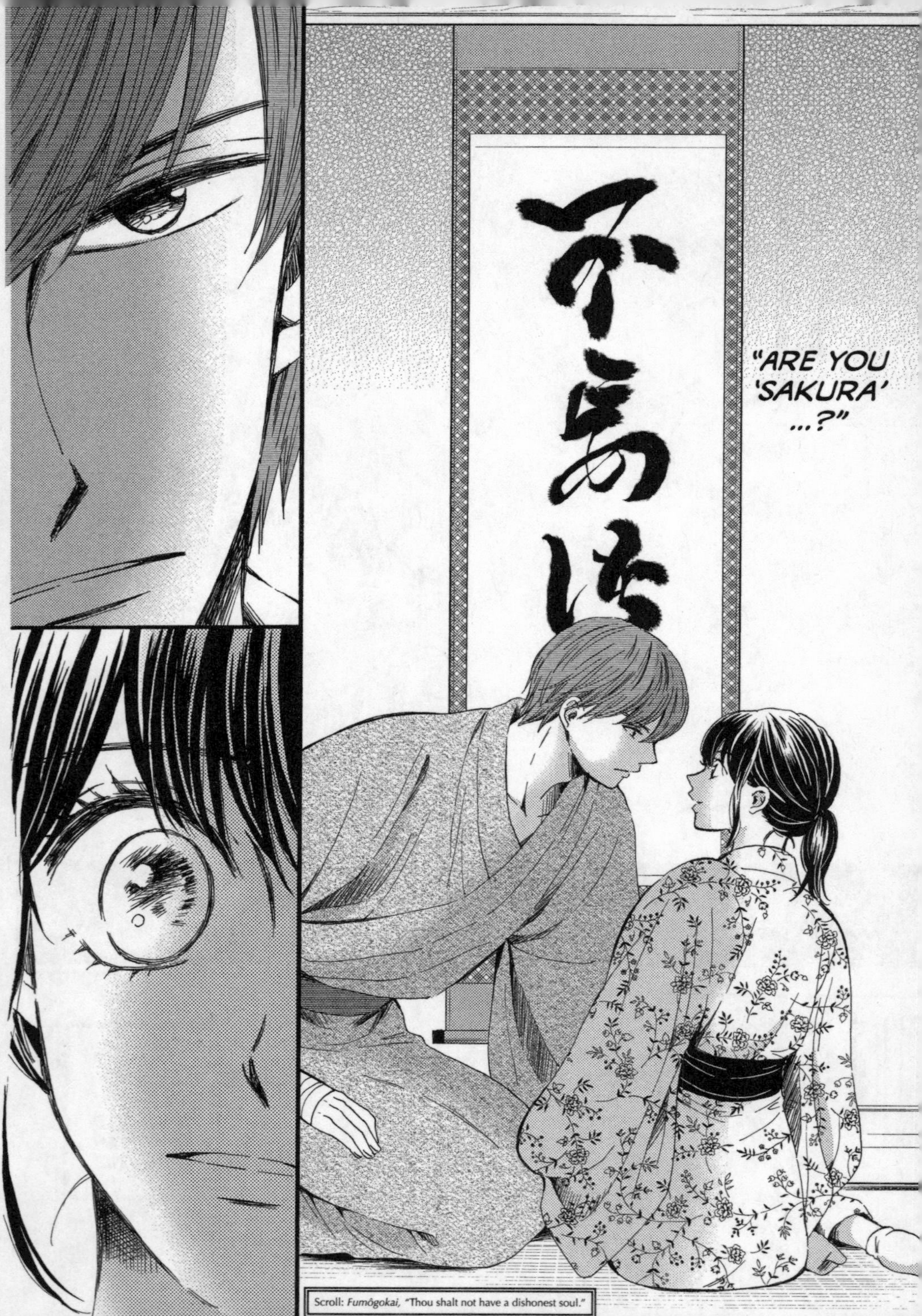
"ARE YOU 'SAKURA' ...?"
Scroll: *Fumôgokai*, "Thou shalt not have a dishonest soul."

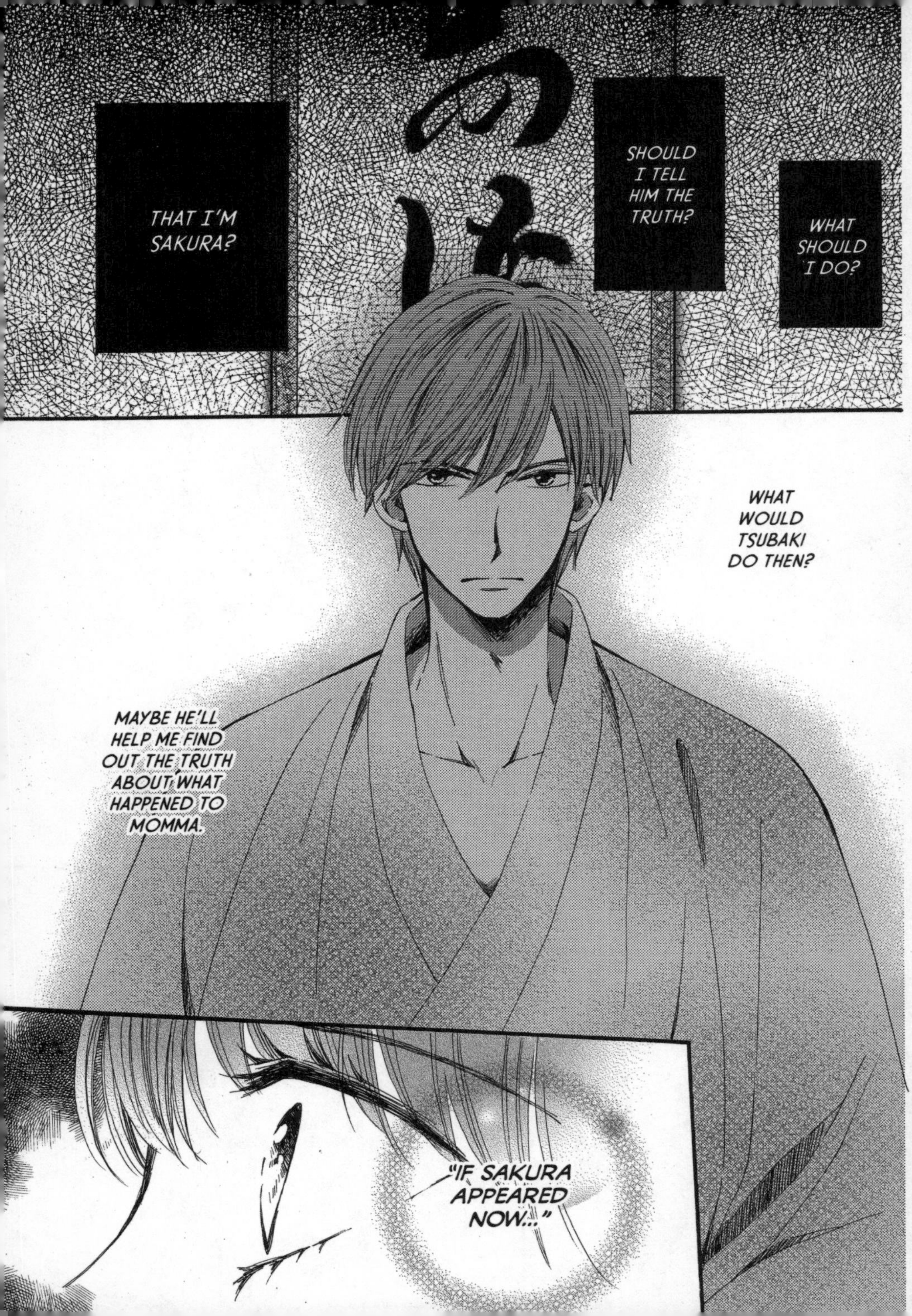
WHAT SHOULD I DO?
SHOULD I TELL HIM THE TRUTH?
THAT I'M SAKURA?
WHAT WOULD TSUBAKI DO THEN?
MAYBE HE'LL HELP ME FIND OUT THE TRUTH ABOUT WHAT HAPPENED TO MOMMA.
"IF SAKURA APPEARED NOW..."

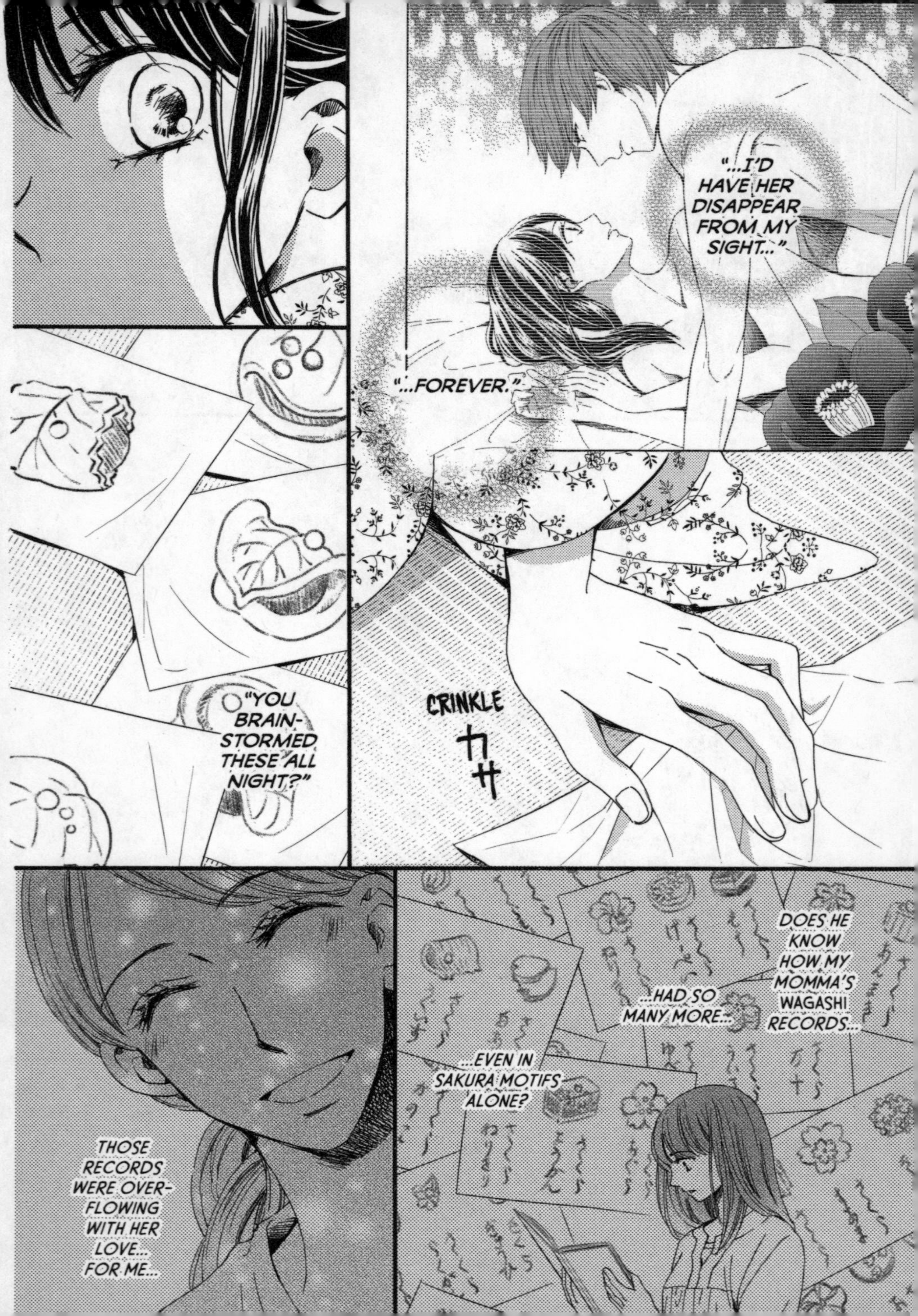
"...I'D HAVE HER DISAPPEAR FROM MY SIGHT..."
"...FOREVER."
CRINKLE
カサ
"YOU BRAIN-STORMED THESE ALL NIGHT?"
DOES HE KNOW HOW MY MOMMA'S WAGASHI RECORDS...
...HAD SO MANY MORE...
...EVEN IN SAKURA MOTIFS ALONE?
THOSE RECORDS WERE OVER-FLOWING WITH HER LOVE... FOR ME...

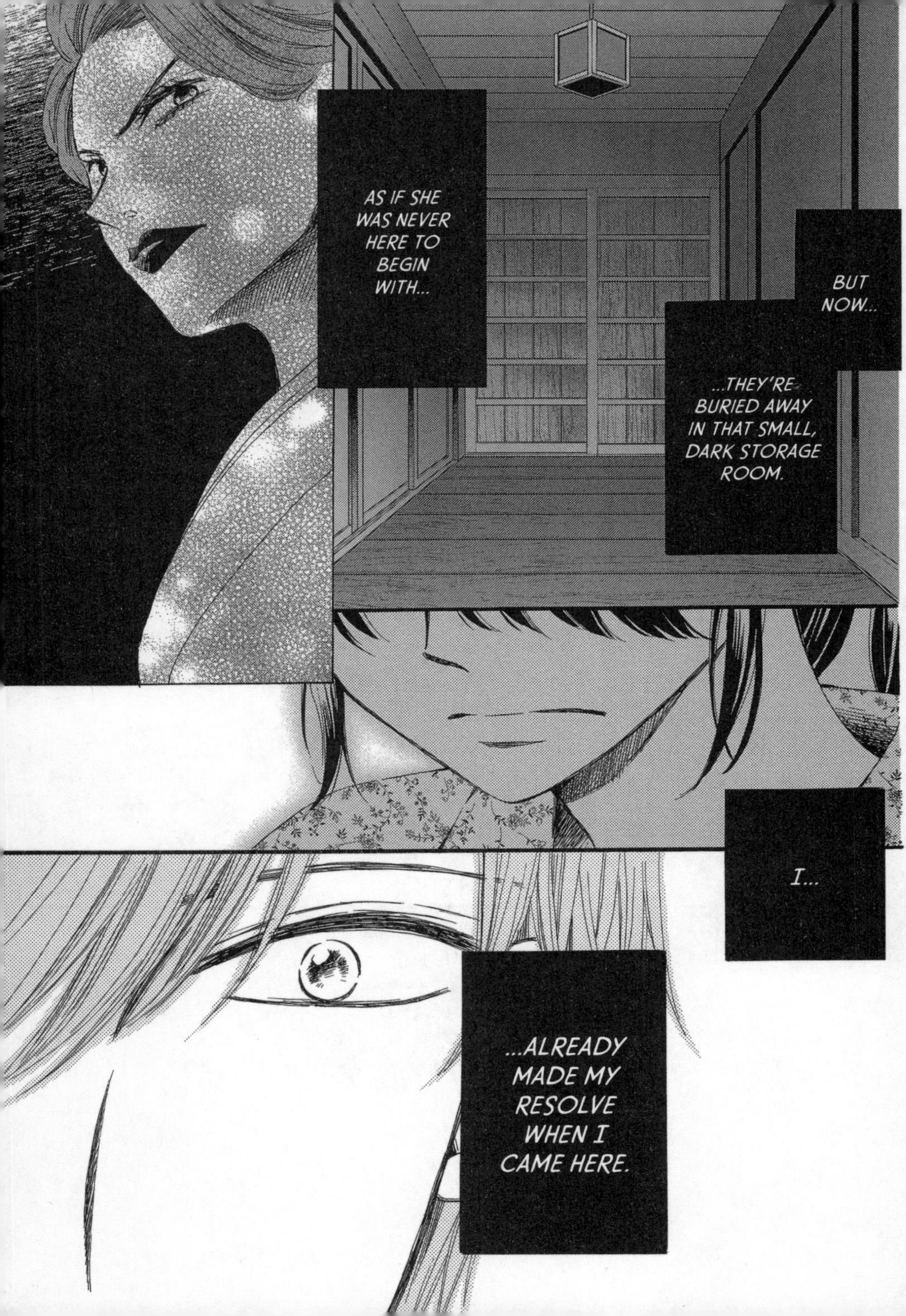
AS IF SHE WAS NEVER HERE TO BEGIN WITH...
BUT NOW...
...THEY'RE BURIED AWAY IN THAT SMALL, DARK STORAGE ROOM.
I...
...ALREADY MADE MY RESOLVE WHEN I CAME HERE.

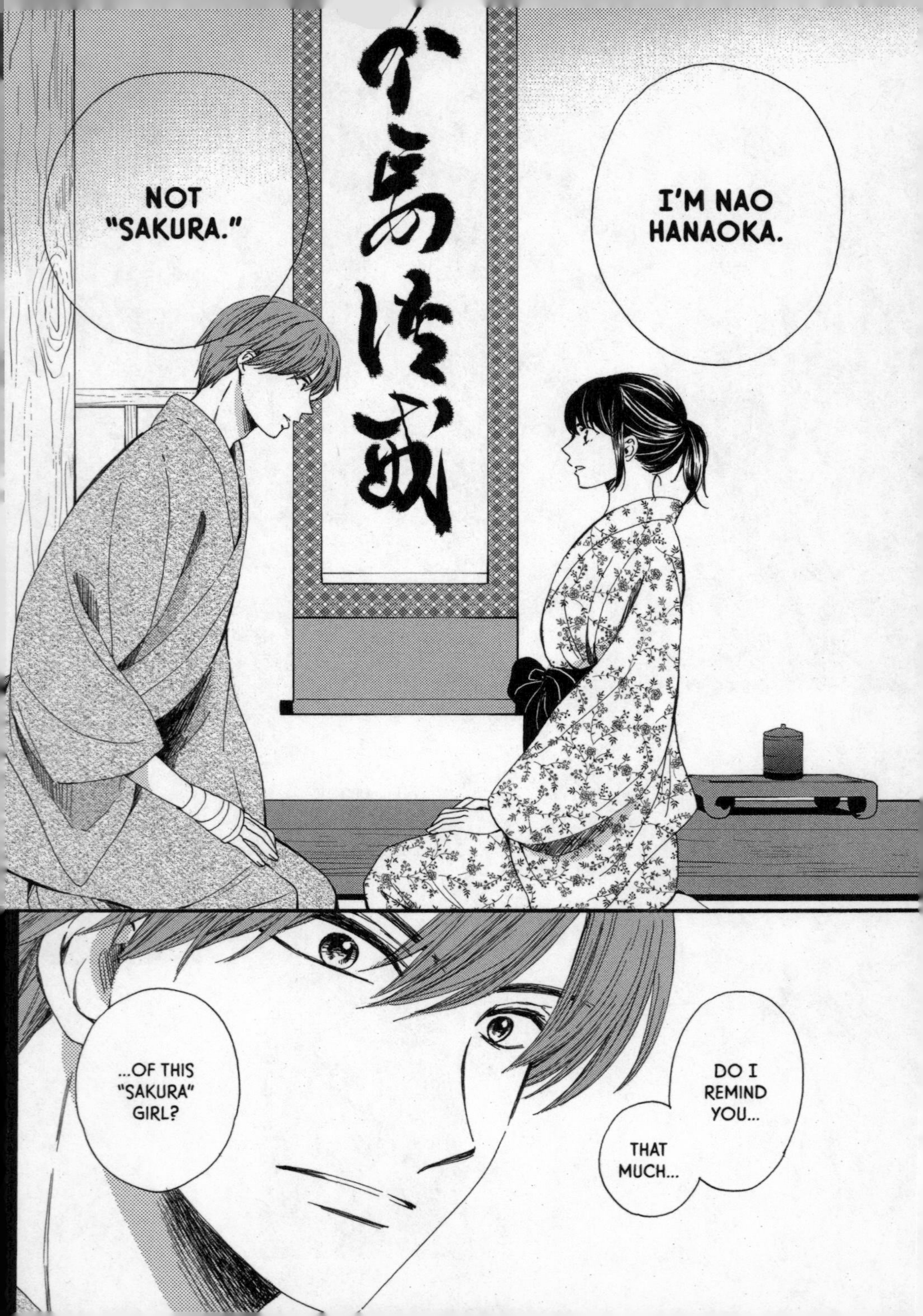
I'M NAO HANAOKA.
NOT "SAKURA."
DO I REMIND YOU...
THAT MUCH...
...OF THIS "SAKURA" GIRL?

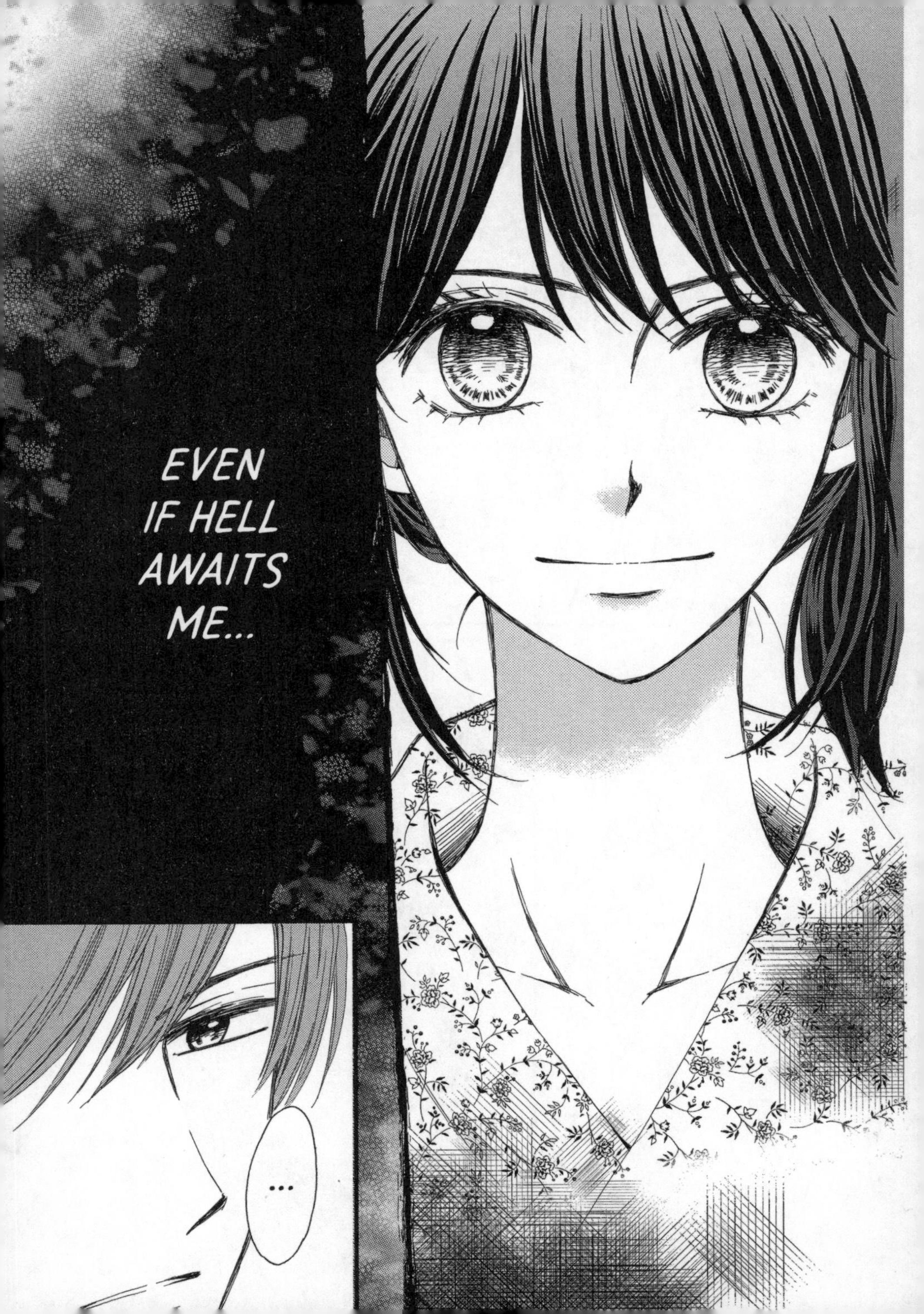
EVEN IF HELL AWAITS ME...
...

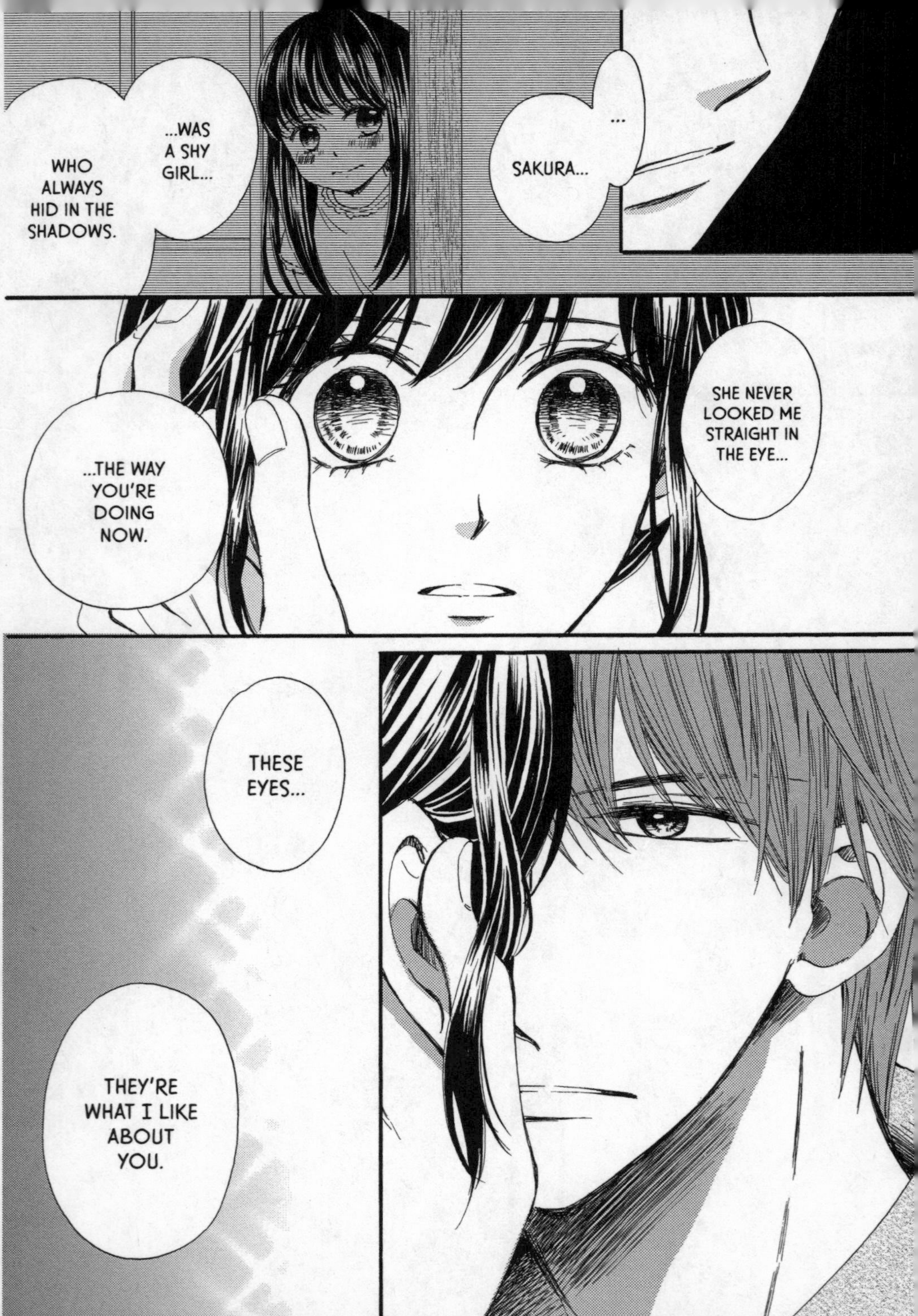
... SAKURA...
...WAS A SHY GIRL...
WHO ALWAYS HID IN THE SHADOWS.
SHE NEVER LOOKED ME STRAIGHT IN THE EYE...
...THE WAY YOU'RE DOING NOW.
THESE EYES...
THEY'RE WHAT I LIKE ABOUT YOU.

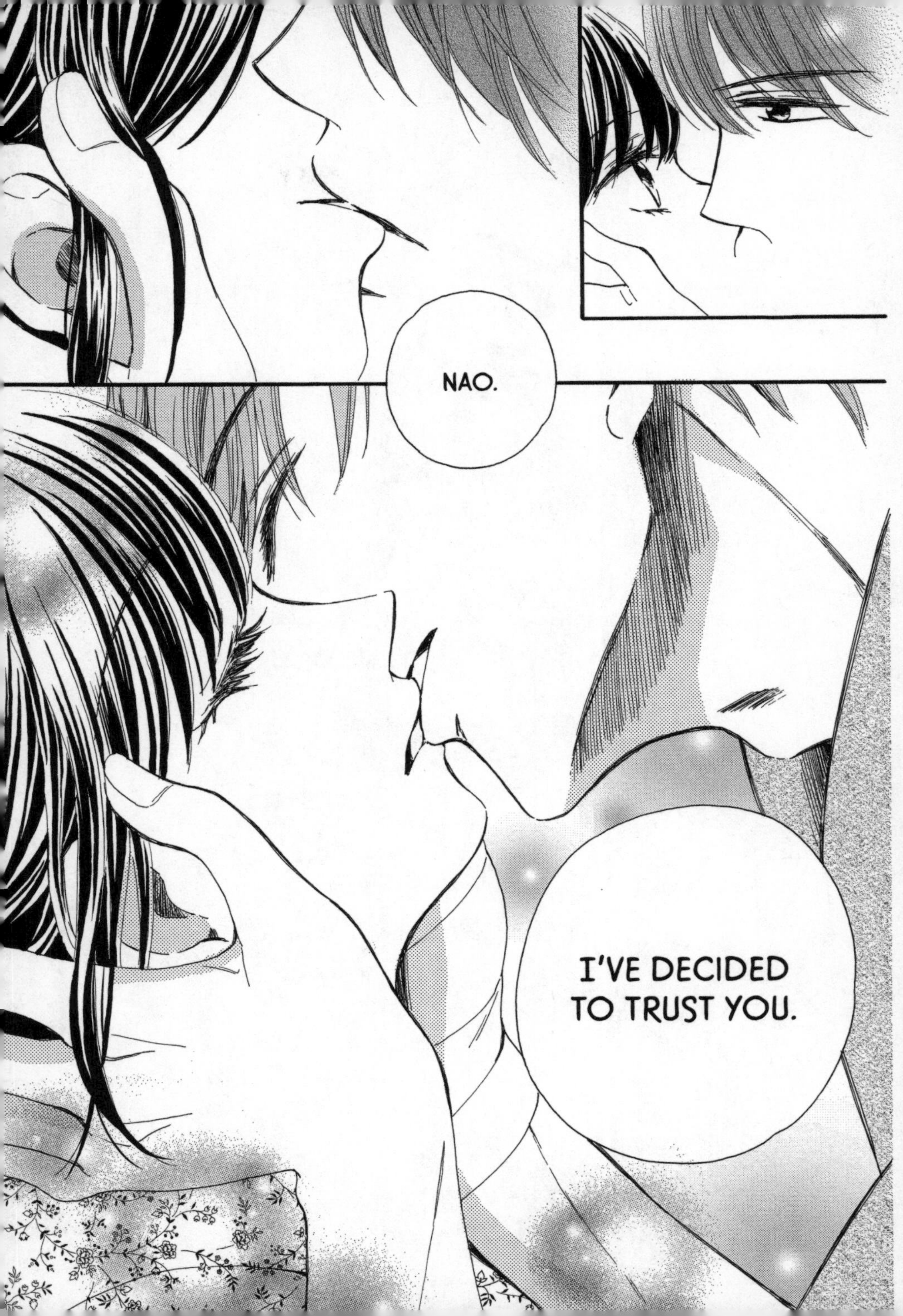
NAO.
I'VE DECIDED TO TRUST YOU.

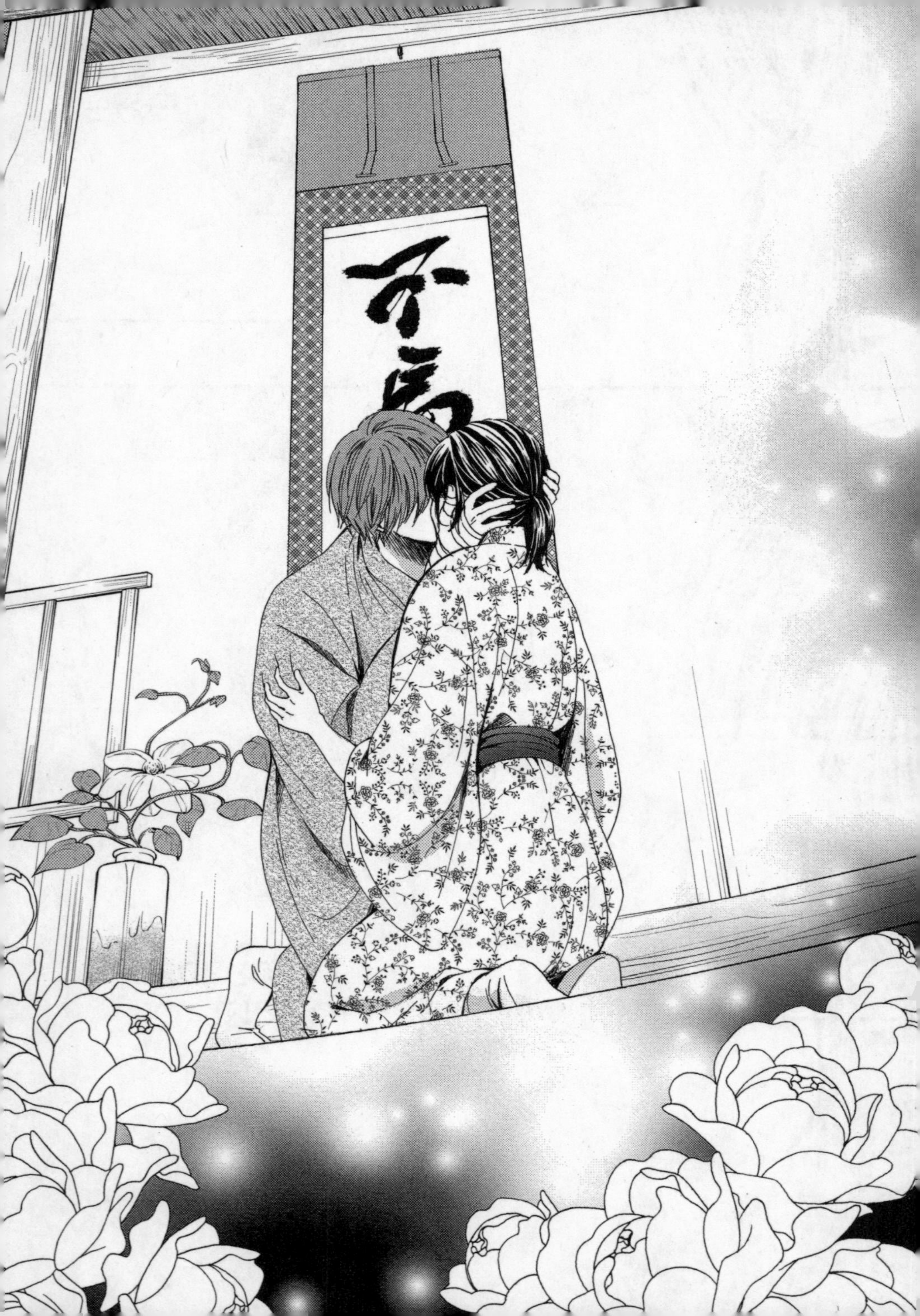

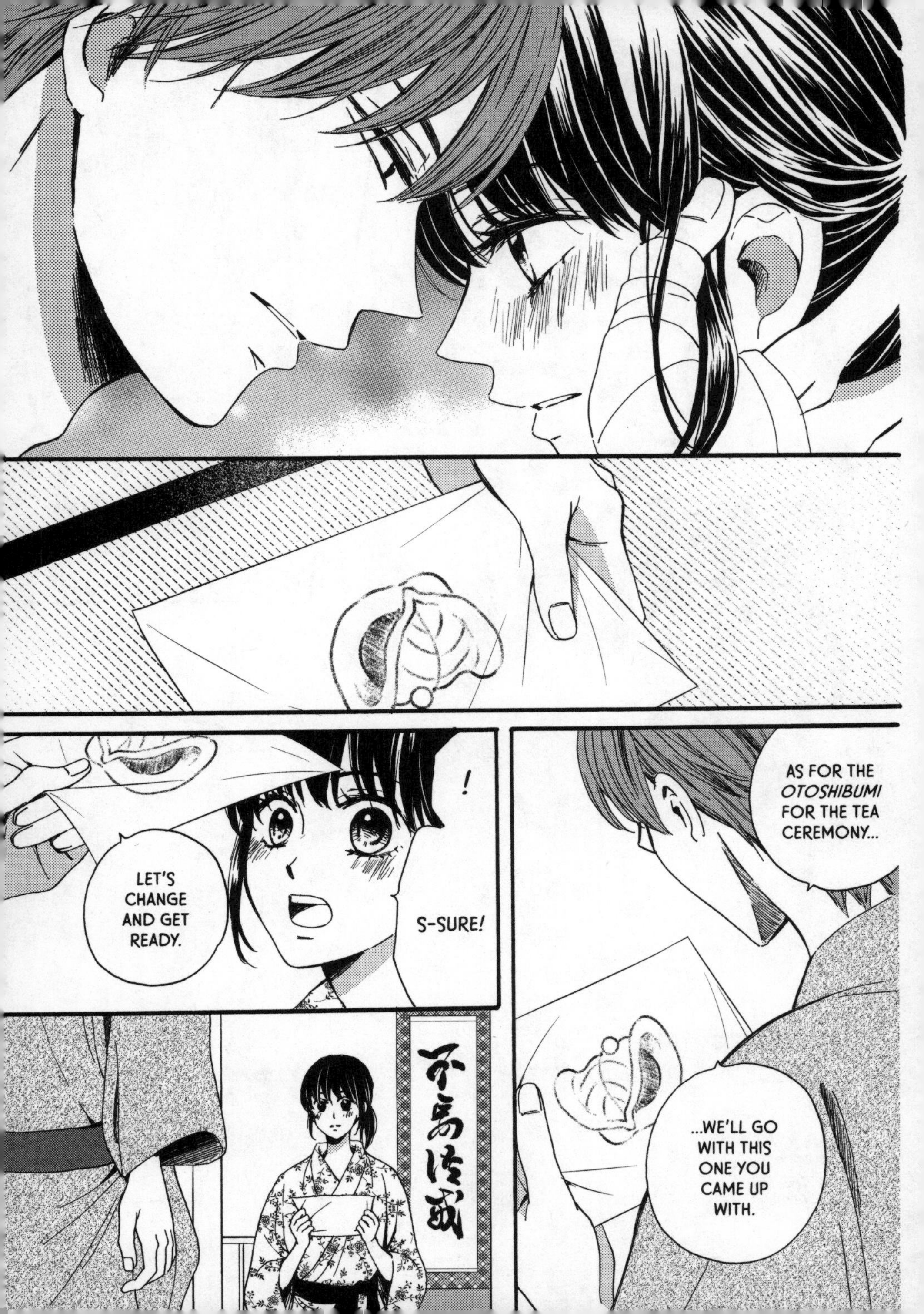
AS FOR THE *OTOSHIBUMI* FOR THE TEA CEREMONY...
...WE'LL GO WITH THIS ONE YOU CAME UP WITH.
!
S-SURE!
LET'S CHANGE AND GET READY.

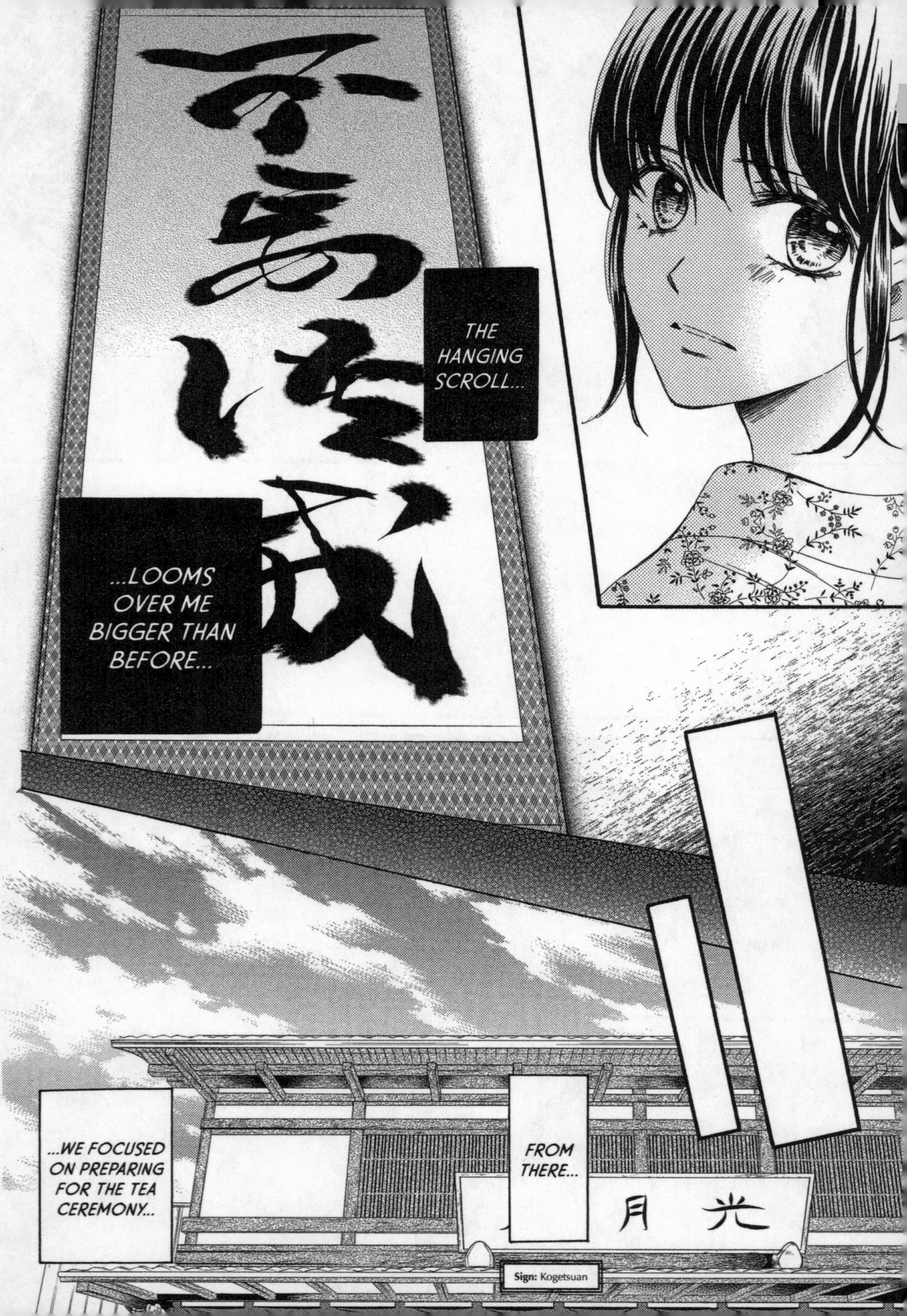
THE HANGING SCROLL...
...LOOMS OVER ME BIGGER THAN BEFORE...
FROM THERE...
...WE FOCUSED ON PREPARING FOR THE TEA CEREMONY...
月 光
Sign: Kogetsuan

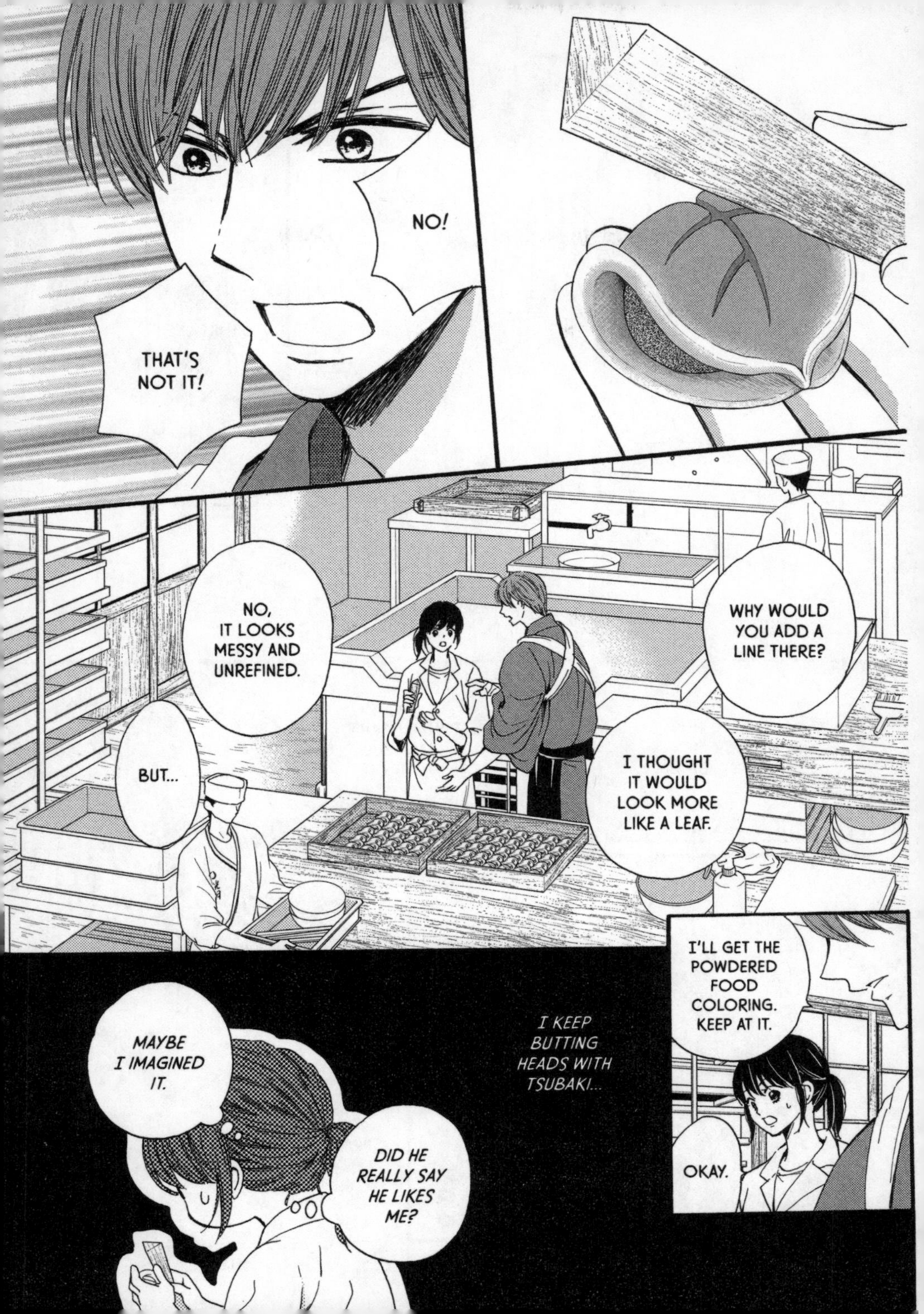
NO!
THAT'S NOT IT!
WHY WOULD YOU ADD A LINE THERE?
I THOUGHT IT WOULD LOOK MORE LIKE A LEAF.
NO, IT LOOKS MESSY AND UNREFINED.
BUT...
I'LL GET THE POWDERED FOOD COLORING. KEEP AT IT.
OKAY.
I KEEP BUTTING HEADS WITH TSUBAKI...
MAYBE I IMAGINED IT.
DID HE REALLY SAY HE LIKES ME?

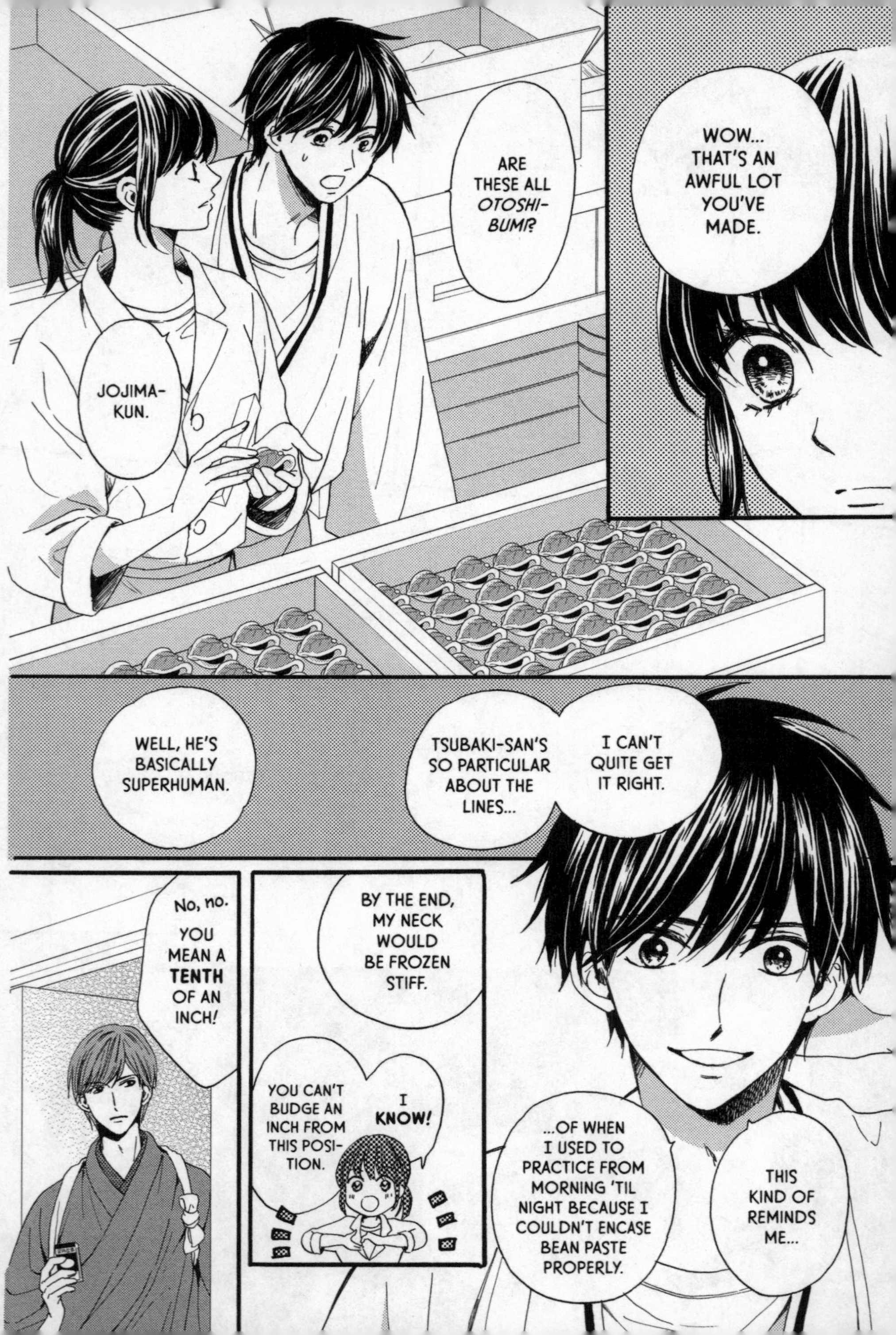
WOW... THAT'S AN AWFUL LOT YOU'VE MADE.
ARE THESE ALL *OTOSHI-BUMI*?
JOJIMA-KUN.
I CAN'T QUITE GET IT RIGHT.
TSUBAKI-SAN'S SO PARTICULAR ABOUT THE LINES...
WELL, HE'S BASICALLY SUPERHUMAN.
THIS KIND OF REMINDS ME...
...OF WHEN I USED TO PRACTICE FROM MORNING 'TIL NIGHT BECAUSE I COULDN'T ENCASE BEAN PASTE PROPERLY.
BY THE END, MY NECK WOULD BE FROZEN STIFF.
YOU CAN'T BUDGE AN INCH FROM THIS POSITION.
I **KNOW!**
No, no.
YOU MEAN A **TENTH** OF AN INCH!

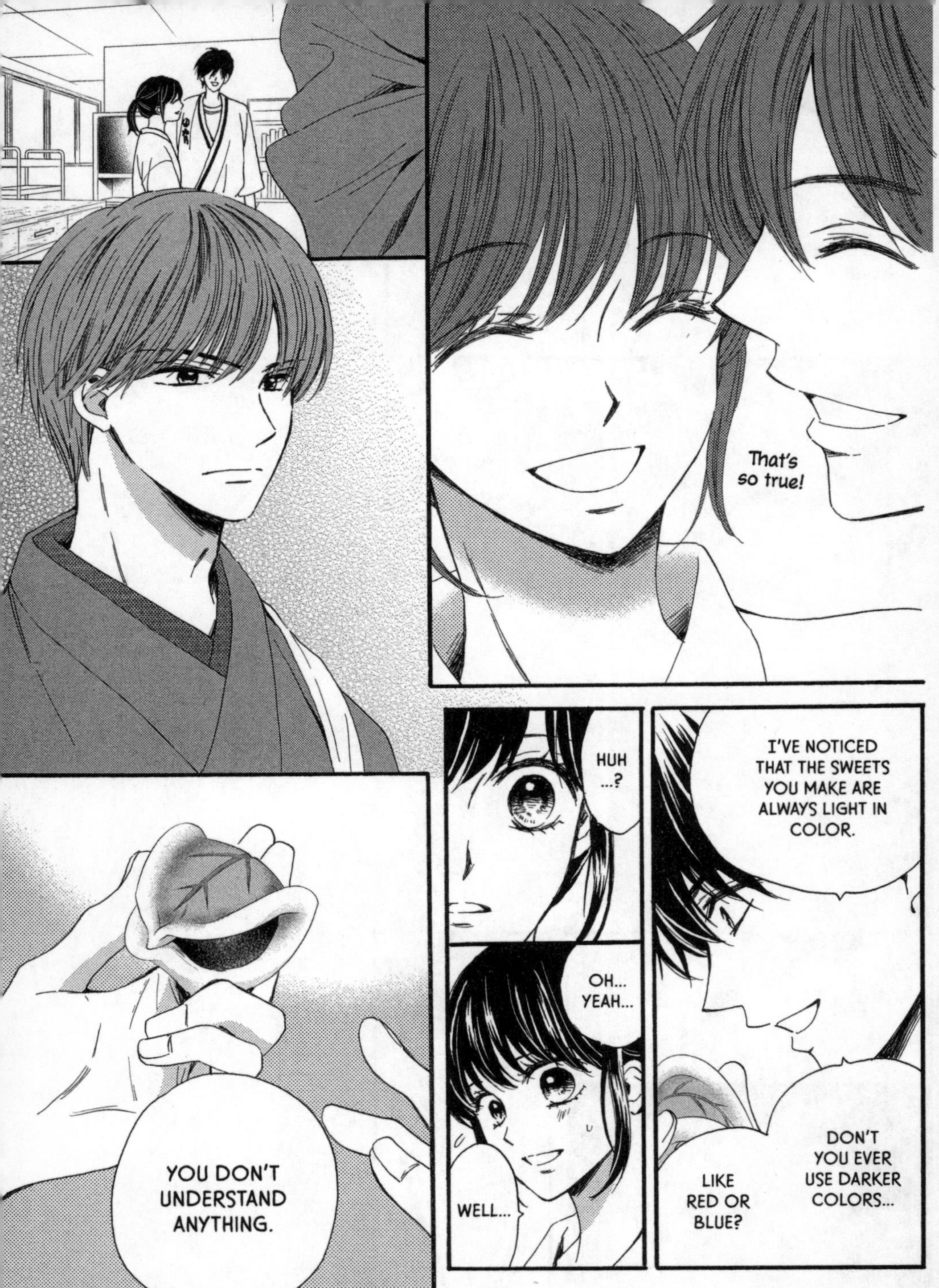
That's so true!
I'VE NOTICED THAT THE SWEETS YOU MAKE ARE ALWAYS LIGHT IN COLOR.
HUH ...?
DON'T YOU EVER USE DARKER COLORS...
LIKE RED OR BLUE?
OH... YEAH...
WELL...
YOU DON'T UNDERSTAND ANYTHING.

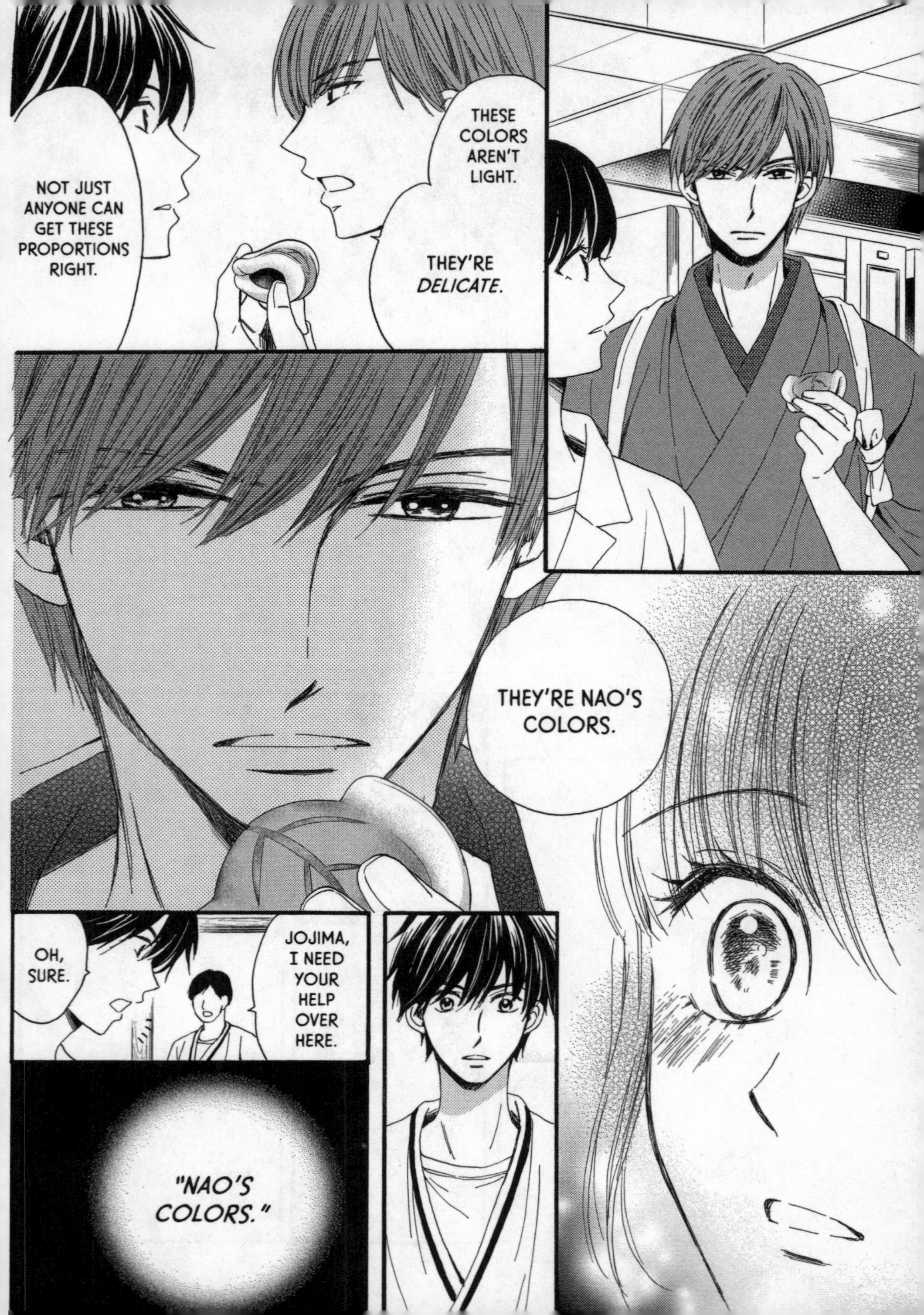
THESE COLORS AREN'T LIGHT.
THEY'RE *DELICATE.*
NOT JUST ANYONE CAN GET THESE PROPORTIONS RIGHT.
THEY'RE NAO'S COLORS.
JOJIMA, I NEED YOUR HELP OVER HERE.
OH, SURE.
"NAO'S COLORS."

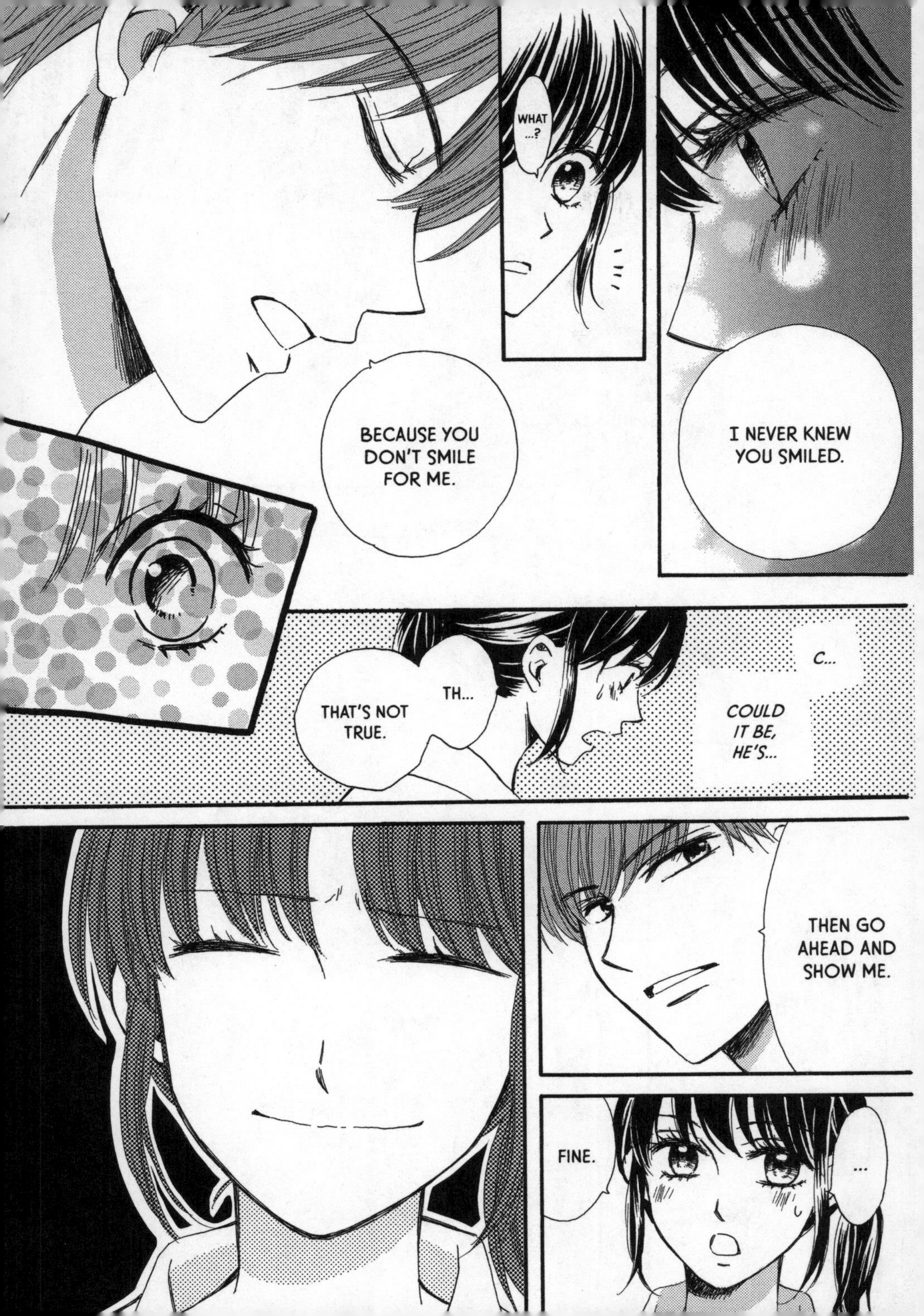
I NEVER KNEW YOU SMILED.
WHAT ...?
BECAUSE YOU DON'T SMILE FOR ME.
C...
COULD IT BE, HE'S...
TH...
THAT'S NOT TRUE.
THEN GO AHEAD AND SHOW ME.
...
FINE.

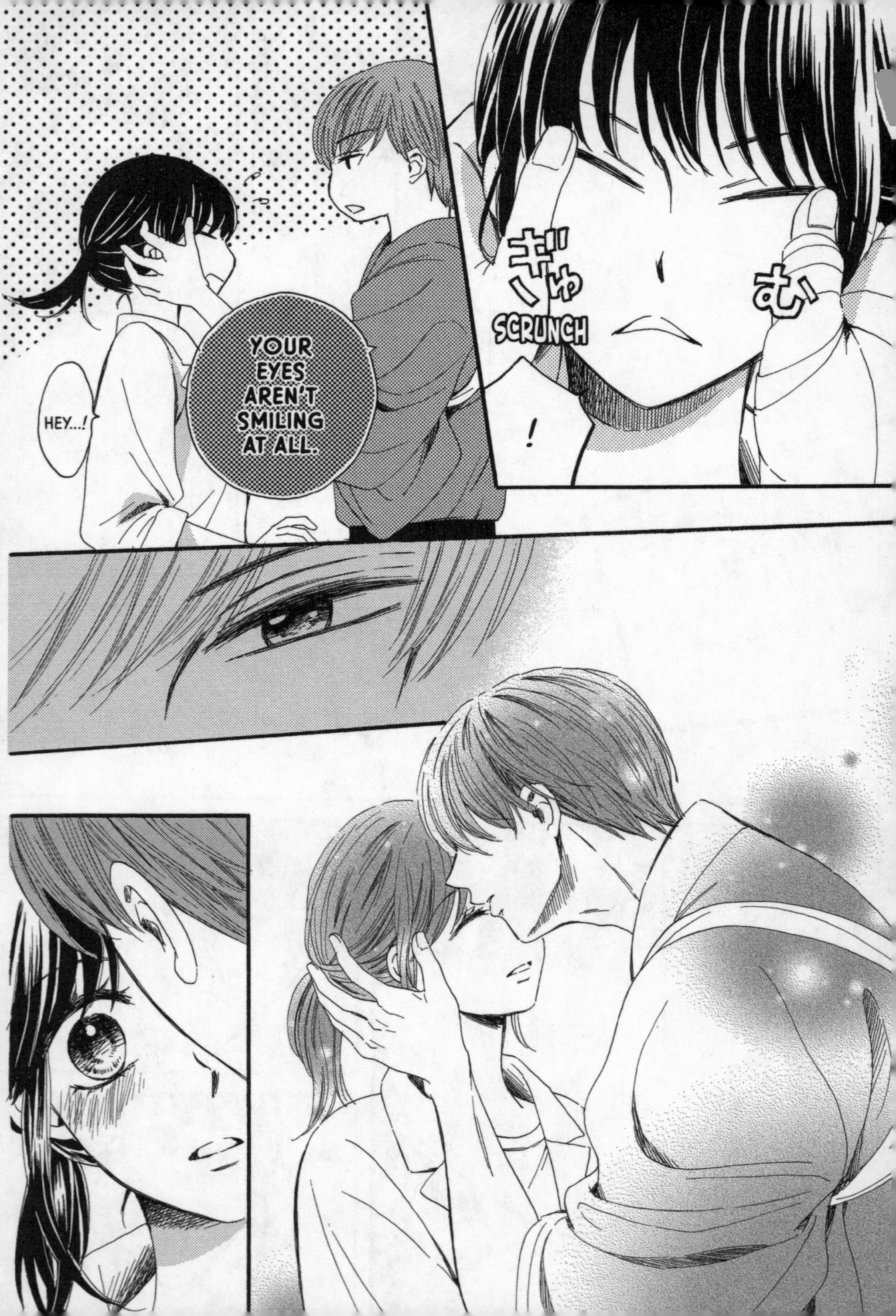
ぎゅむ
SCRUNCH
!
YOUR EYES AREN'T SMILING AT ALL.
HEY...!

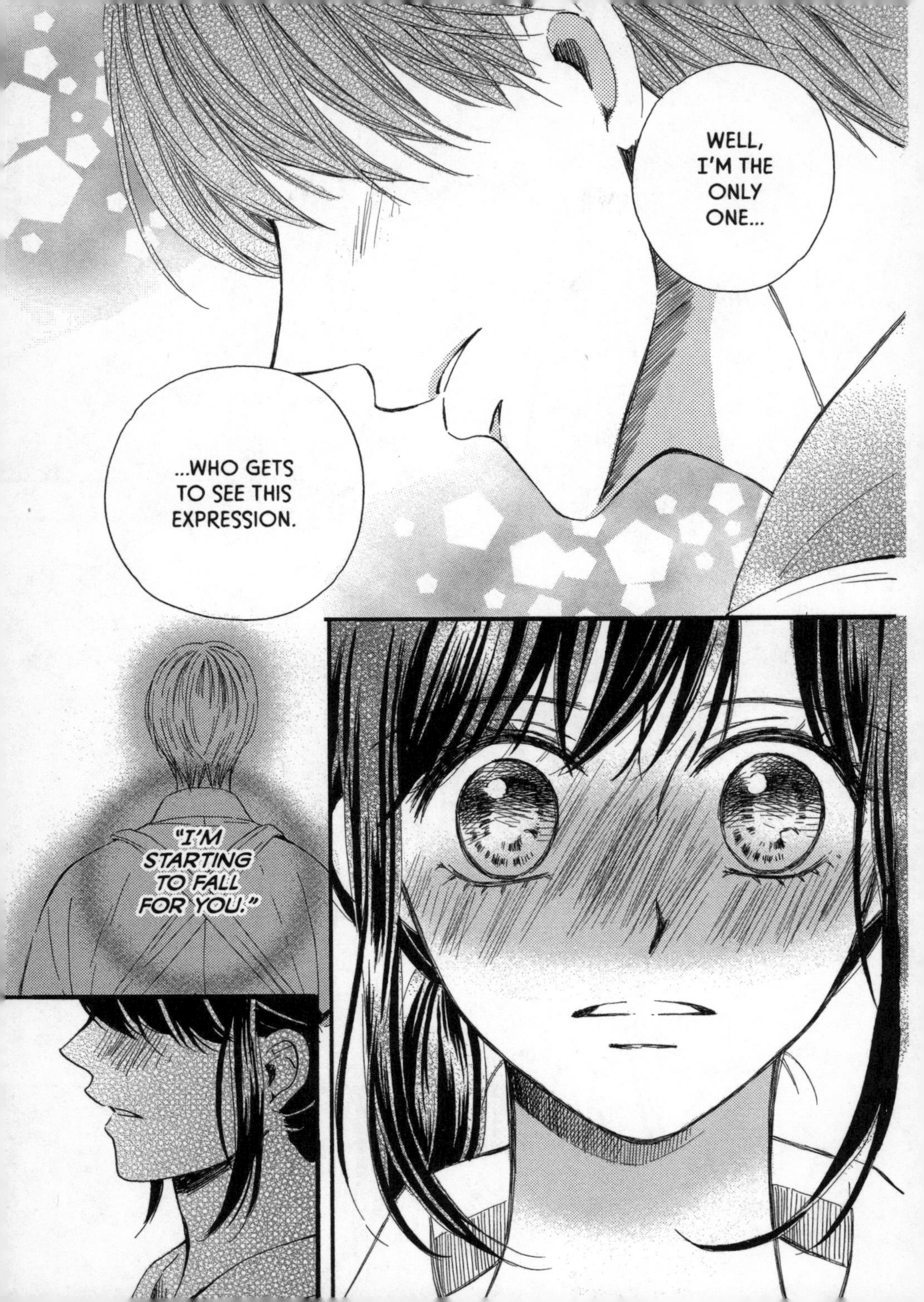
WELL, I'M THE ONLY ONE...
...WHO GETS TO SEE THIS EXPRESSION.
"I'M STARTING TO FALL FOR YOU."

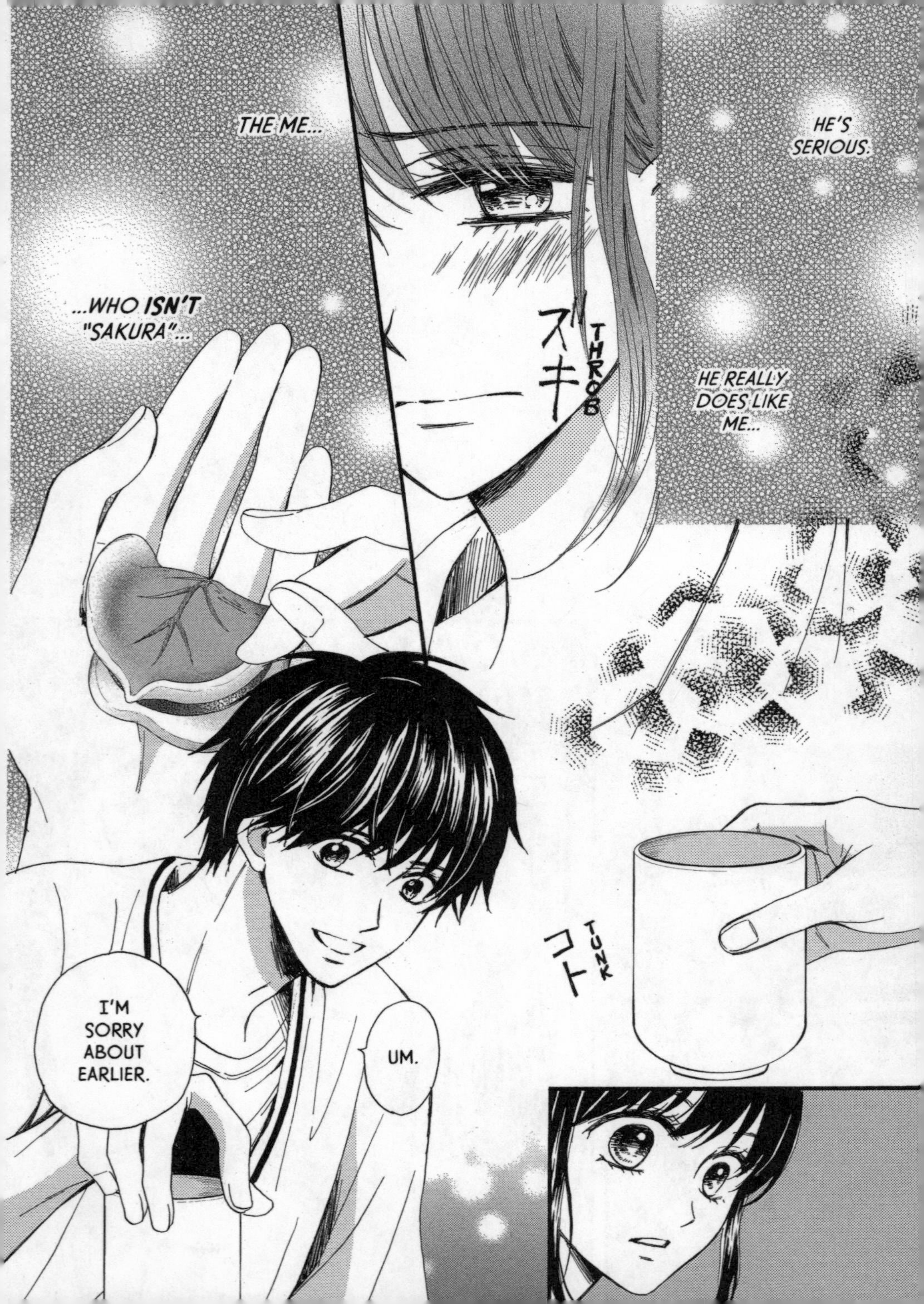
HE'S SERIOUS.
HE REALLY DOES LIKE ME...
ズキ THROB
THE ME...
...WHO ISN'T "SAKURA"...
コト TUNK
UM.
I'M SORRY ABOUT EARLIER.

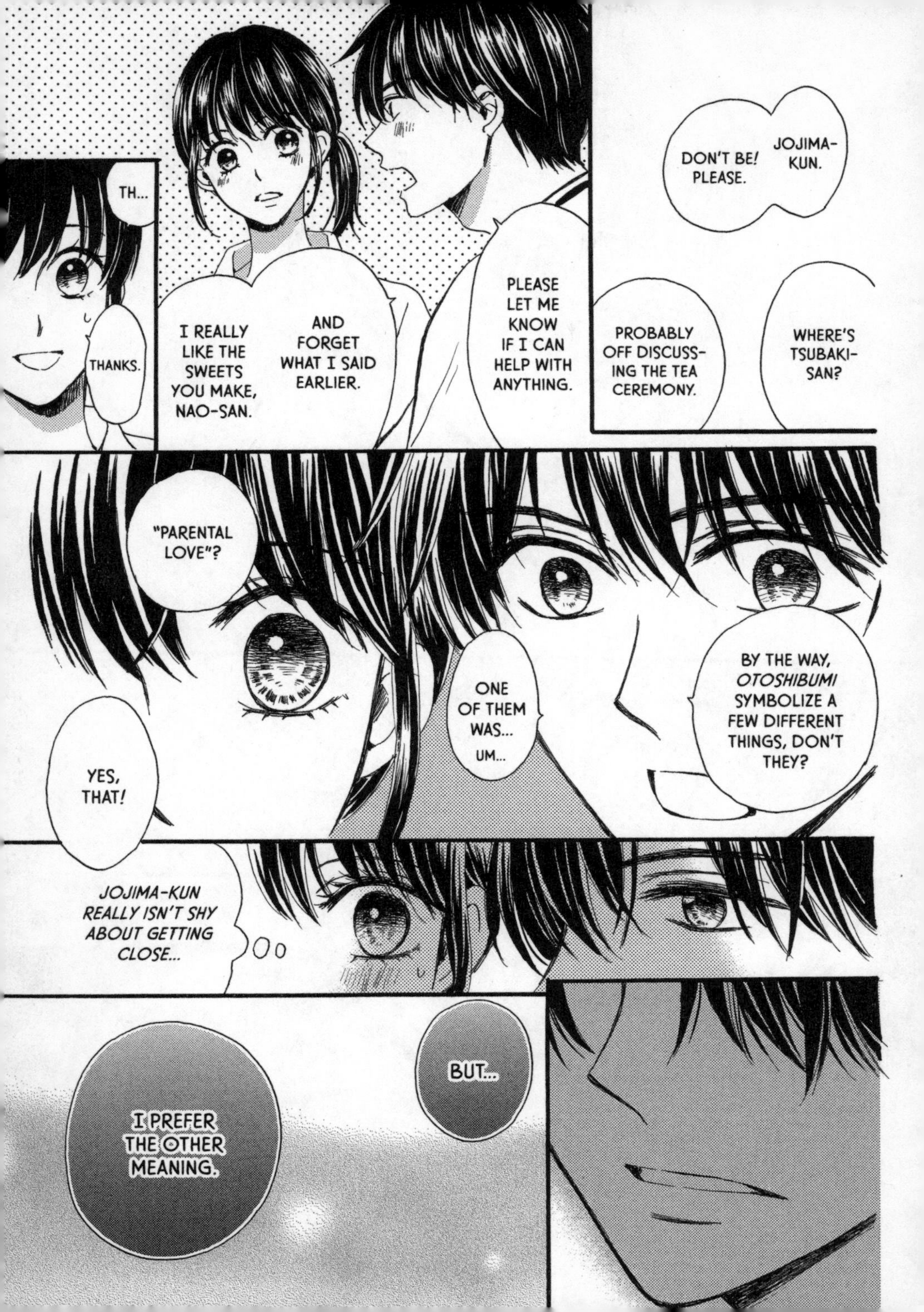
JOJIMA-KUN.
DON'T BE! PLEASE.
WHERE'S TSUBAKI-SAN?
PROBABLY OFF DISCUSSING THE TEA CEREMONY.
PLEASE LET ME KNOW IF I CAN HELP WITH ANYTHING.
AND FORGET WHAT I SAID EARLIER.
I REALLY LIKE THE SWEETS YOU MAKE, NAO-SAN.
TH...
THANKS.
BY THE WAY, *OTOSHIBUMI* SYMBOLIZE A FEW DIFFERENT THINGS, DON'T THEY?
ONE OF THEM WAS... UM...
"PARENTAL LOVE"?
YES, THAT!
JOJIMA-KUN REALLY ISN'T SHY ABOUT GETTING CLOSE...
BUT...
I PREFER THE OTHER MEANING.

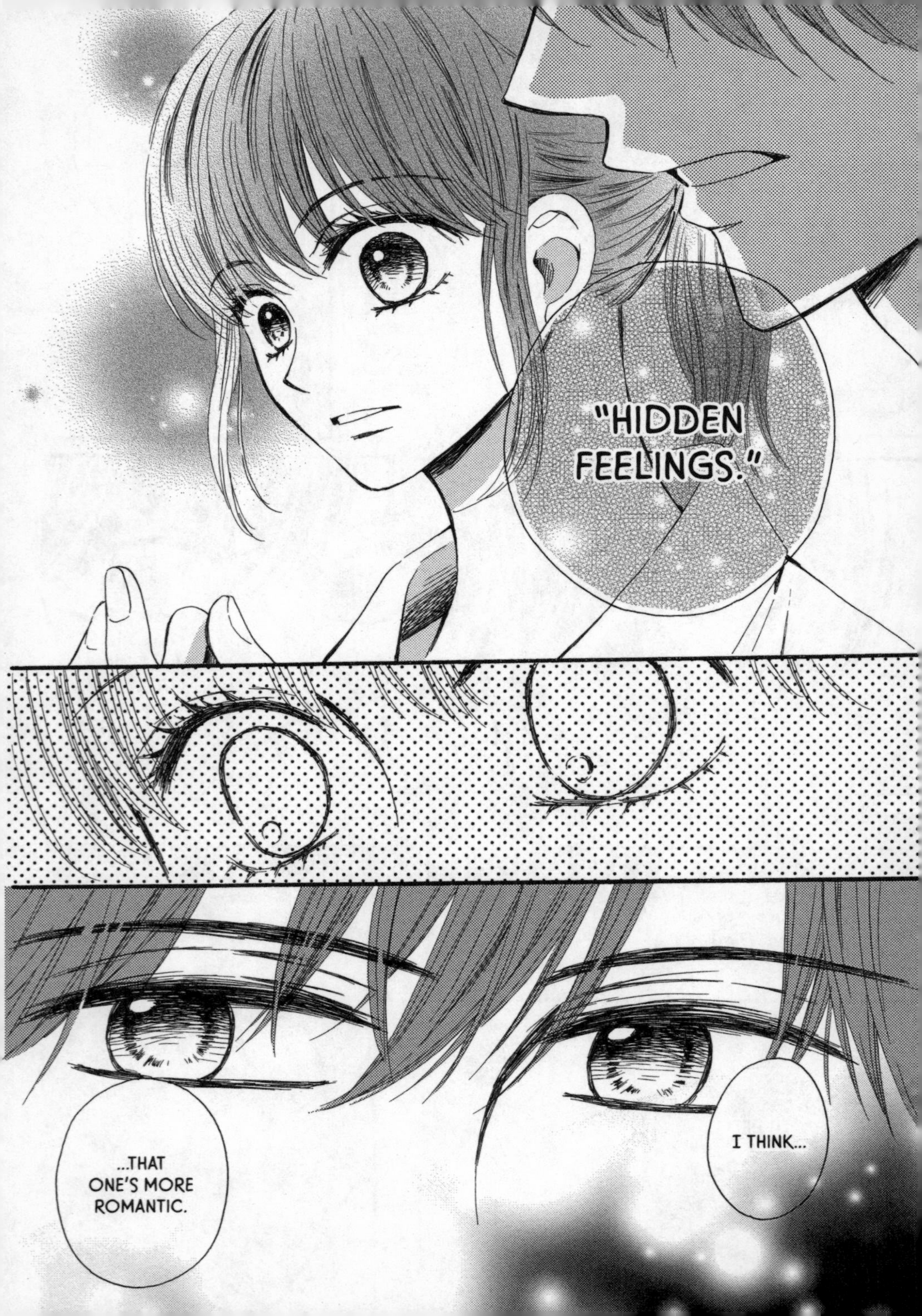
"HIDDEN FEELINGS."
I THINK...
...THAT ONE'S MORE ROMANTIC.

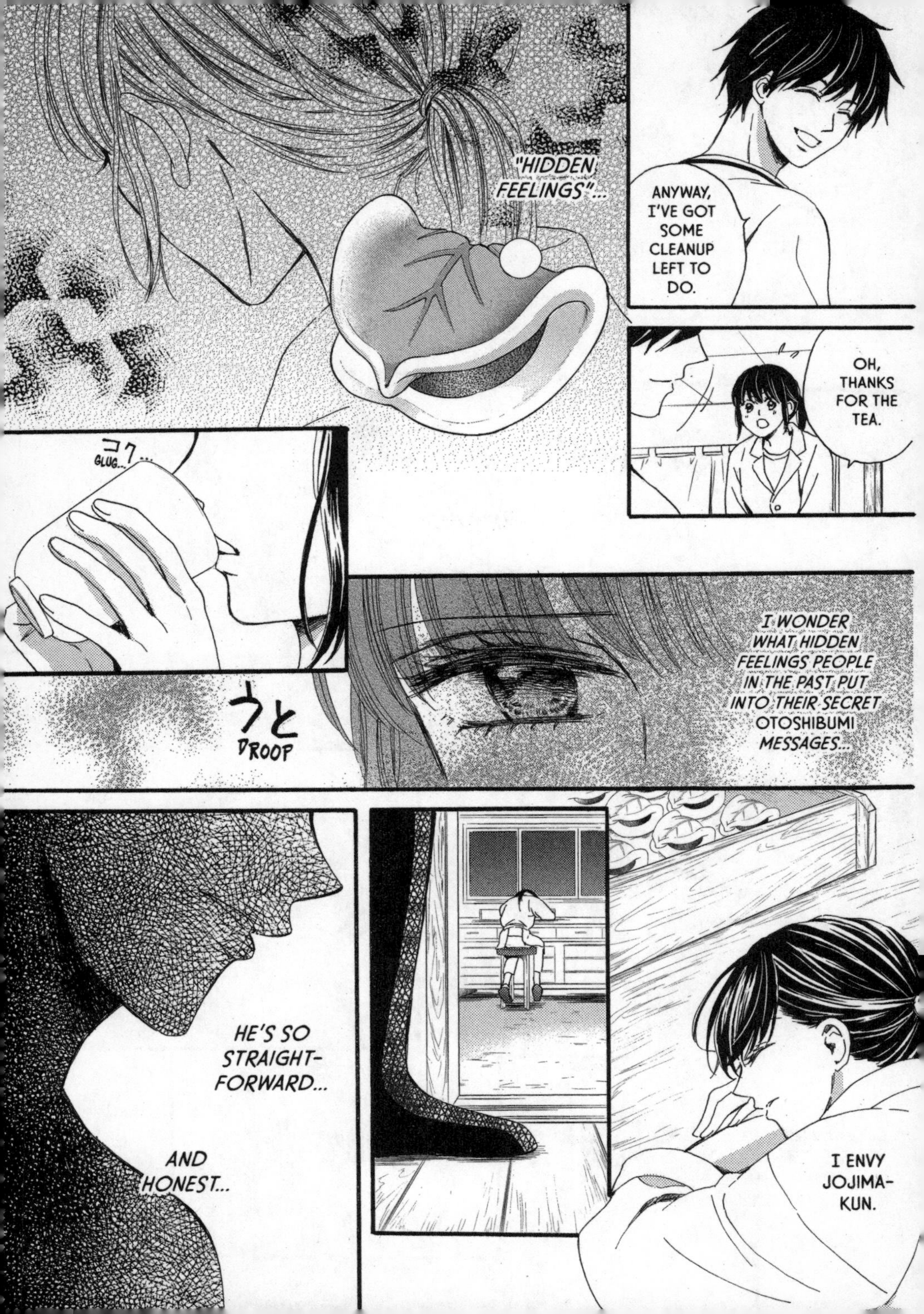
ANYWAY, I'VE GOT SOME CLEANUP LEFT TO DO.
OH, THANKS FOR THE TEA.
"HIDDEN FEELINGS"...
コク... GLUG...
I WONDER WHAT HIDDEN FEELINGS PEOPLE IN THE PAST PUT INTO THEIR SECRET OTOSHIBUMI MESSAGES...
うと DROOP
I ENVY JOJIMA-KUN.
HE'S SO STRAIGHT-FORWARD...
AND HONEST...

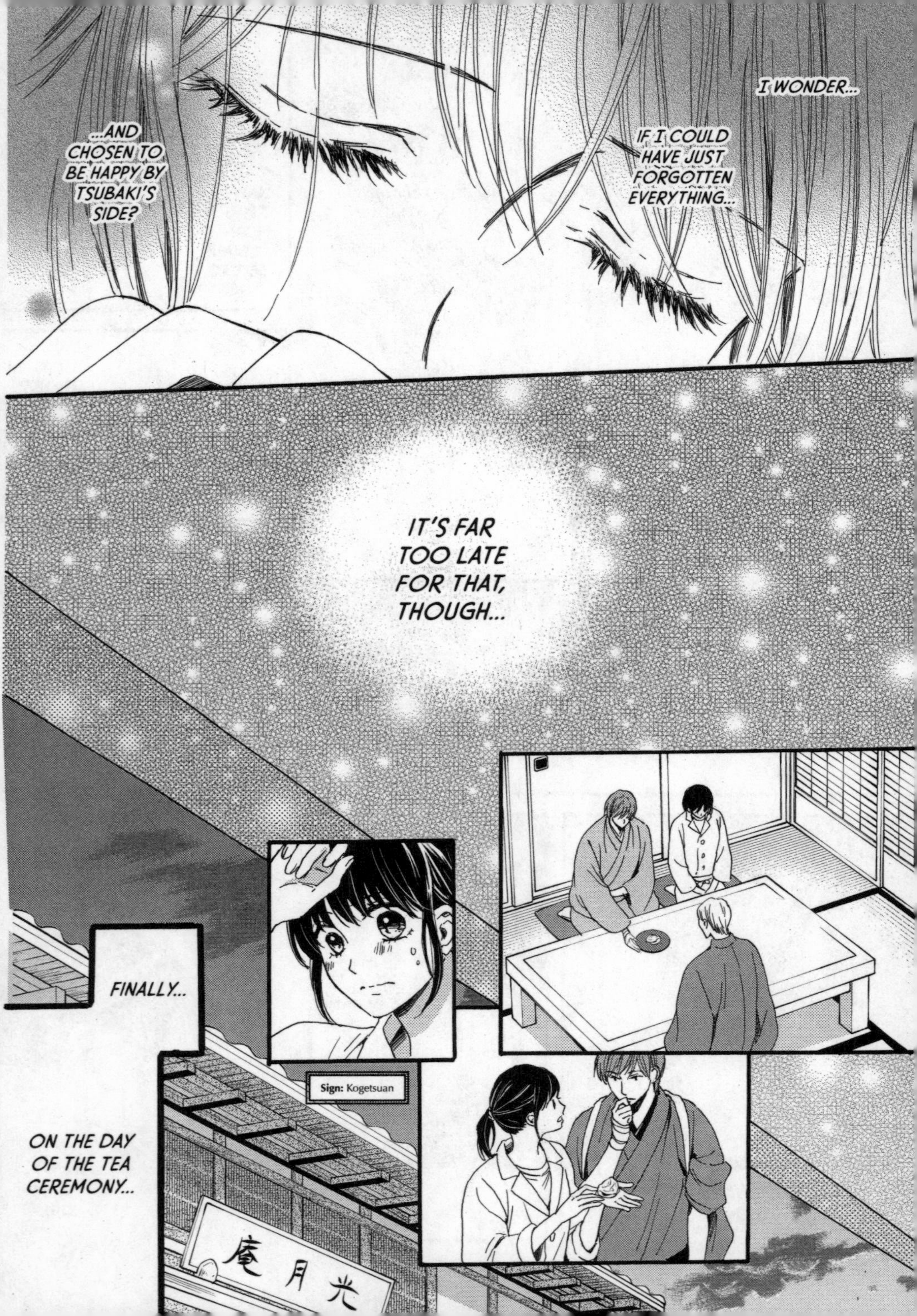

I WONDER...
IF I COULD HAVE JUST FORGOTTEN EVERYTHING...
...AND CHOSEN TO BE HAPPY BY TSUBAKI'S SIDE?
IT'S FAR TOO LATE FOR THAT, THOUGH...
FINALLY...
Sign: Kogetsuan
光月庵
ON THE DAY OF THE TEA CEREMONY...

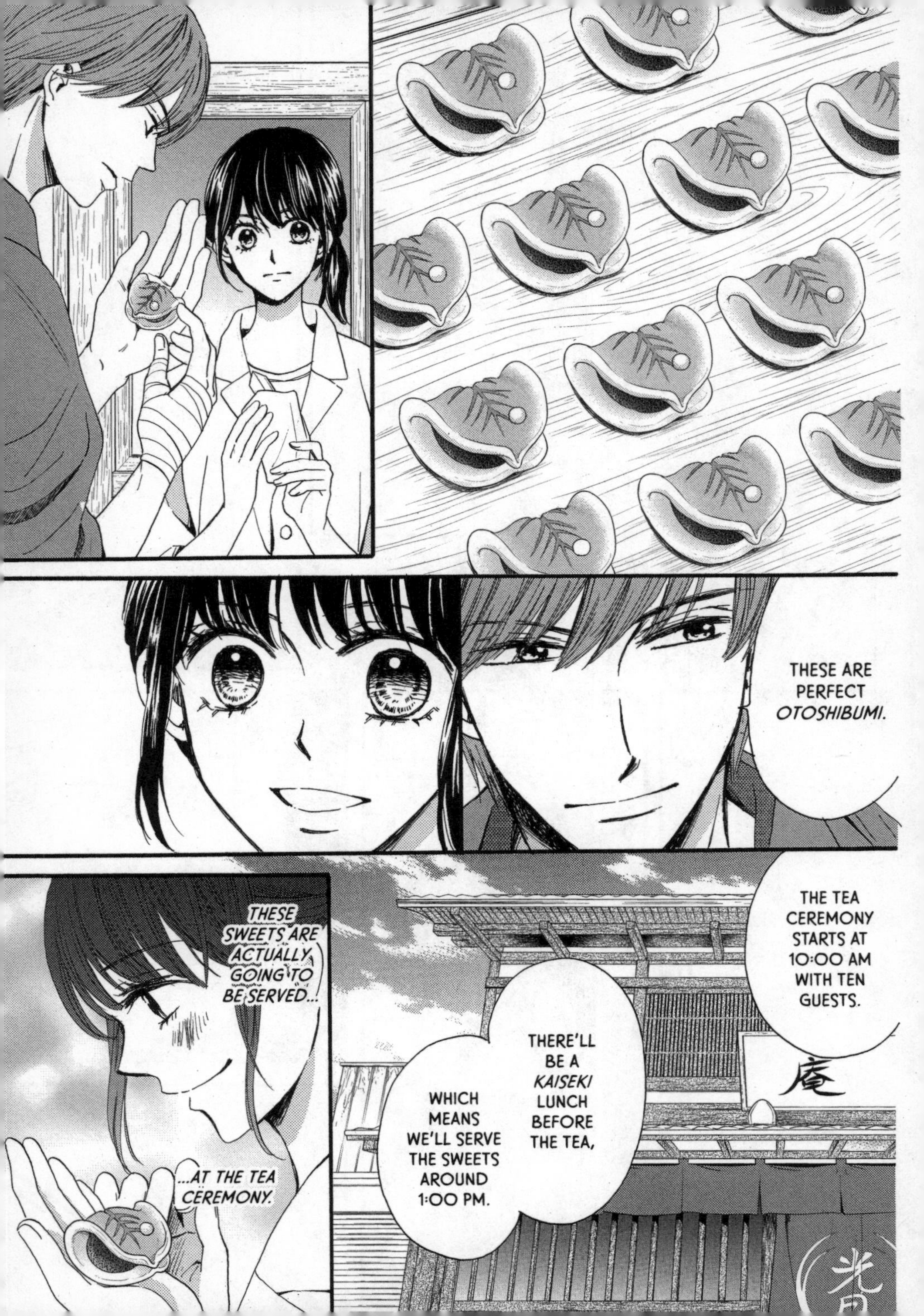
THESE ARE PERFECT *OTOSHIBUMI*.
THE TEA CEREMONY STARTS AT 10:00 AM WITH TEN GUESTS.
THERE'LL BE A *KAISEKI* LUNCH BEFORE THE TEA,
WHICH MEANS WE'LL SERVE THE SWEETS AROUND 1:00 PM.
庵
THESE SWEETS ARE ACTUALLY GOING TO BE SERVED...
...AT THE TEA CEREMONY.

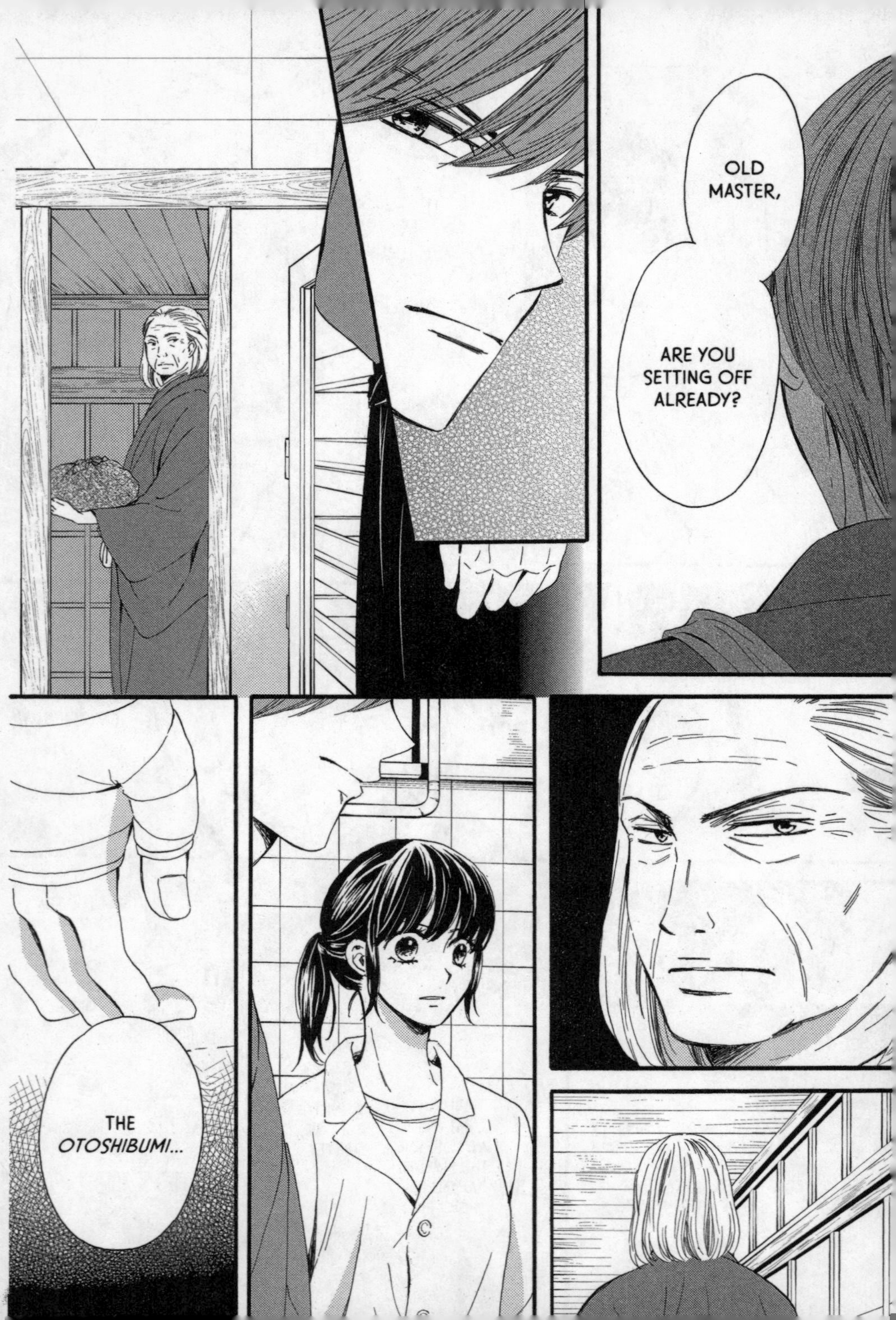
OLD MASTER,
ARE YOU SETTING OFF ALREADY?
THE *OTOSHIBUMI*...

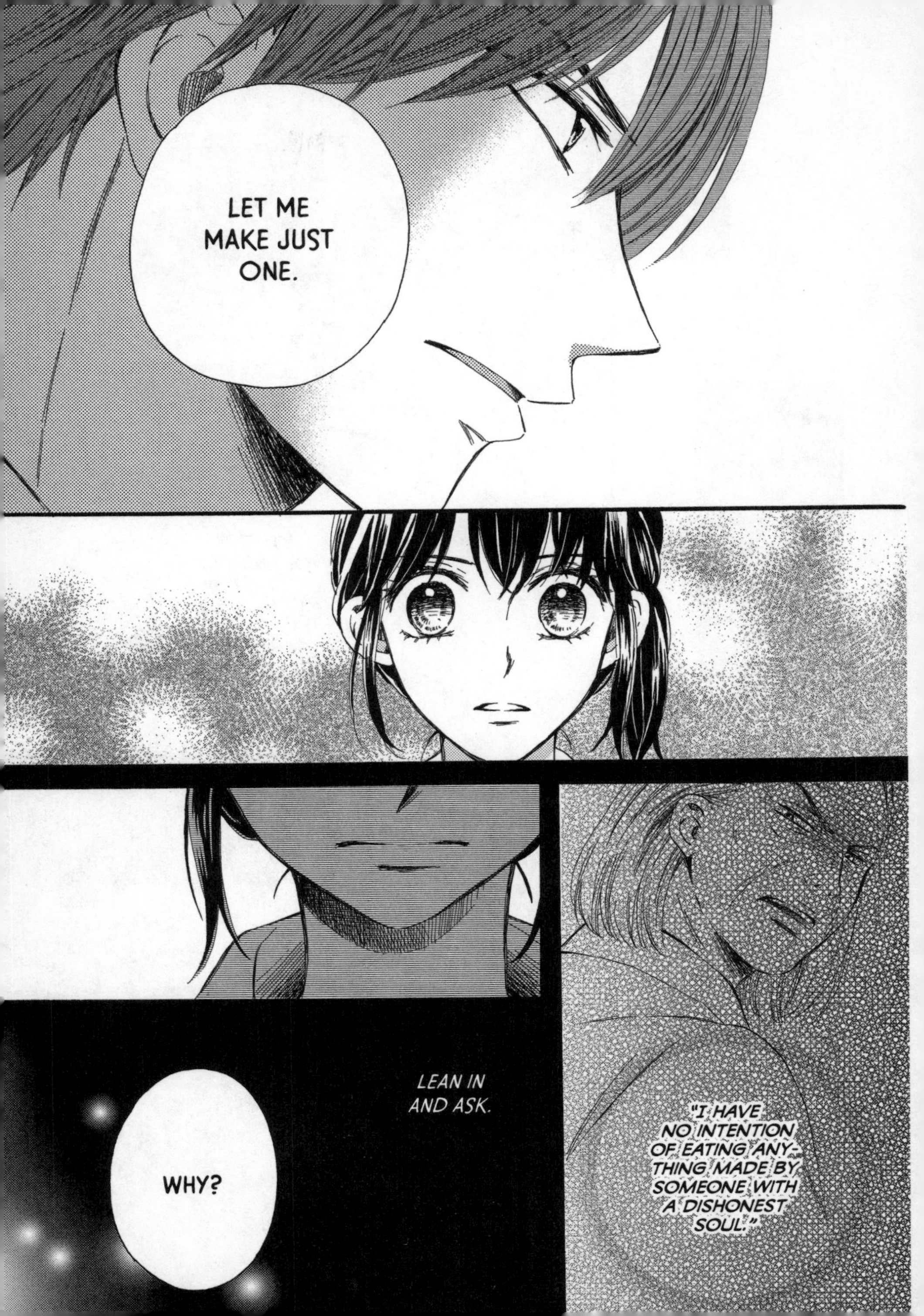
LET ME MAKE JUST ONE.
"I HAVE NO INTENTION OF EATING ANYTHING MADE BY SOMEONE WITH A DISHONEST SOUL."
LEAN IN AND ASK.
WHY?

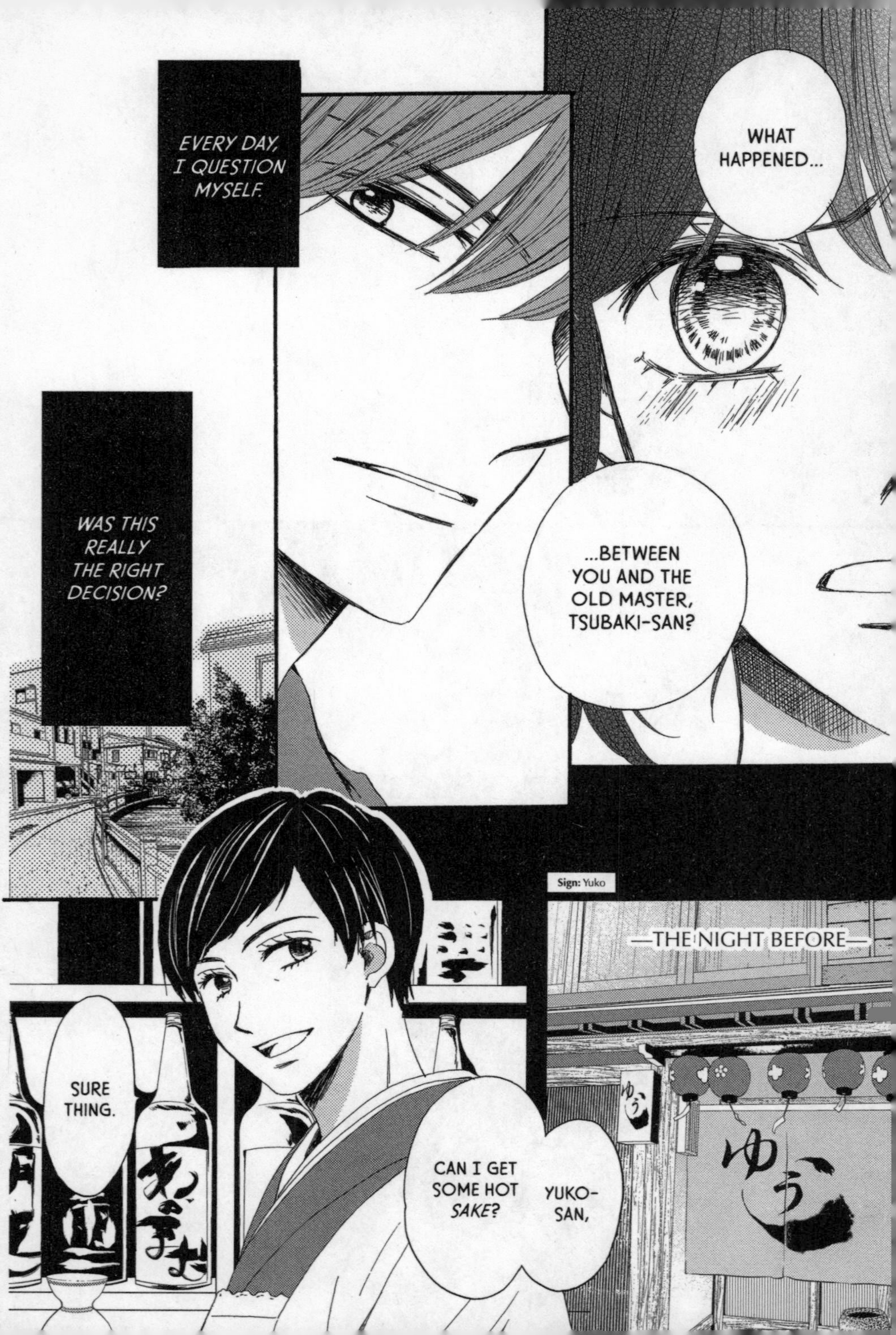
WHAT HAPPENED...
...BETWEEN YOU AND THE OLD MASTER, TSUBAKI-SAN?
EVERY DAY, I QUESTION MYSELF.
WAS THIS REALLY THE RIGHT DECISION?
Sign: Yuko
—THE NIGHT BEFORE—
YUKO-SAN,
CAN I GET SOME HOT *SAKE?*
SURE THING.

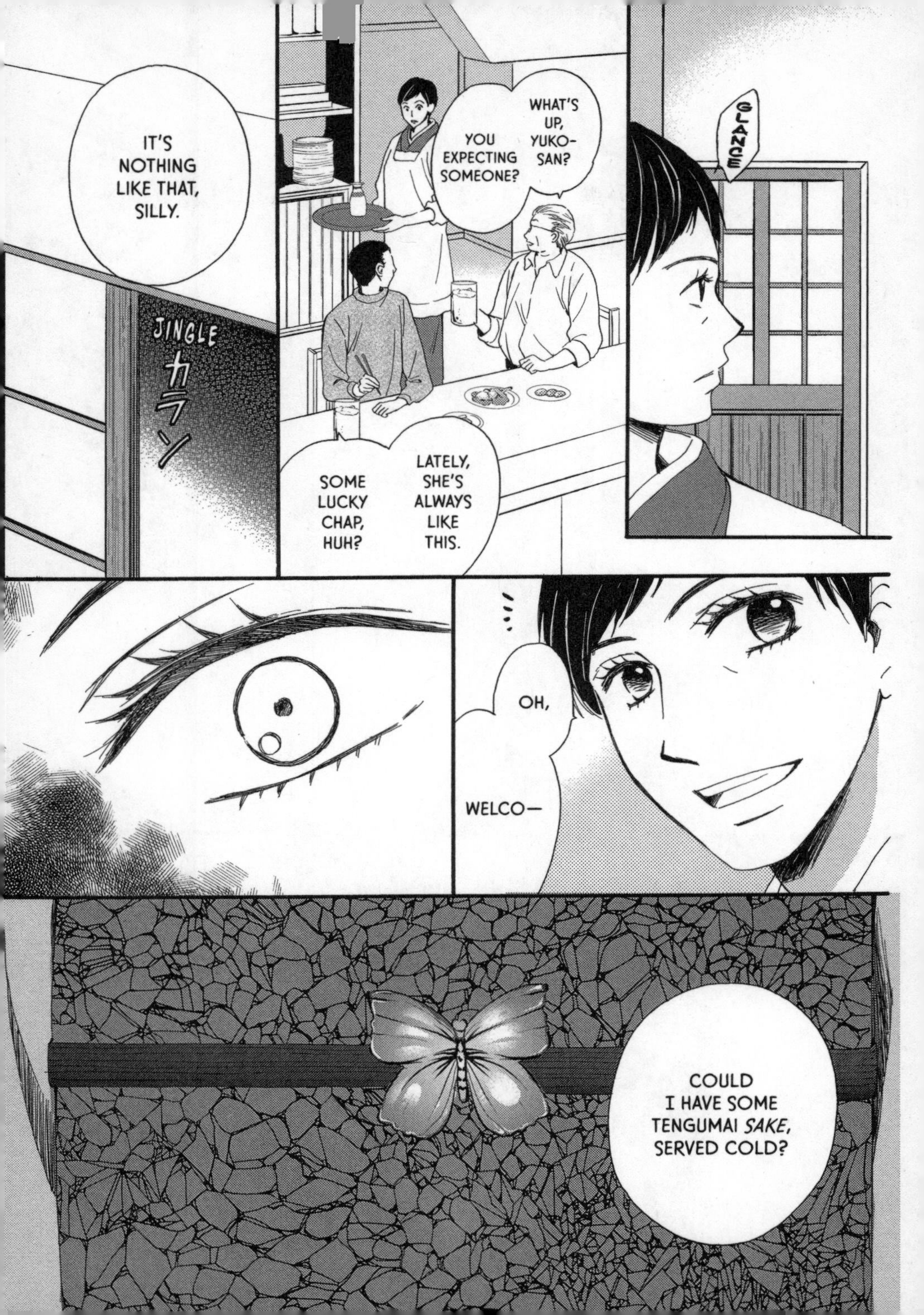
GLANCE
WHAT'S UP, YUKO-SAN?
YOU EXPECTING SOMEONE?
LATELY, SHE'S ALWAYS LIKE THIS.
SOME LUCKY CHAP, HUH?
IT'S NOTHING LIKE THAT, SILLY.
JINGLE
カラン
...
OH,
WELCO—
COULD I HAVE SOME TENGUMAI *SAKE*, SERVED COLD?

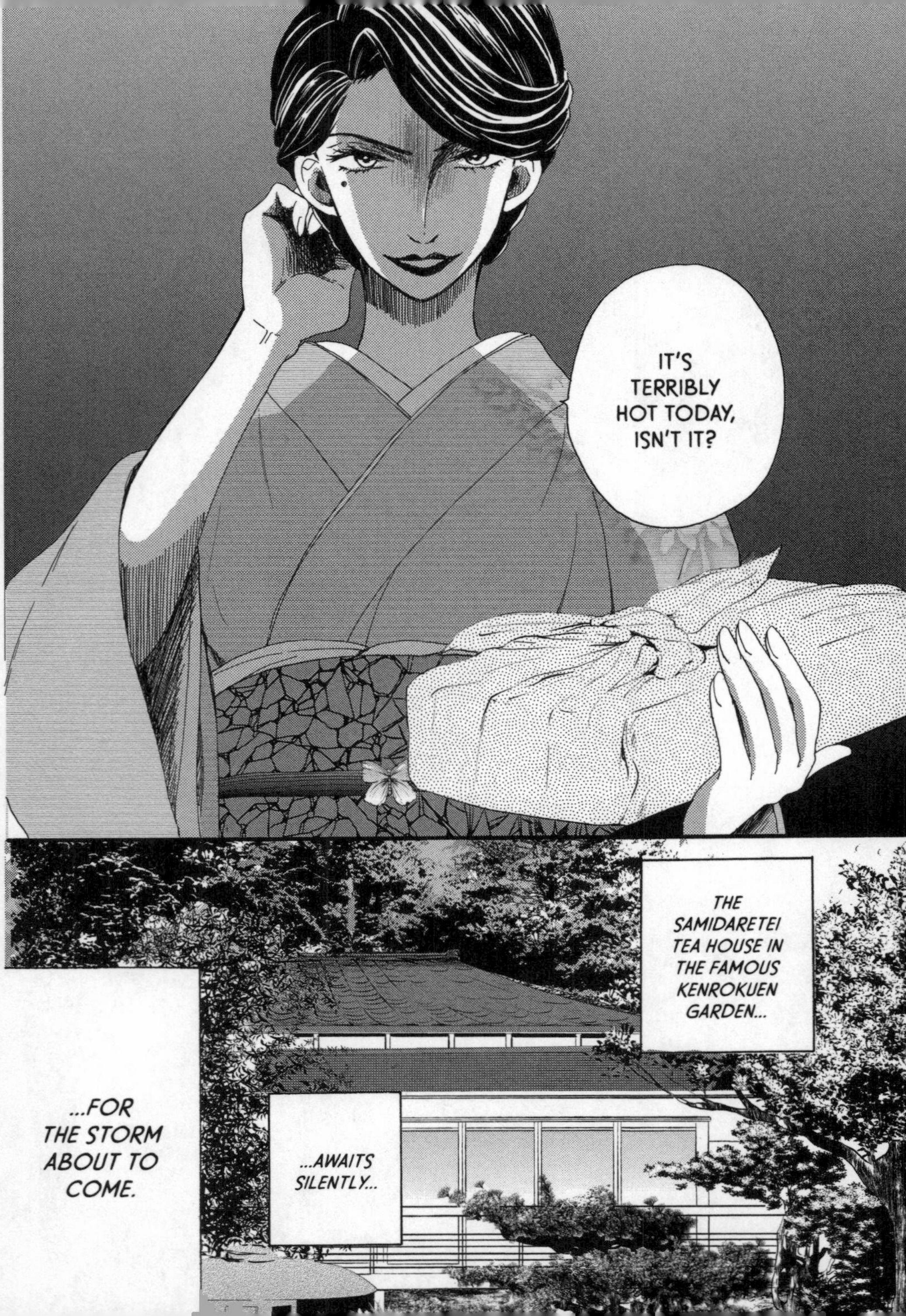
IT'S TERRIBLY HOT TODAY, ISN'T IT?
THE SAMIDARETEI TEA HOUSE IN THE FAMOUS KENROKUEN GARDEN...
...AWAITS SILENTLY...
...FOR THE STORM ABOUT TO COME.

Something's
Wrong
With Us

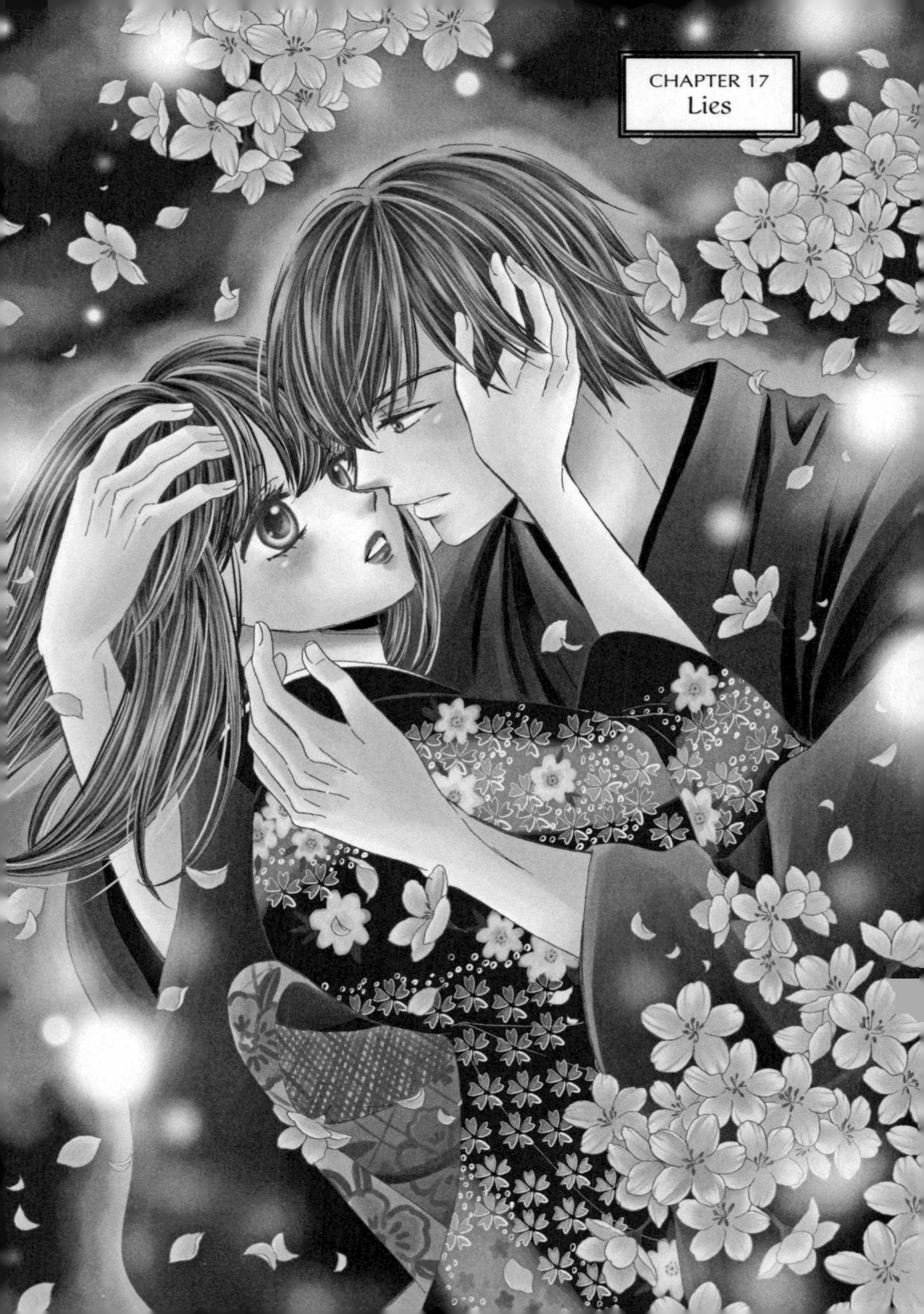
CHAPTER 17
Lies

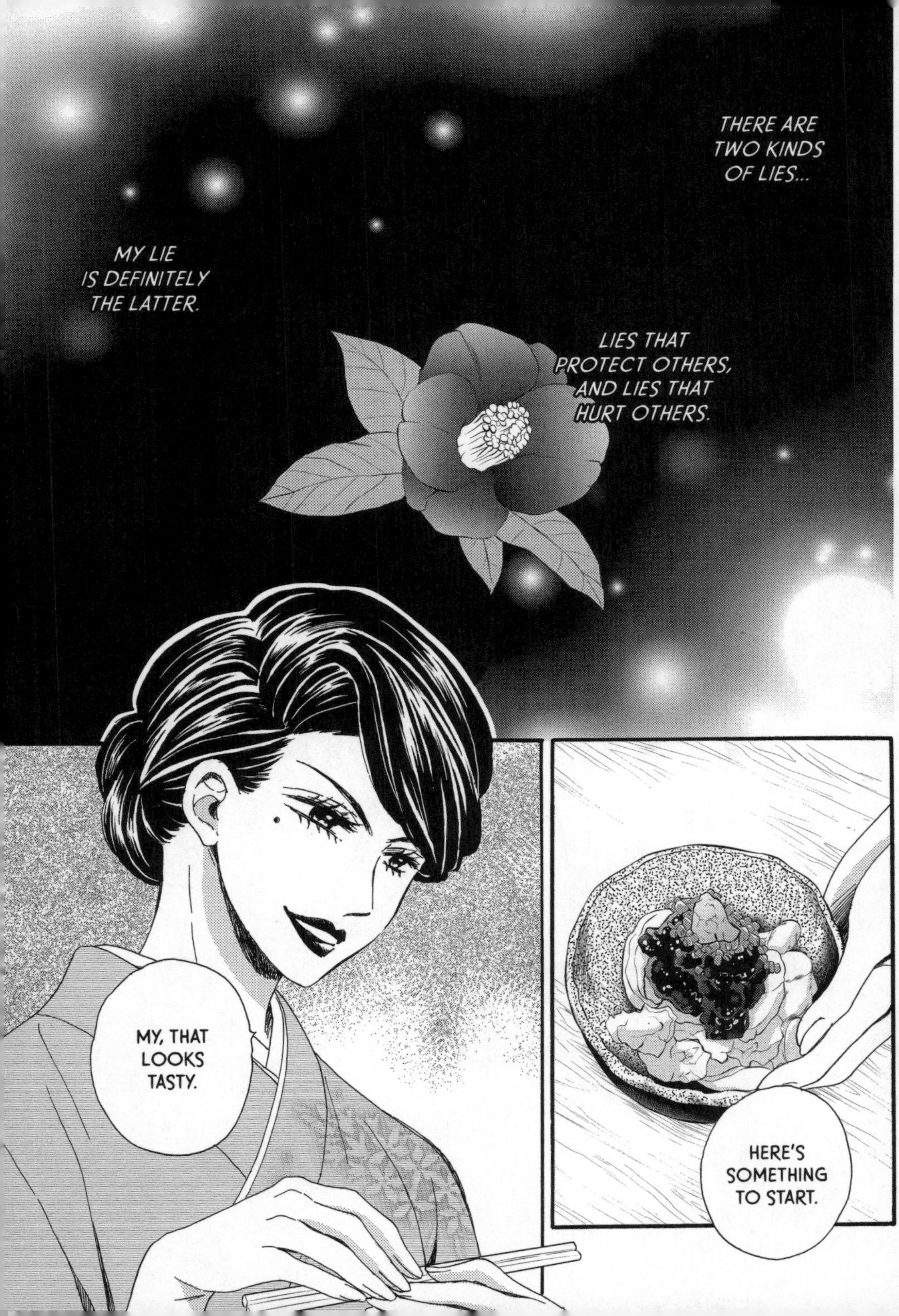
THERE ARE TWO KINDS OF LIES...
LIES THAT PROTECT OTHERS, AND LIES THAT HURT OTHERS.
MY LIE IS DEFINITELY THE LATTER.
HERE'S SOMETHING TO START.
MY, THAT LOOKS TASTY.

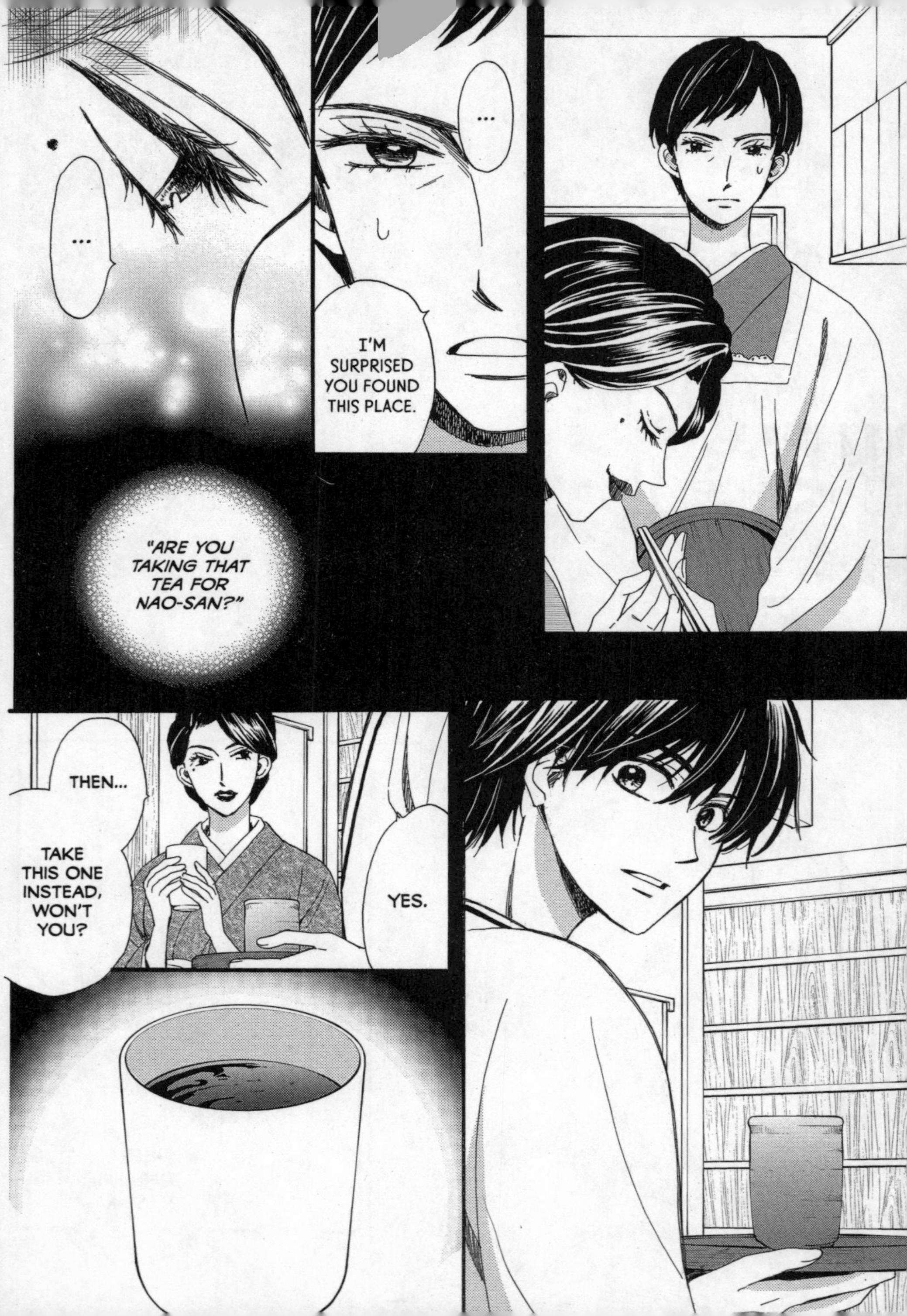
...
I'M SURPRISED YOU FOUND THIS PLACE.
...
"ARE YOU TAKING THAT TEA FOR NAO-SAN?"
YES.
THEN...
TAKE THIS ONE INSTEAD, WON'T YOU?

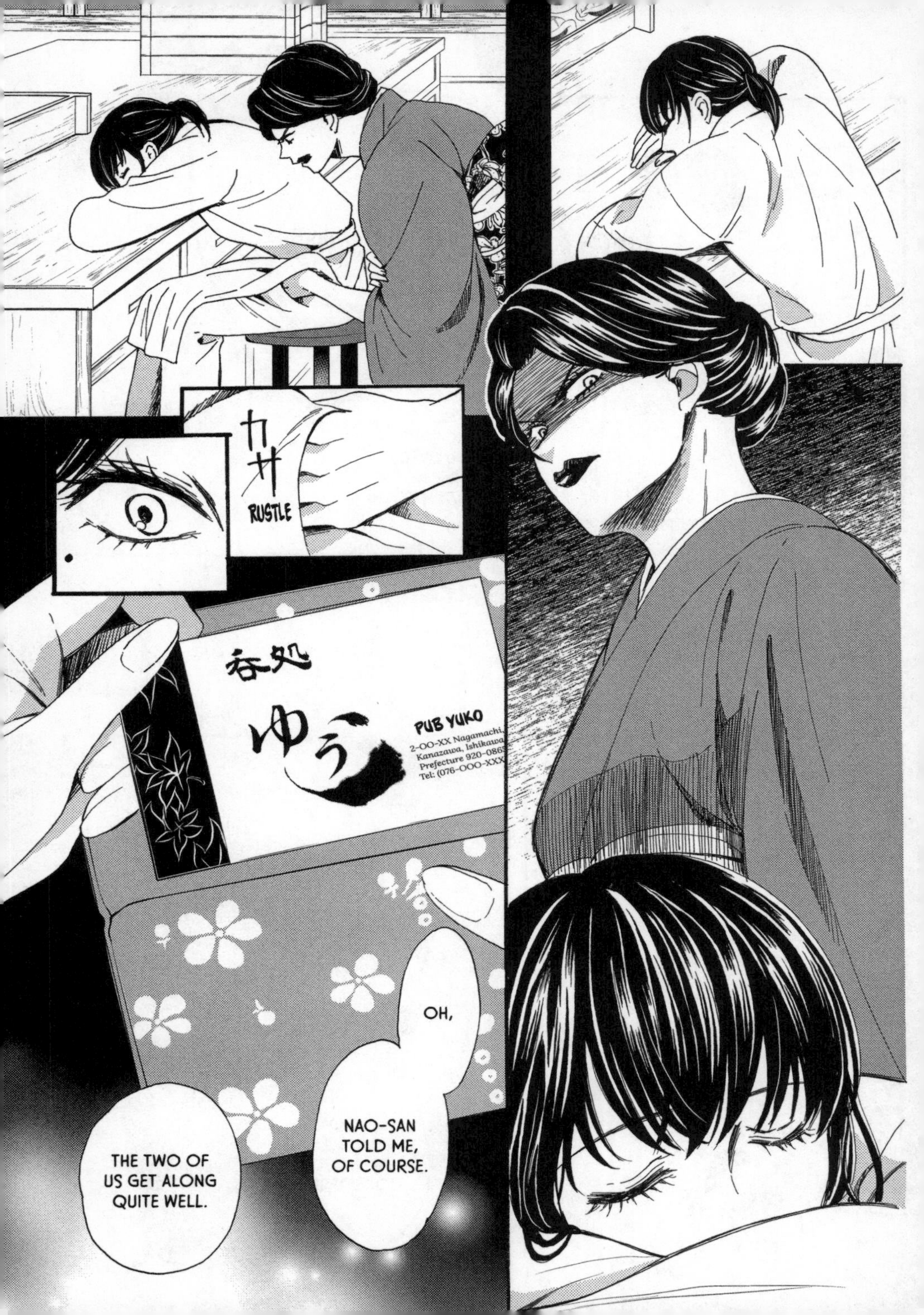

カサ
RUSTLE
呑処
ゆう
PUB YUKO
2-OO-XX Nagamachi,
Kanazawa, Ishikawa
Prefecture 920-086
Tel: (076-OOO-XXX
OH,
NAO-SAN TOLD ME, OF COURSE.
THE TWO OF US GET ALONG QUITE WELL.

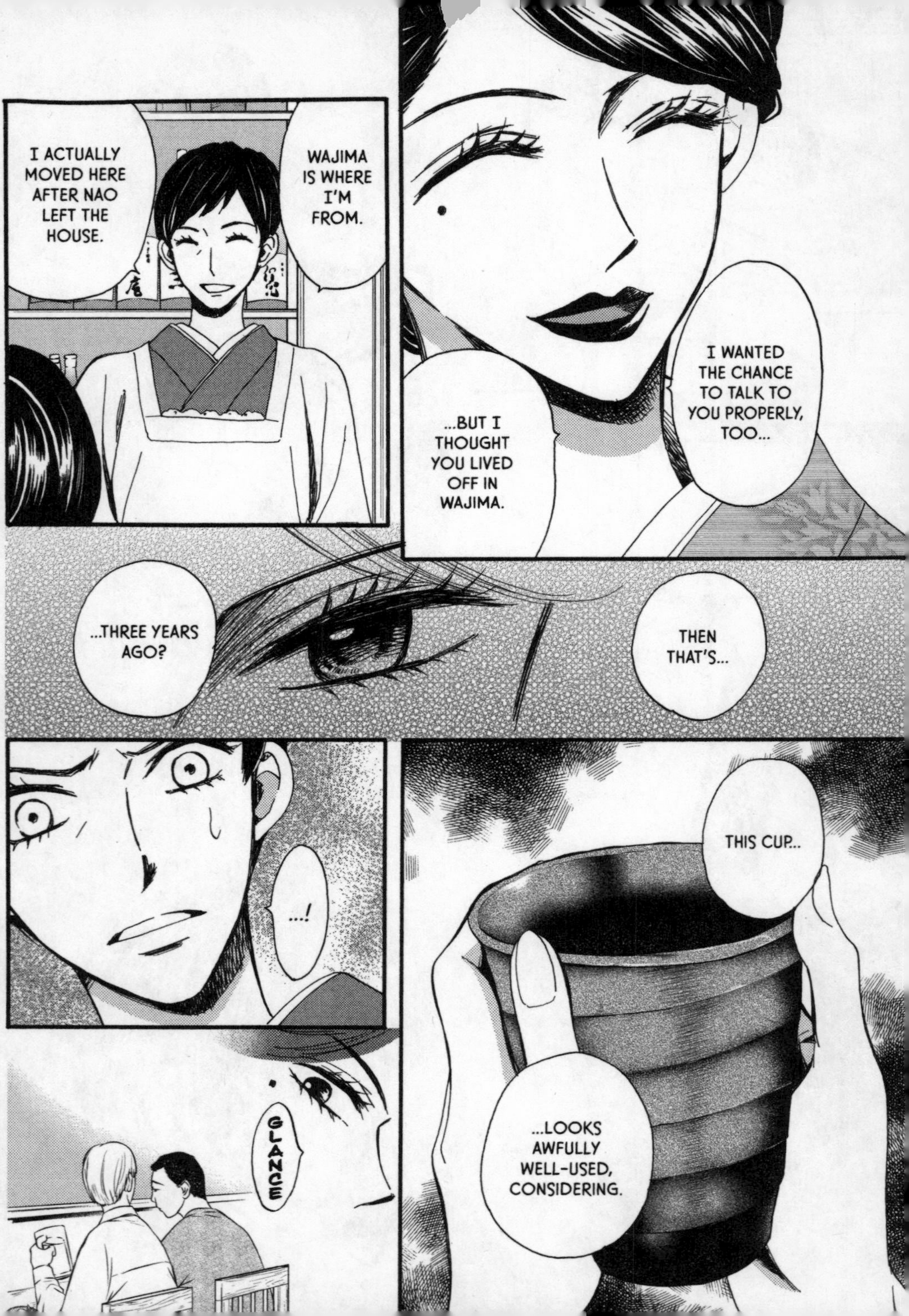
I WANTED THE CHANCE TO TALK TO YOU PROPERLY, TOO...
...BUT I THOUGHT YOU LIVED OFF IN WAJIMA.
WAJIMA IS WHERE I'M FROM.
I ACTUALLY MOVED HERE AFTER NAO LEFT THE HOUSE.
THEN THAT'S...
...THREE YEARS AGO?
THIS CUP...
...LOOKS AWFULLY WELL-USED, CONSIDERING.
...!
GLANCE

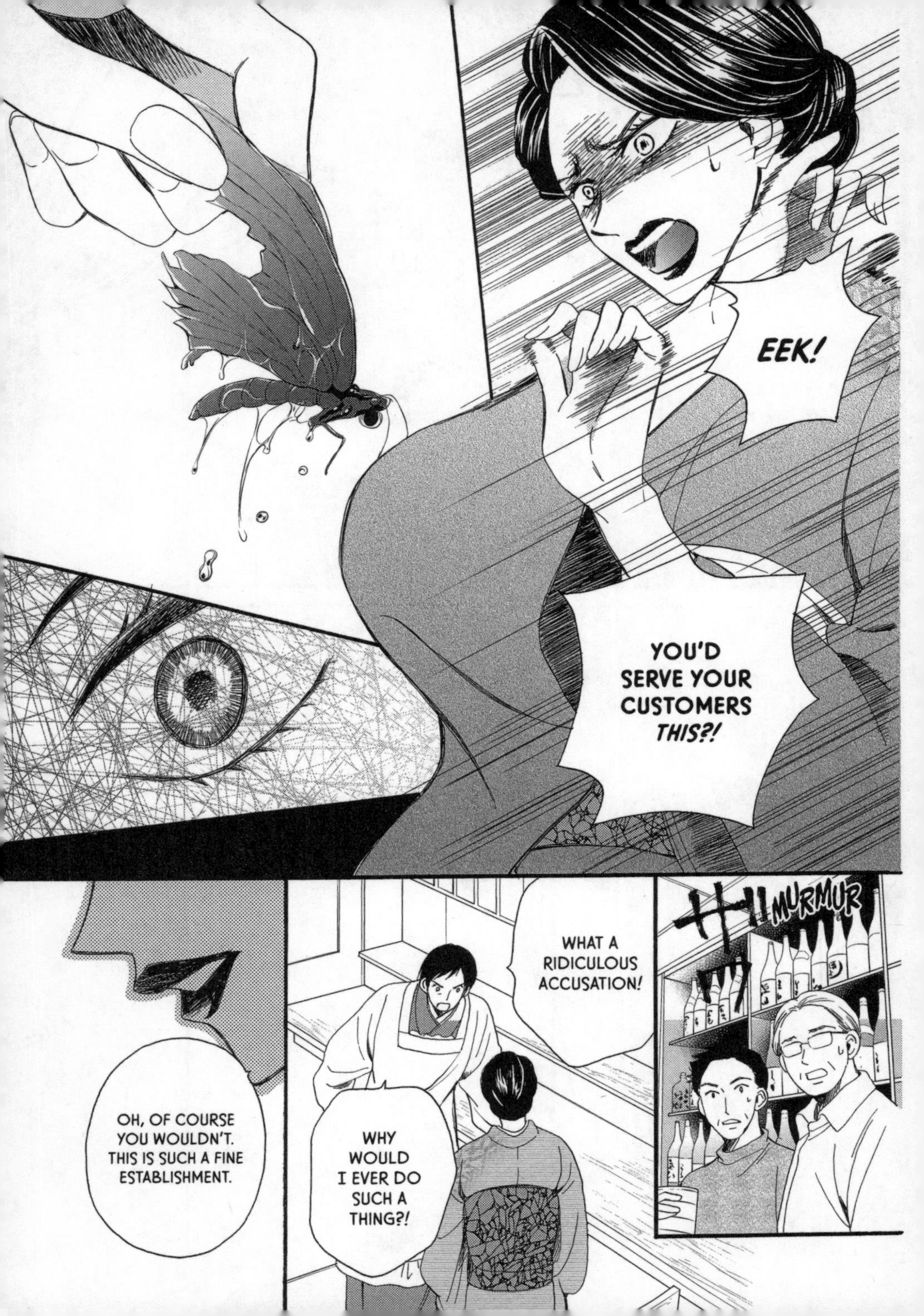
EEK!
YOU'D SERVE YOUR CUSTOMERS *THIS?!*
MURMUR
WHAT A RIDICULOUS ACCUSATION!
WHY WOULD I EVER DO SUCH A THING?!
OH, OF COURSE YOU WOULDN'T. THIS IS SUCH A FINE ESTABLISHMENT.

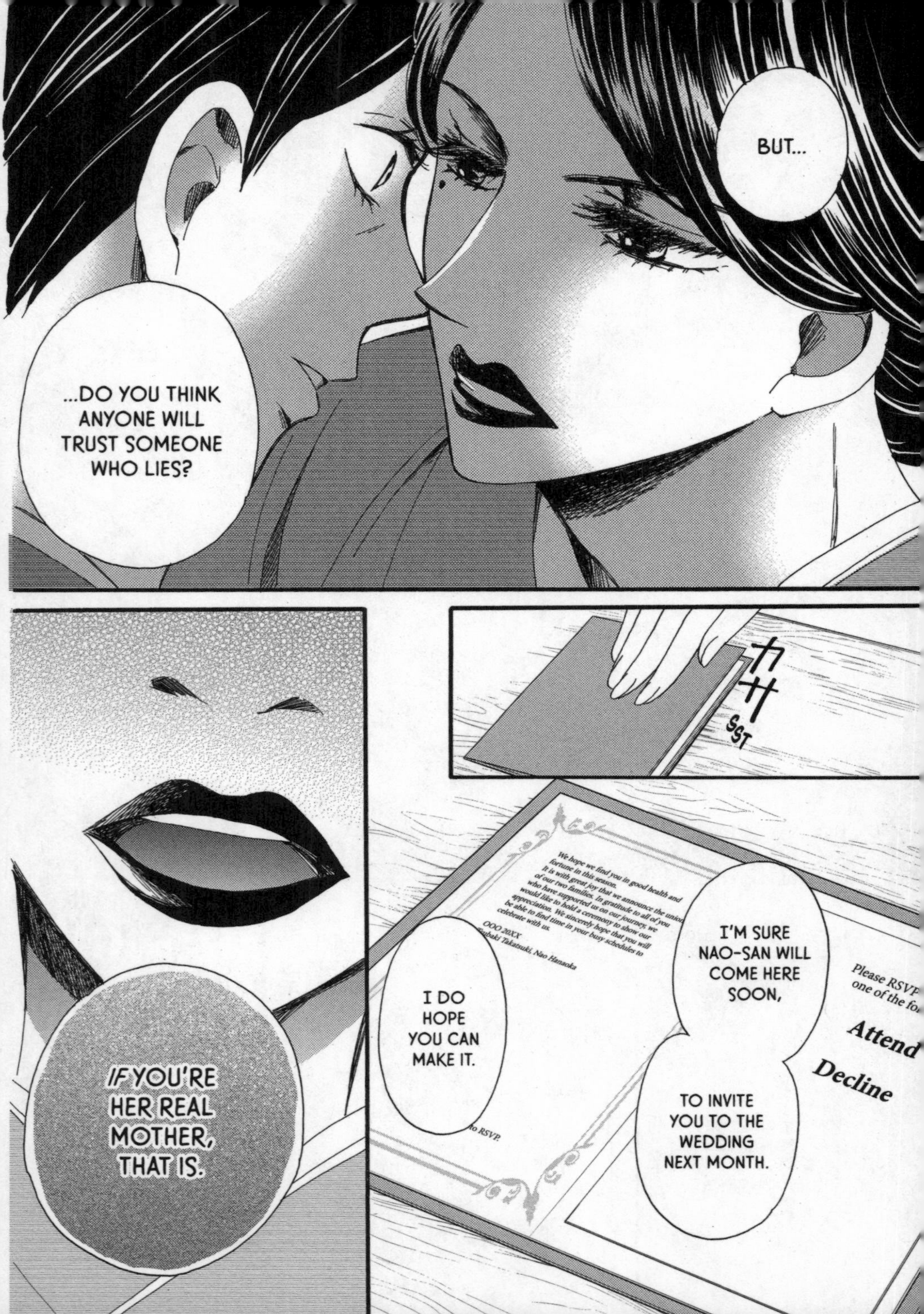
BUT...
...DO YOU THINK ANYONE WILL TRUST SOMEONE WHO LIES?
SST
We hope we find you in good health and fortune in this season. It is with great joy that we announce the union of our two families. In gratitude to all of you who have supported us on our journey, we would like to hold a ceremony to show our appreciation. We sincerely hope that you will be able to find time in your busy schedules to celebrate with us.
OOO 20XX
Attend
Decline
I'M SURE NAO-SAN WILL COME HERE SOON,
TO INVITE YOU TO THE WEDDING NEXT MONTH.
I DO HOPE YOU CAN MAKE IT.
IF YOU'RE HER REAL MOTHER, THAT IS.

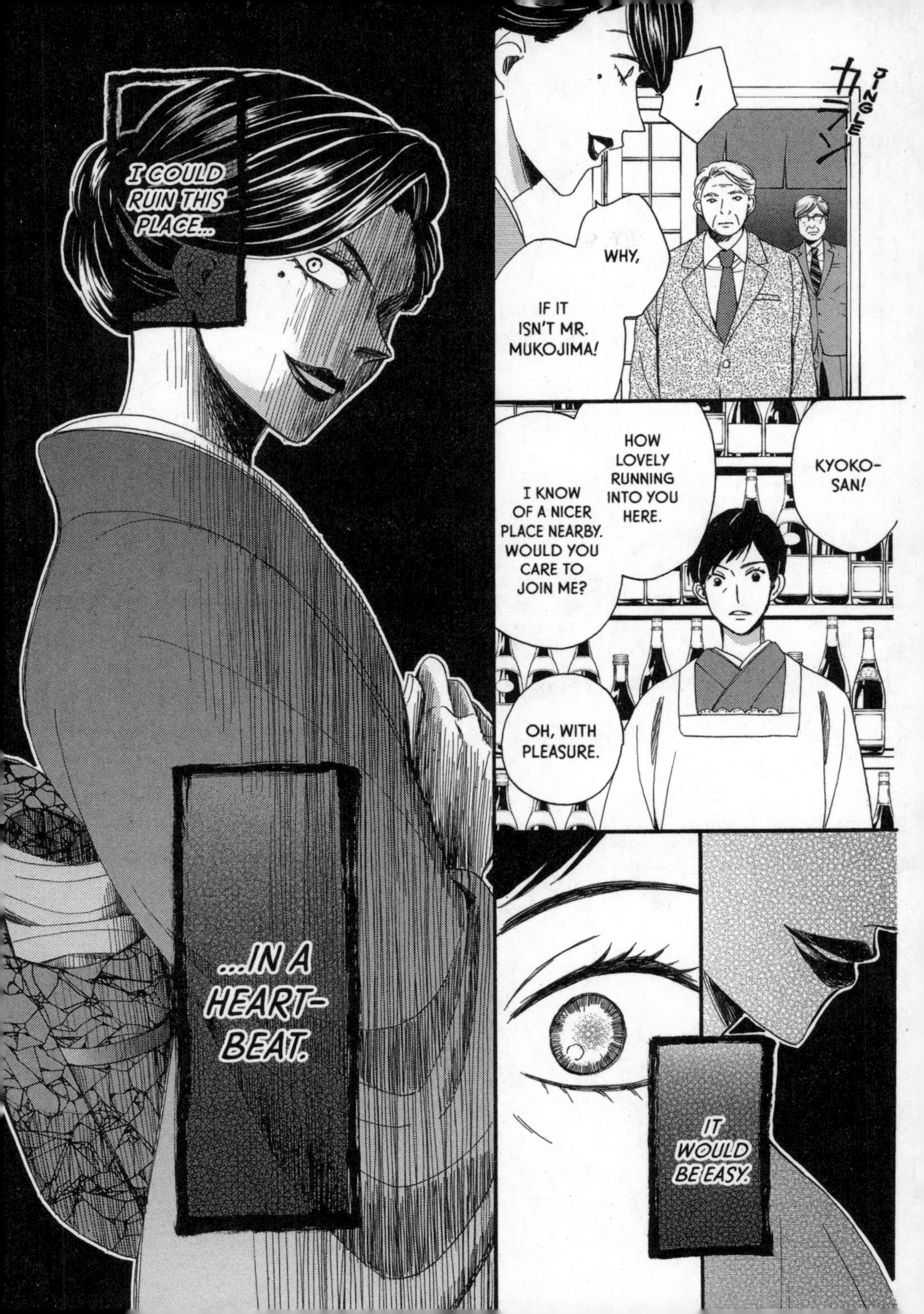
JINGLE
!
WHY,
IF IT ISN'T MR. MUKOJIMA!
KYOKO-SAN!
HOW LOVELY RUNNING INTO YOU HERE.
I KNOW OF A NICER PLACE NEARBY. WOULD YOU CARE TO JOIN ME?
OH, WITH PLEASURE.
IT WOULD BE EASY.
I COULD RUIN THIS PLACE...
...IN A HEART-BEAT.

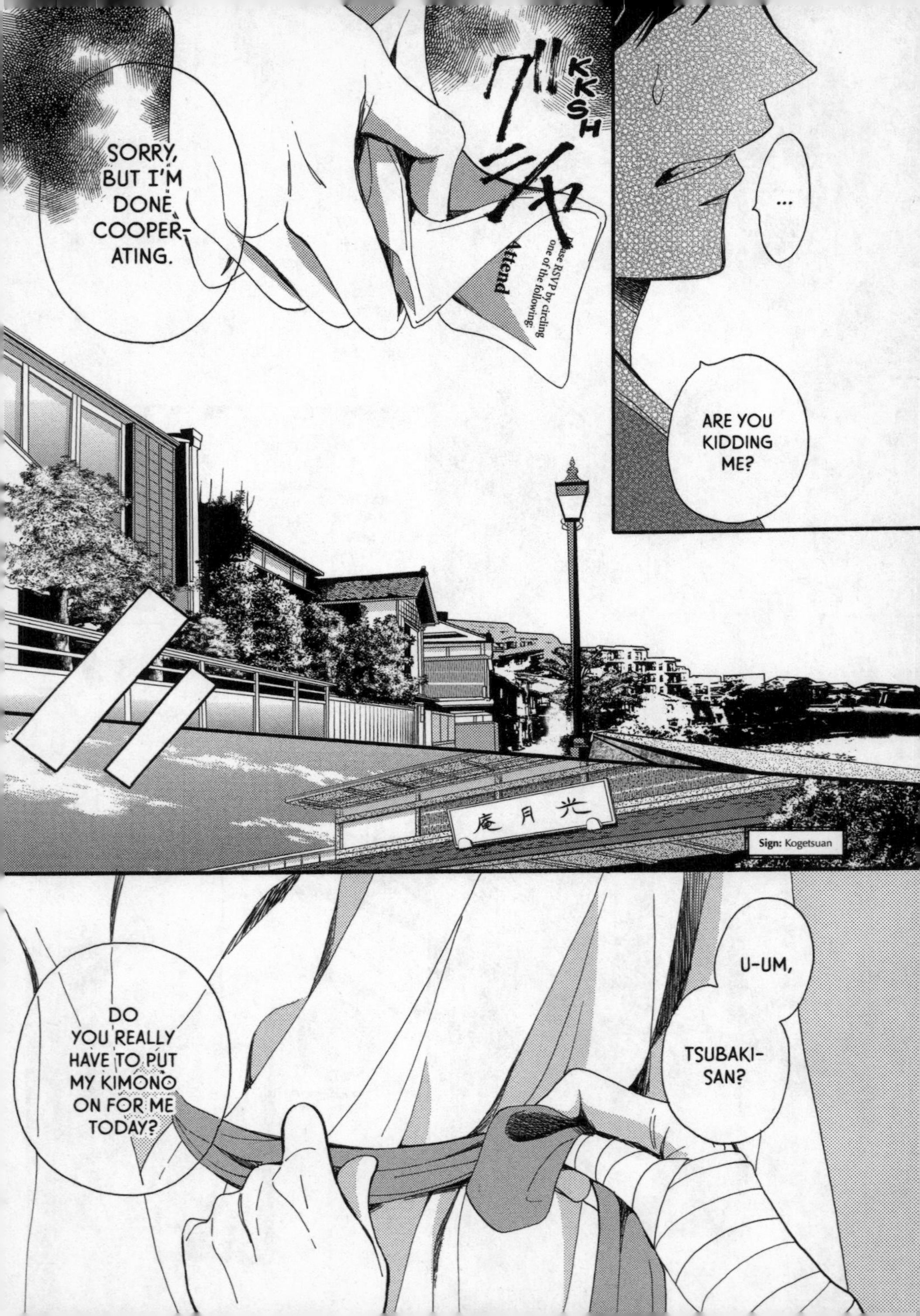
...
ARE YOU KIDDING ME?
KKSH
SORRY, BUT I'M DONE COOPERATING.
Attend
ase RSVP by circling one of the following:
Sign: Kogetsuan
U-UM,
TSUBAKI-SAN?
DO YOU REALLY HAVE TO PUT MY KIMONO ON FOR ME TODAY?

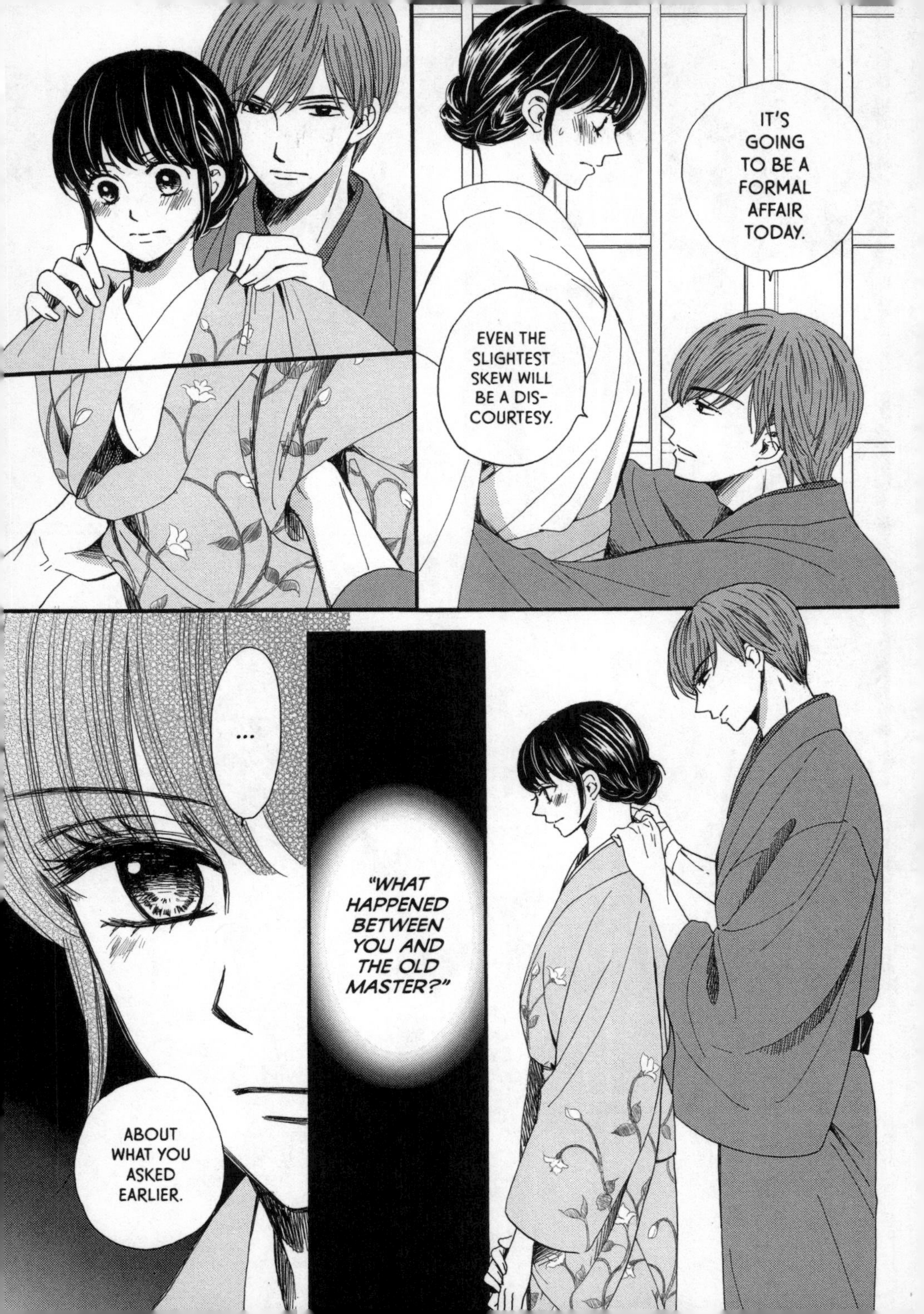
IT'S GOING TO BE A FORMAL AFFAIR TODAY.
EVEN THE SLIGHTEST SKEW WILL BE A DIS-COURTESY.
"WHAT HAPPENED BETWEEN YOU AND THE OLD MASTER?"
...
ABOUT WHAT YOU ASKED EARLIER.

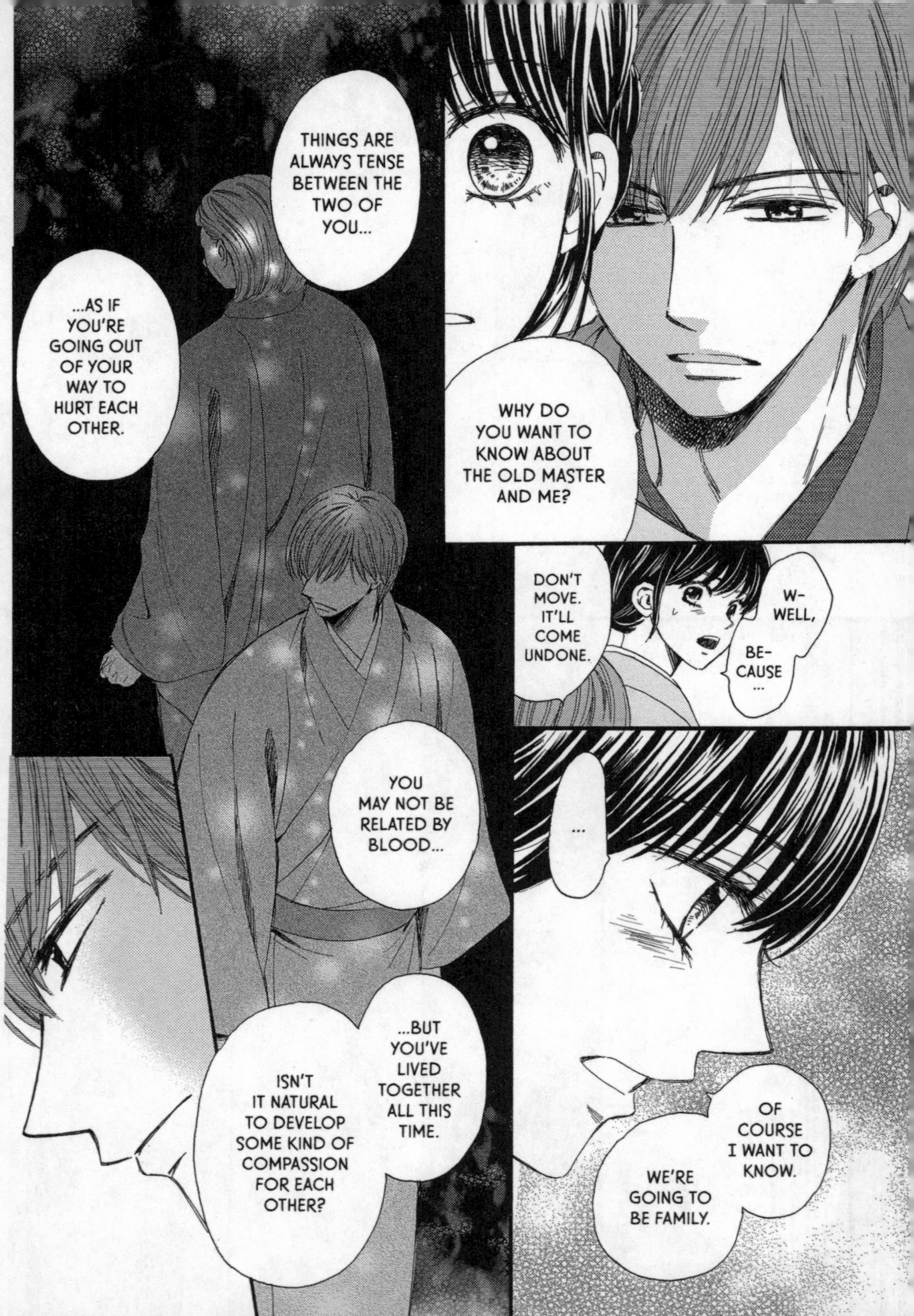
THINGS ARE ALWAYS TENSE BETWEEN THE TWO OF YOU...
...AS IF YOU'RE GOING OUT OF YOUR WAY TO HURT EACH OTHER.
WHY DO YOU WANT TO KNOW ABOUT THE OLD MASTER AND ME?
W-WELL, BE-CAUSE...
DON'T MOVE. IT'LL COME UNDONE.
...
OF COURSE I WANT TO KNOW.
WE'RE GOING TO BE FAMILY.
YOU MAY NOT BE RELATED BY BLOOD...
...BUT YOU'VE LIVED TOGETHER ALL THIS TIME.
ISN'T IT NATURAL TO DEVELOP SOME KIND OF COMPASSION FOR EACH OTHER?

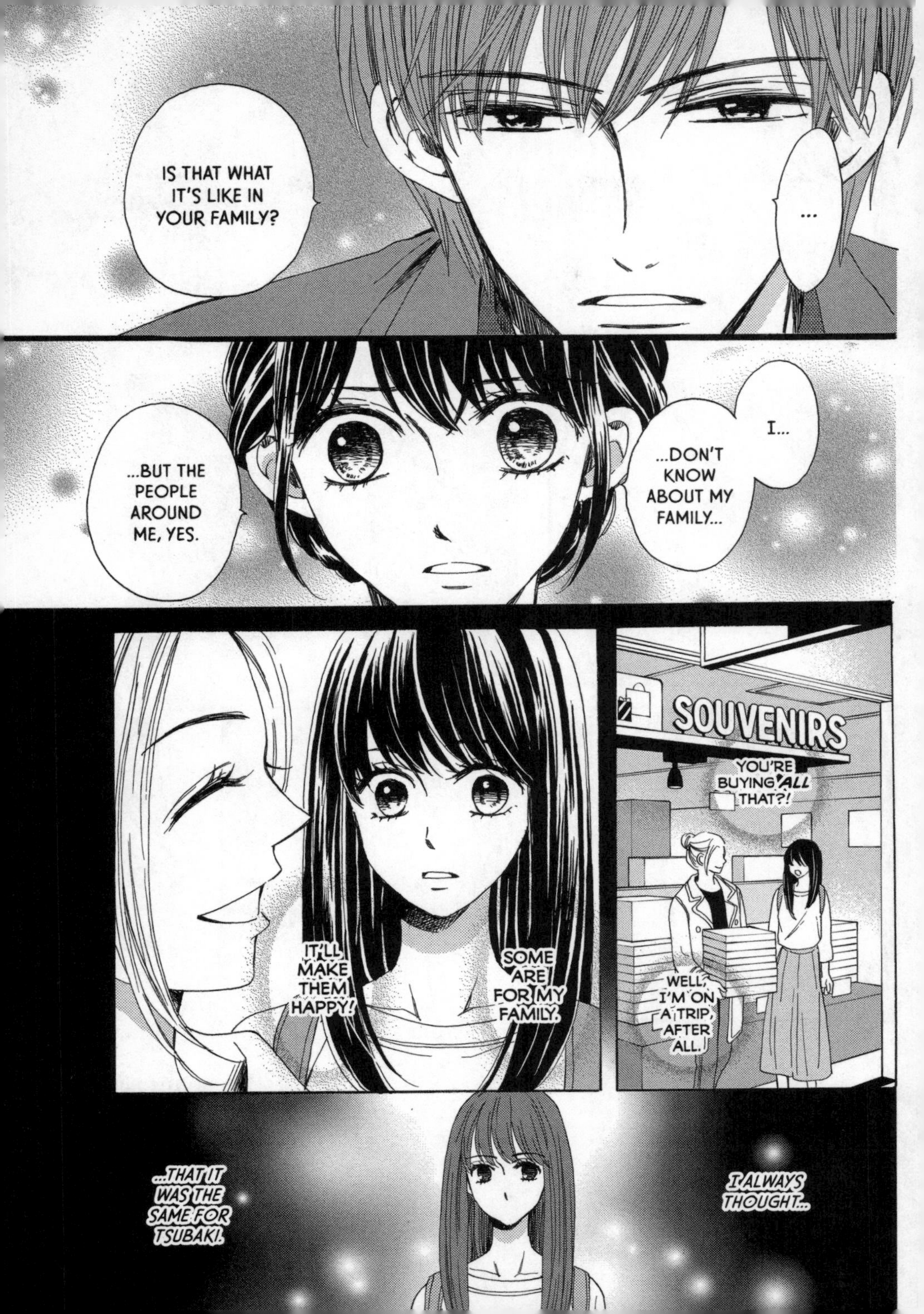
...
IS THAT WHAT IT'S LIKE IN YOUR FAMILY?
I...
...DON'T KNOW ABOUT MY FAMILY...
...BUT THE PEOPLE AROUND ME, YES.
SOUVENIRS
YOU'RE BUYING ALL THAT?!
WELL, I'M ON A TRIP, AFTER ALL.
SOME ARE FOR MY FAMILY.
IT'LL MAKE THEM HAPPY!
I ALWAYS THOUGHT...
...THAT IT WAS THE SAME FOR TSUBAKI.

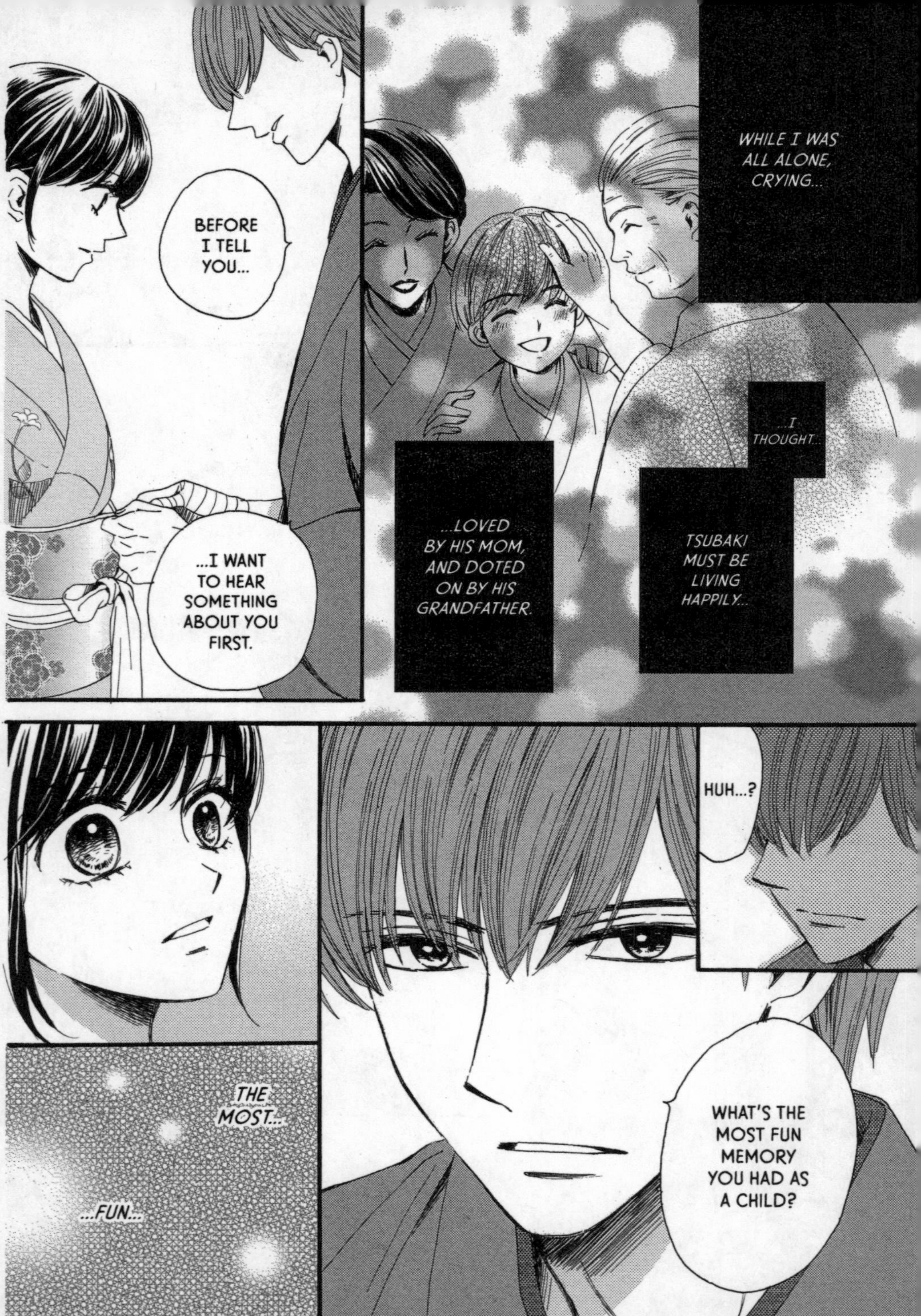
WHILE I WAS ALL ALONE, CRYING...
...I THOUGHT...
TSUBAKI MUST BE LIVING HAPPILY...
...LOVED BY HIS MOM, AND DOTED ON BY HIS GRANDFATHER.
BEFORE I TELL YOU...
...I WANT TO HEAR SOMETHING ABOUT YOU FIRST.
HUH...?
WHAT'S THE MOST FUN MEMORY YOU HAD AS A CHILD?
THE MOST...
...FUN...

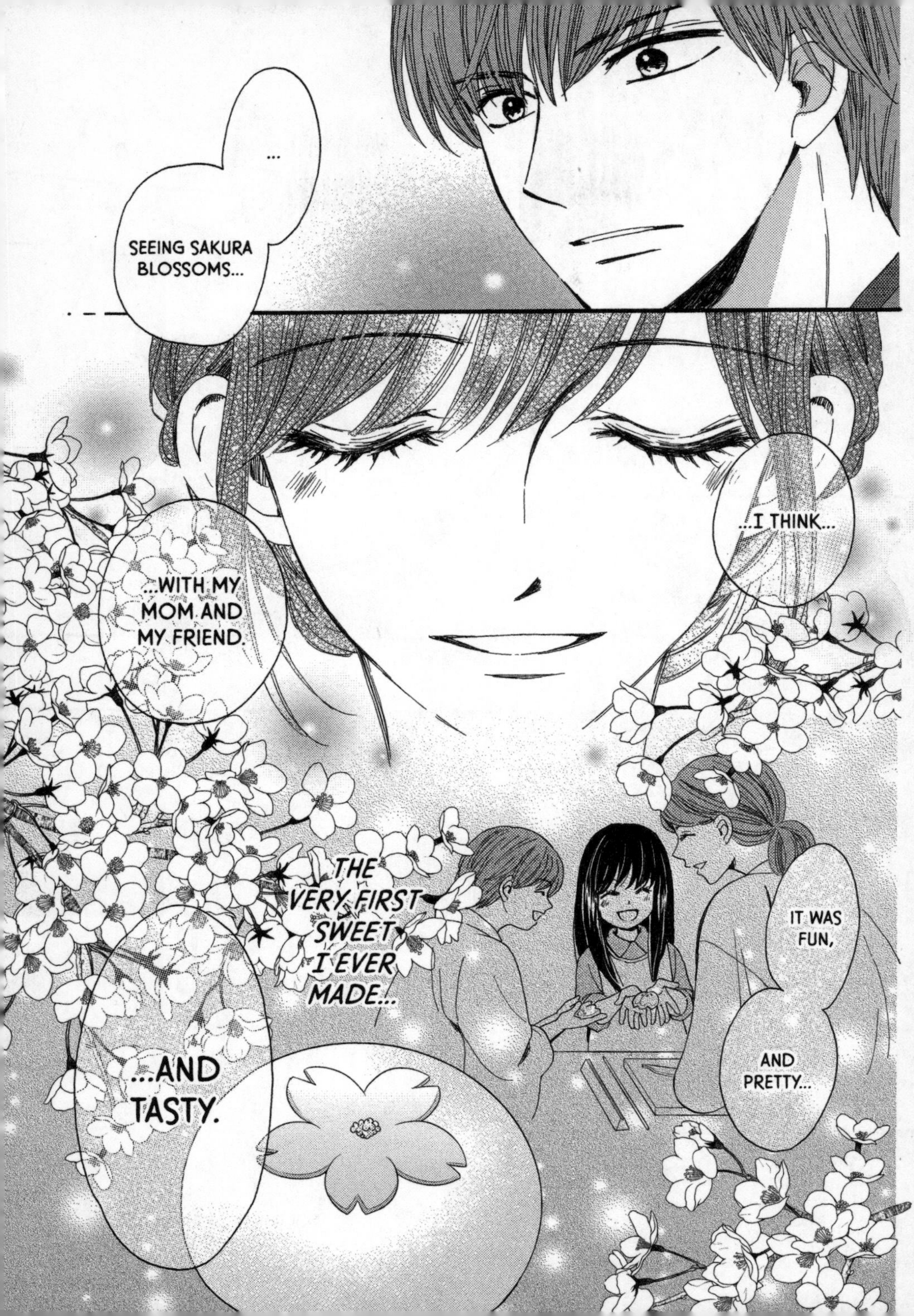
...
SEEING SAKURA BLOSSOMS...
...I THINK...
...WITH MY MOM AND MY FRIEND.
IT WAS FUN,
AND PRETTY...
THE VERY FIRST SWEET I EVER MADE...
...AND TASTY.

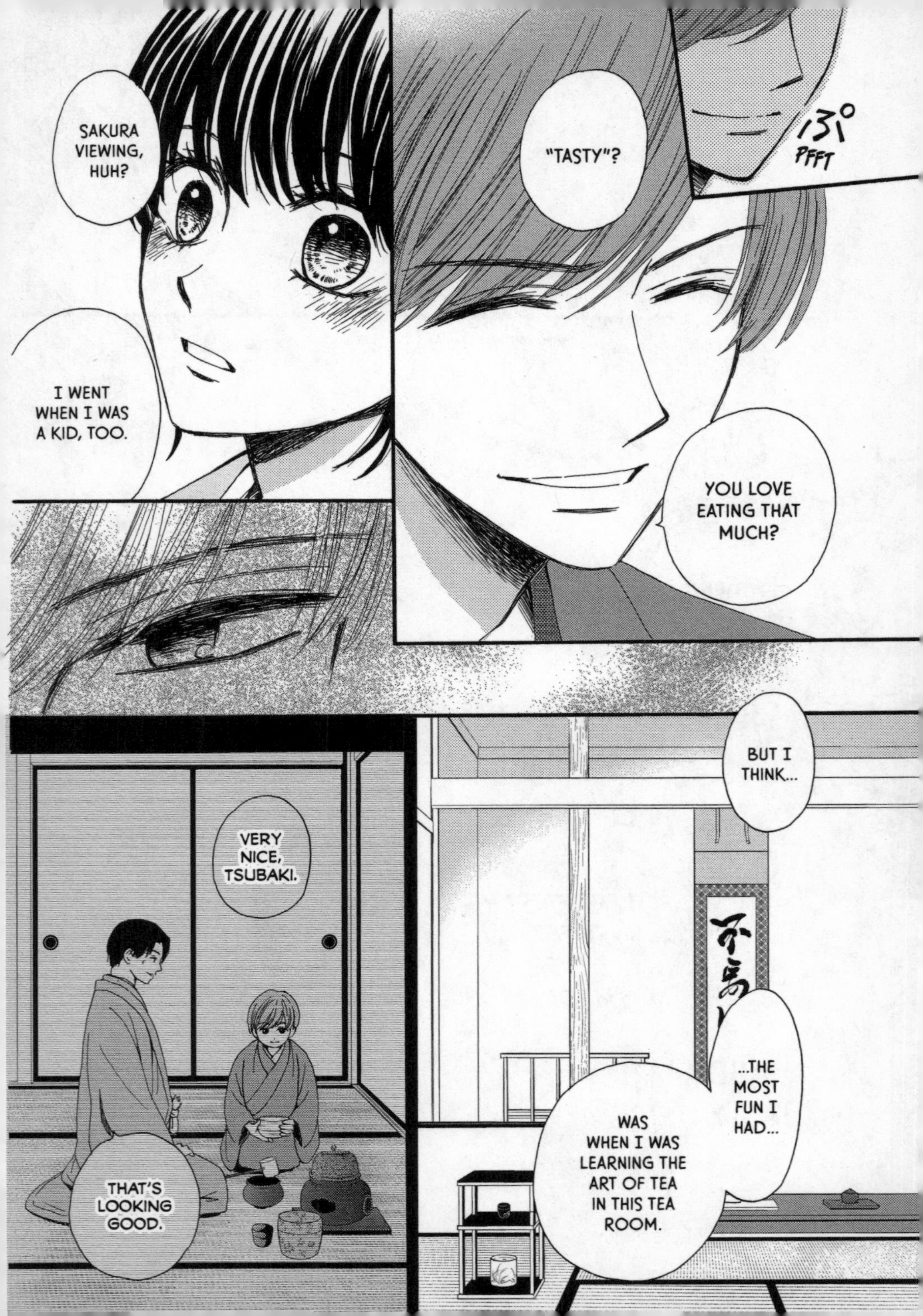
"TASTY"?
ぷ
PFFT
YOU LOVE EATING THAT MUCH?
SAKURA VIEWING, HUH?
I WENT WHEN I WAS A KID, TOO.
BUT I THINK...
...THE MOST FUN I HAD...
WAS WHEN I WAS LEARNING THE ART OF TEA IN THIS TEA ROOM.
VERY NICE, TSUBAKI.
THAT'S LOOKING GOOD.

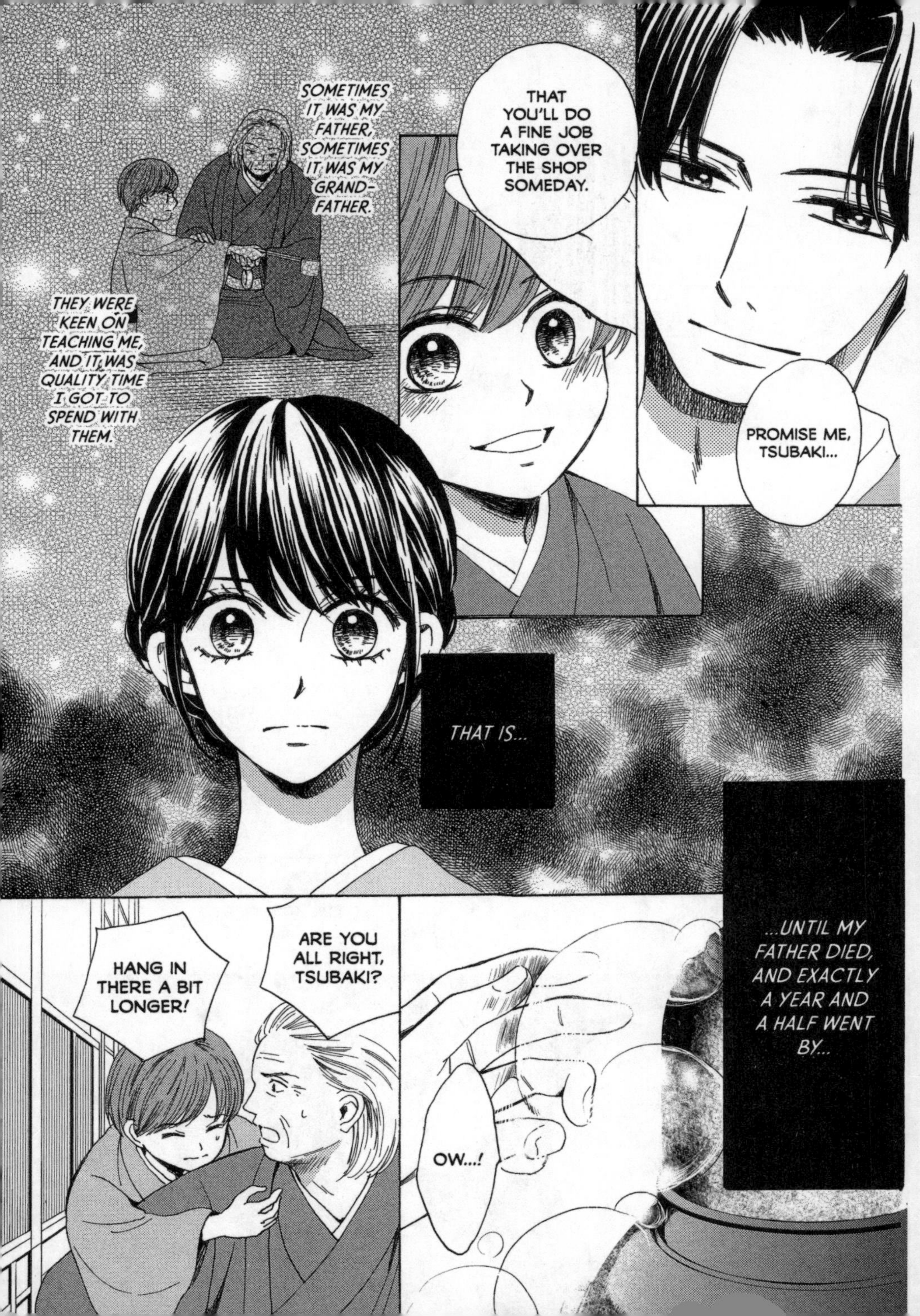
PROMISE ME, TSUBAKI...
THAT YOU'LL DO A FINE JOB TAKING OVER THE SHOP SOMEDAY.
SOMETIMES IT WAS MY FATHER, SOMETIMES IT WAS MY GRAND-FATHER.
THEY WERE KEEN ON TEACHING ME, AND IT WAS QUALITY TIME I GOT TO SPEND WITH THEM.
THAT IS...
...UNTIL MY FATHER DIED, AND EXACTLY A YEAR AND A HALF WENT BY...
OW...!
ARE YOU ALL RIGHT, TSUBAKI?
HANG IN THERE A BIT LONGER!

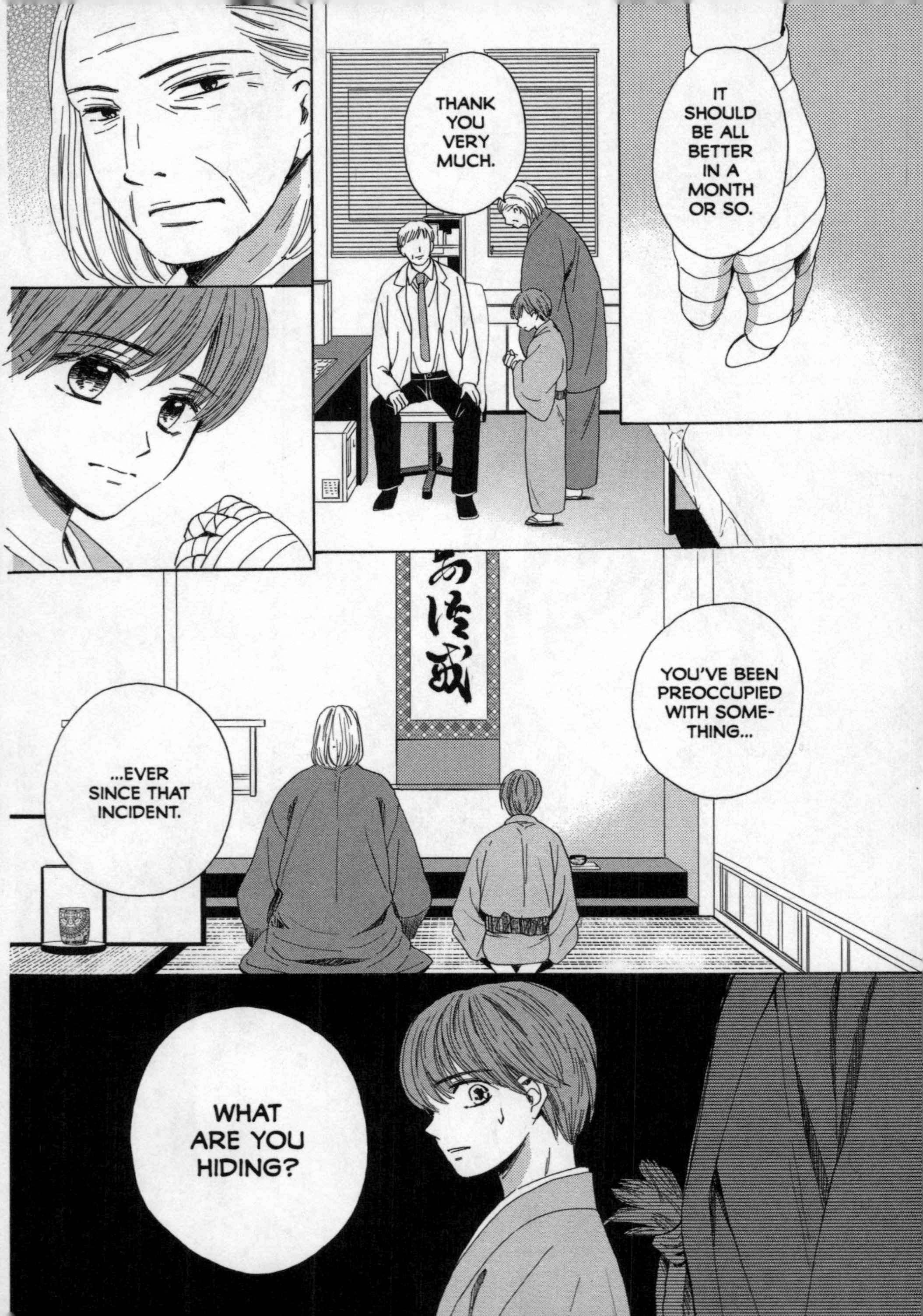
IT SHOULD BE ALL BETTER IN A MONTH OR SO.
THANK YOU VERY MUCH.
YOU'VE BEEN PREOCCUPIED WITH SOME-THING...
...EVER SINCE THAT INCIDENT.
WHAT ARE YOU HIDING?

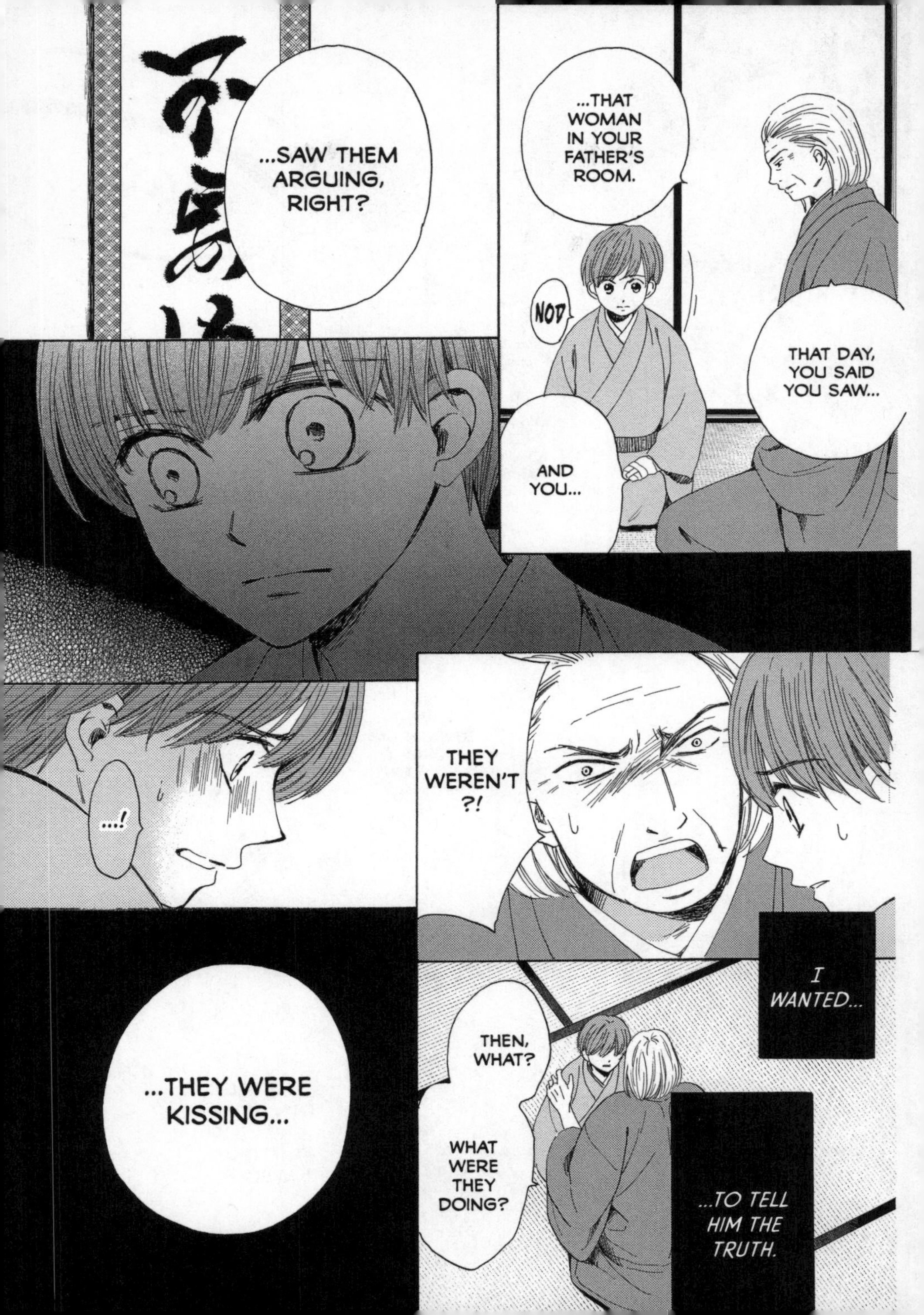
THAT DAY, YOU SAID YOU SAW...
...THAT WOMAN IN YOUR FATHER'S ROOM.
NOD
AND YOU...
...SAW THEM ARGUING, RIGHT?
THEY WEREN'T ?!
...!
I WANTED...
THEN, WHAT?
WHAT WERE THEY DOING?
...TO TELL HIM THE TRUTH.
...THEY WERE KISSING...

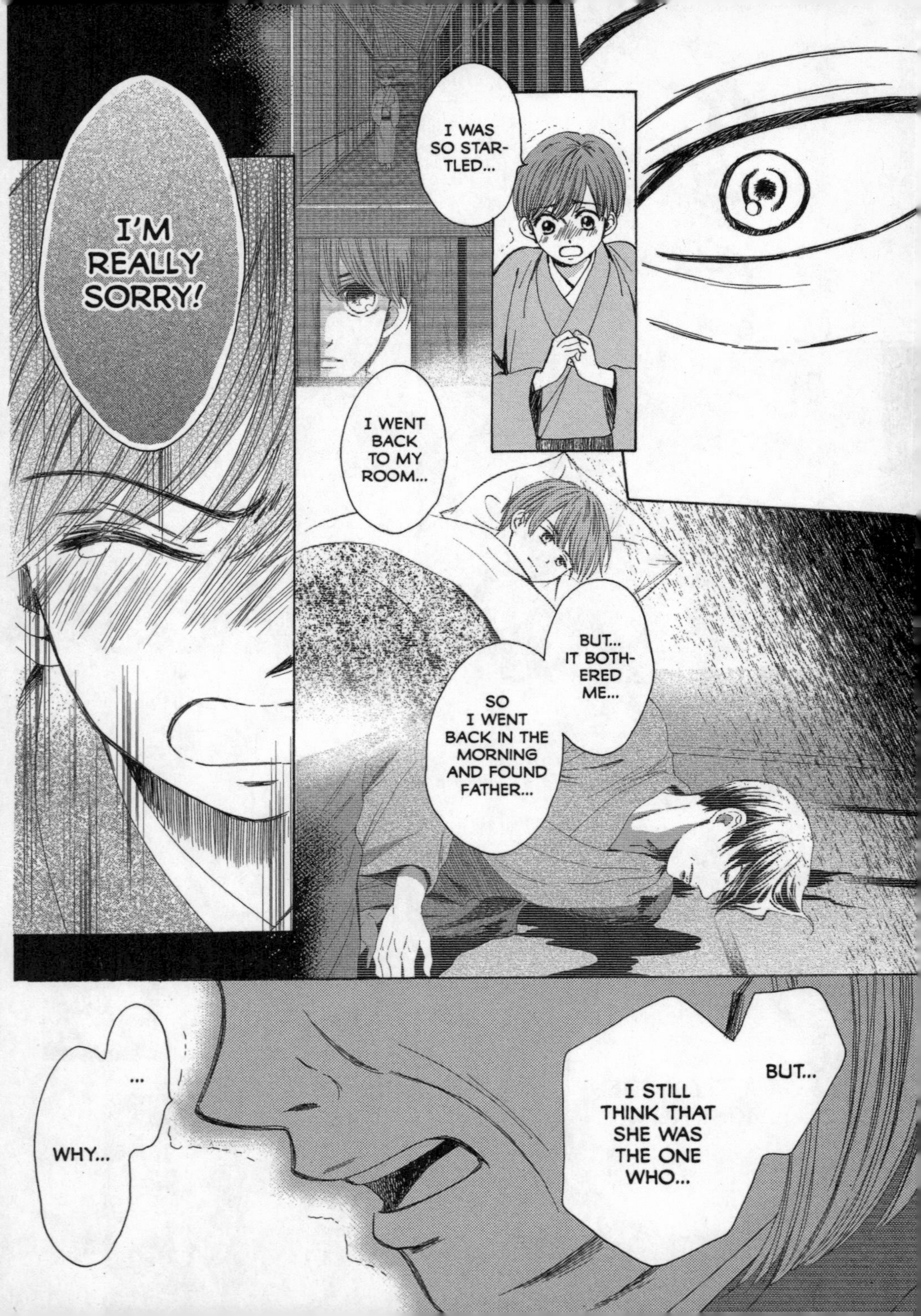
I WAS SO STAR-TLED...
I WENT BACK TO MY ROOM...
BUT... IT BOTH-ERED ME...
SO I WENT BACK IN THE MORNING AND FOUND FATHER...
I'M REALLY SORRY!
BUT...
I STILL THINK THAT SHE WAS THE ONE WHO...
...
WHY...

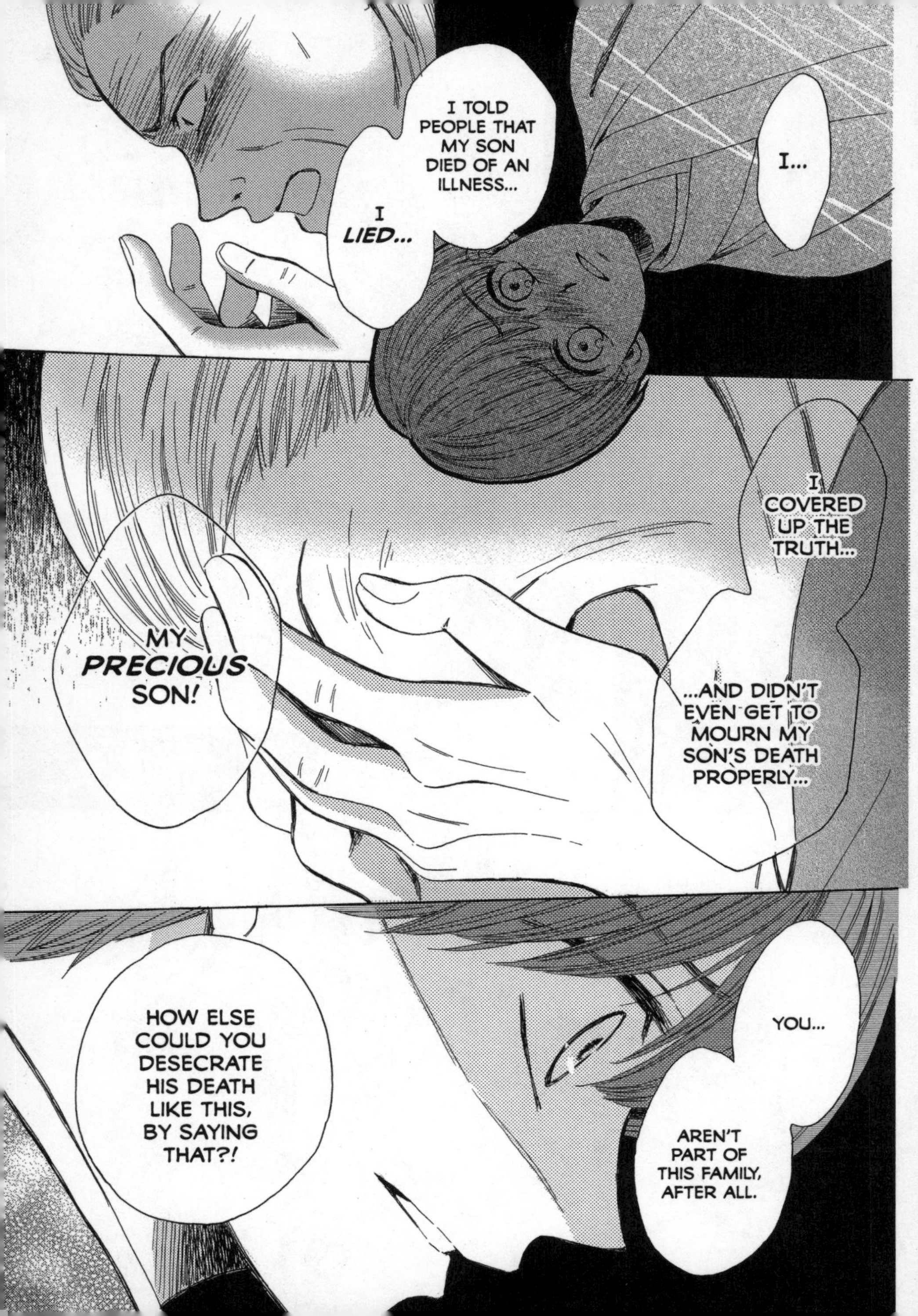
I...
I TOLD PEOPLE THAT MY SON DIED OF AN ILLNESS...
I *LIED*...
I COVERED UP THE TRUTH...
...AND DIDN'T EVEN GET TO MOURN MY SON'S DEATH PROPERLY...
MY *PRECIOUS* SON!
YOU...
AREN'T PART OF THIS FAMILY, AFTER ALL.
HOW ELSE COULD YOU DESECRATE HIS DEATH LIKE THIS, BY SAYING THAT?!

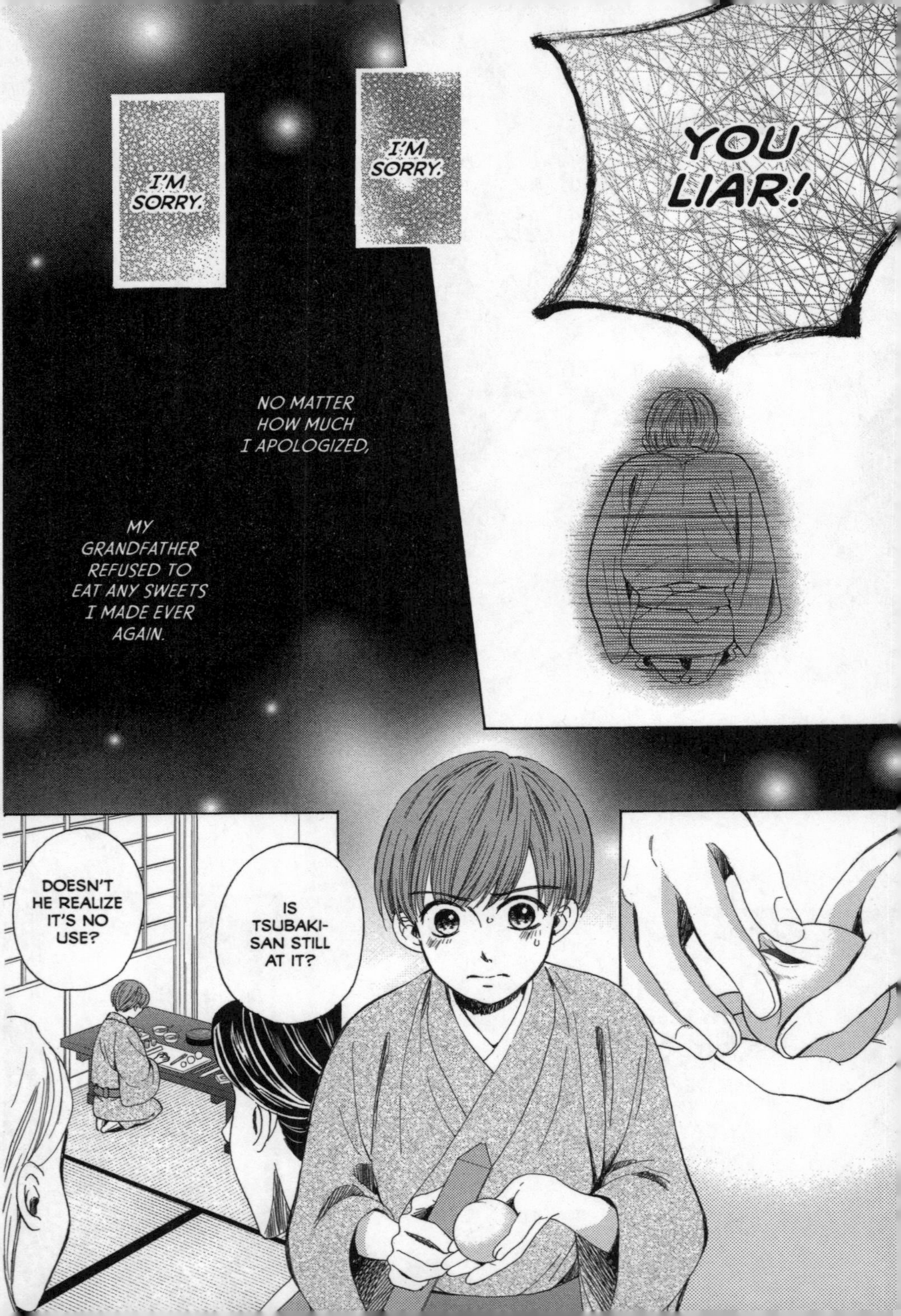
YOU LIAR!
I'M SORRY.
I'M SORRY.
NO MATTER HOW MUCH I APOLOGIZED,
MY GRANDFATHER REFUSED TO EAT ANY SWEETS I MADE EVER AGAIN.
IS TSUBAKI-SAN STILL AT IT?
DOESN'T HE REALIZE IT'S NO USE?

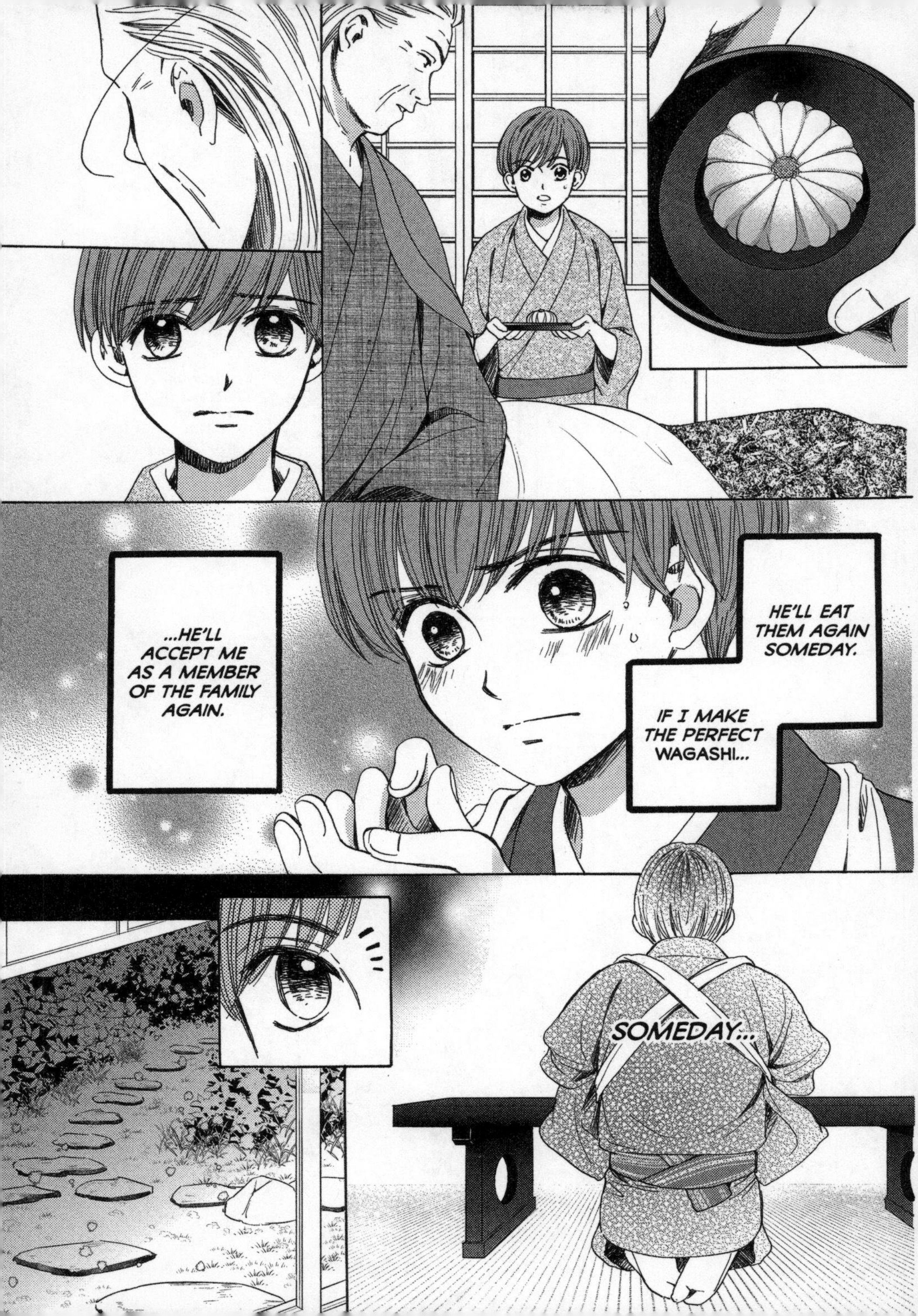
HE'LL EAT THEM AGAIN SOMEDAY.
IF I MAKE THE PERFECT WAGASHI...
...HE'LL ACCEPT ME AS A MEMBER OF THE FAMILY AGAIN.
SOMEDAY...

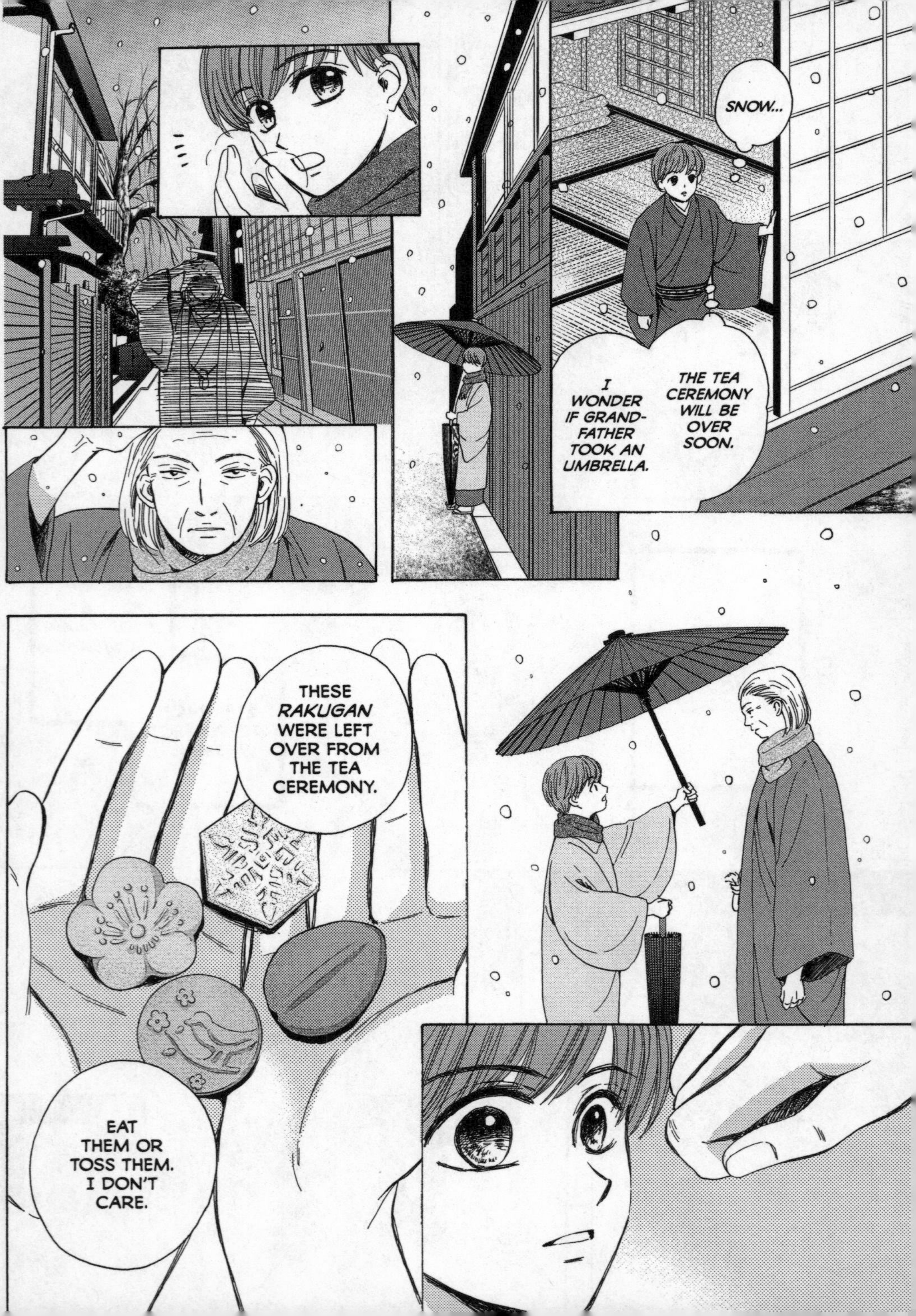
SNOW...
THE TEA CEREMONY WILL BE OVER SOON.
I WONDER IF GRAND-FATHER TOOK AN UMBRELLA.
THESE *RAKUGAN* WERE LEFT OVER FROM THE TEA CEREMONY.
EAT THEM OR TOSS THEM. I DON'T CARE.

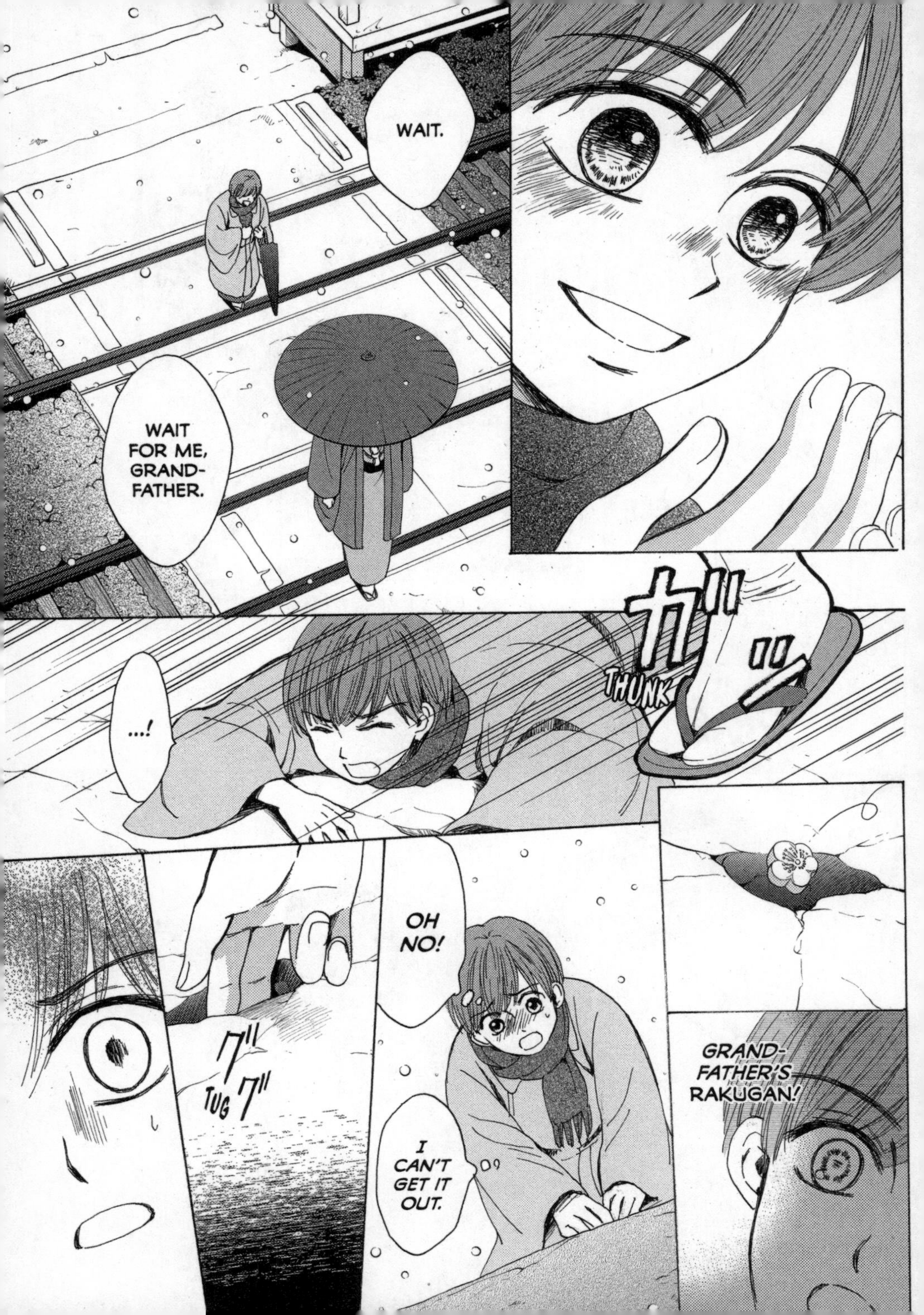
WAIT.
WAIT FOR ME, GRAND-FATHER.
ガッ
THUNK
...!
GRAND-FATHER'S RAKUGAN!
OH NO!
I CAN'T GET IT OUT.
グッ グッ
TUG

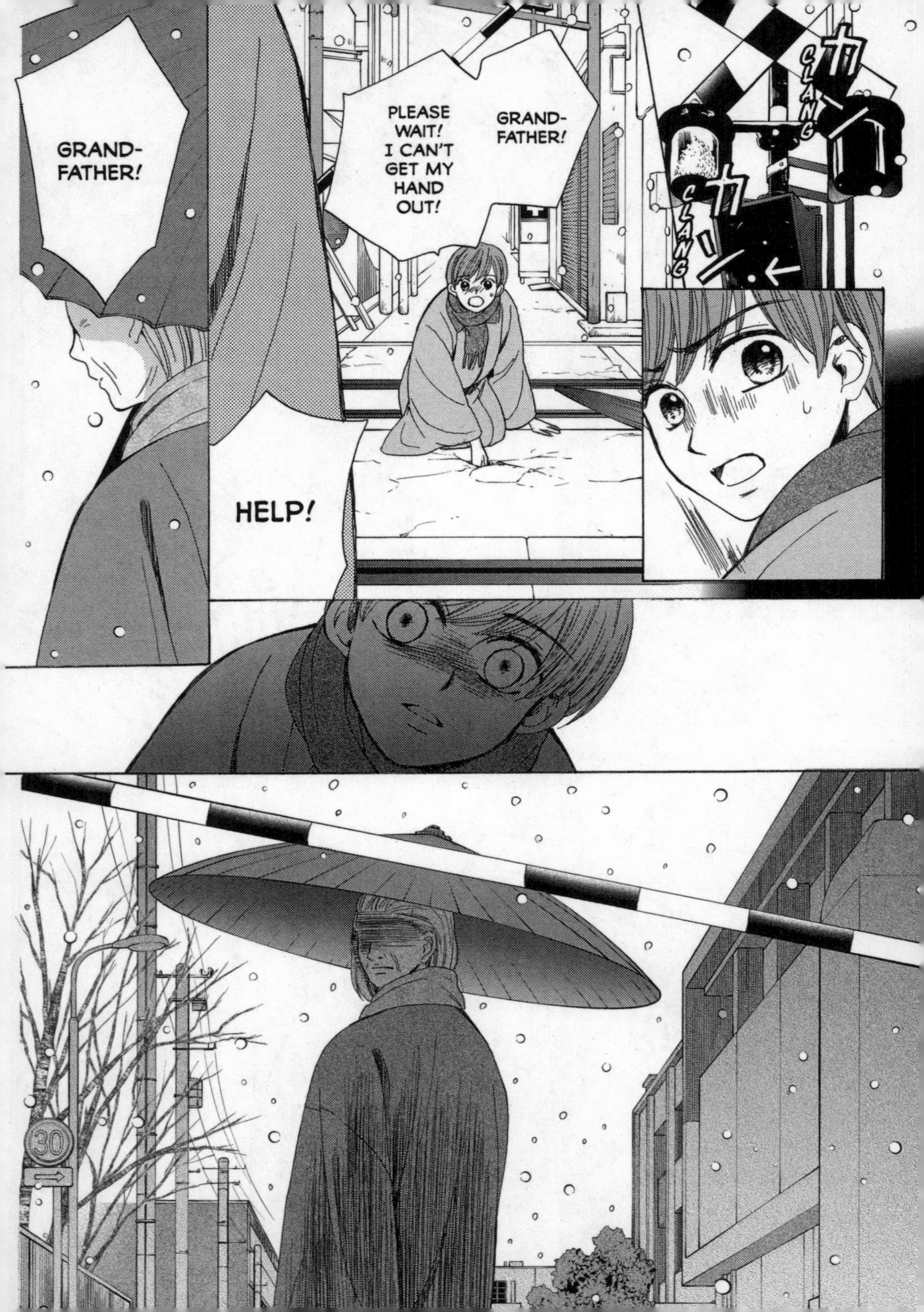
CLANG
CLANG
GRAND-FATHER!
PLEASE WAIT! I CAN'T GET MY HAND OUT!
HELP!
GRAND-FATHER!
30

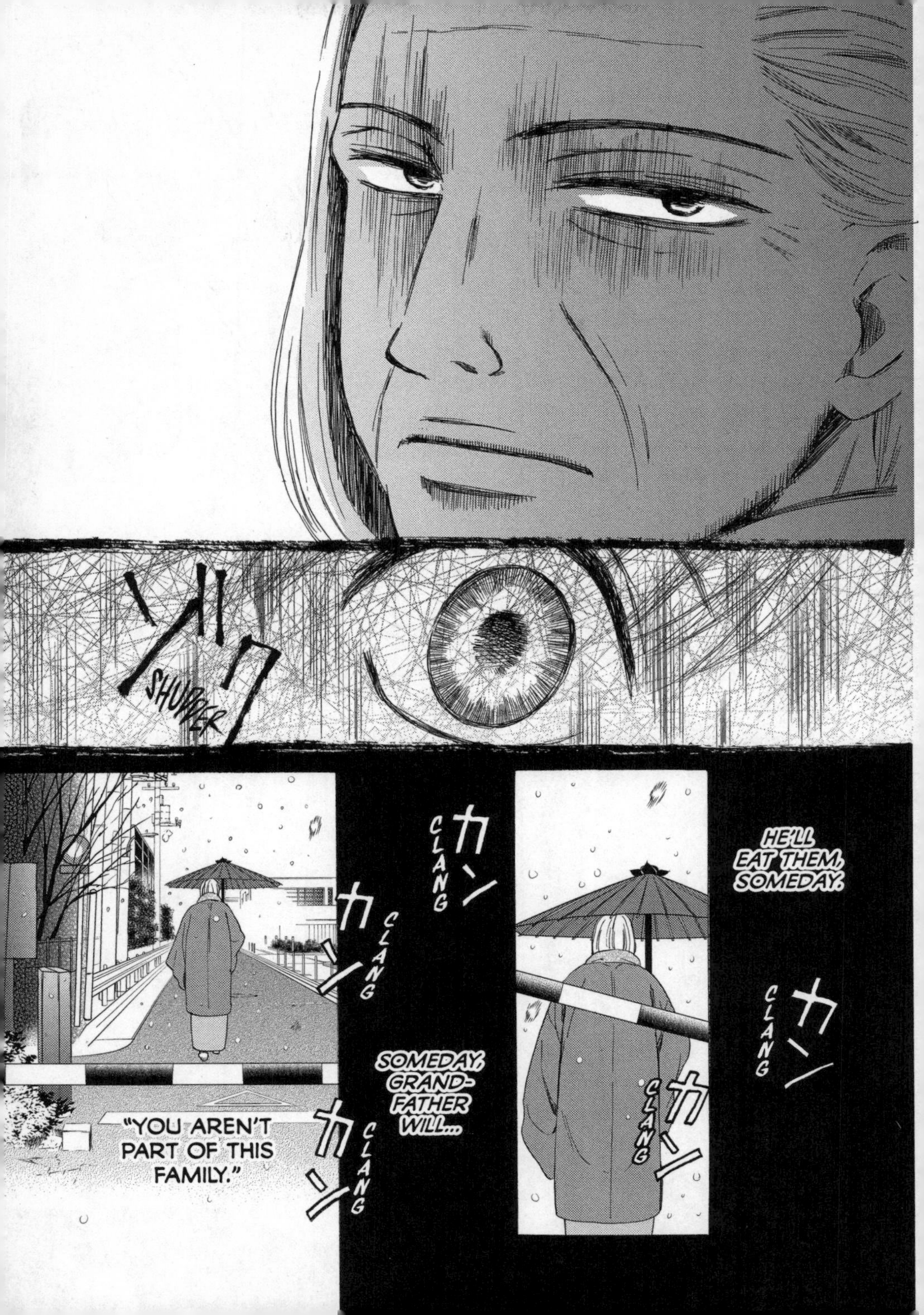
ゾク
SHUDDER
HE'LL EAT THEM, SOMEDAY.
カン
CLANG
カン
CLANG
SOMEDAY, GRAND-FATHER WILL...
カン
CLANG
カン
CLANG
カン
CLANG
"YOU AREN'T PART OF THIS FAMILY."
カン
CLANG

"MY PRECIOUS SON!"
LIAR.
HOONK
OH NO!
THE EMERGENCY BUTTON!
PRESSING AS A PRANK IS ILLEGAL AND ... WILL BE PUNISHED.

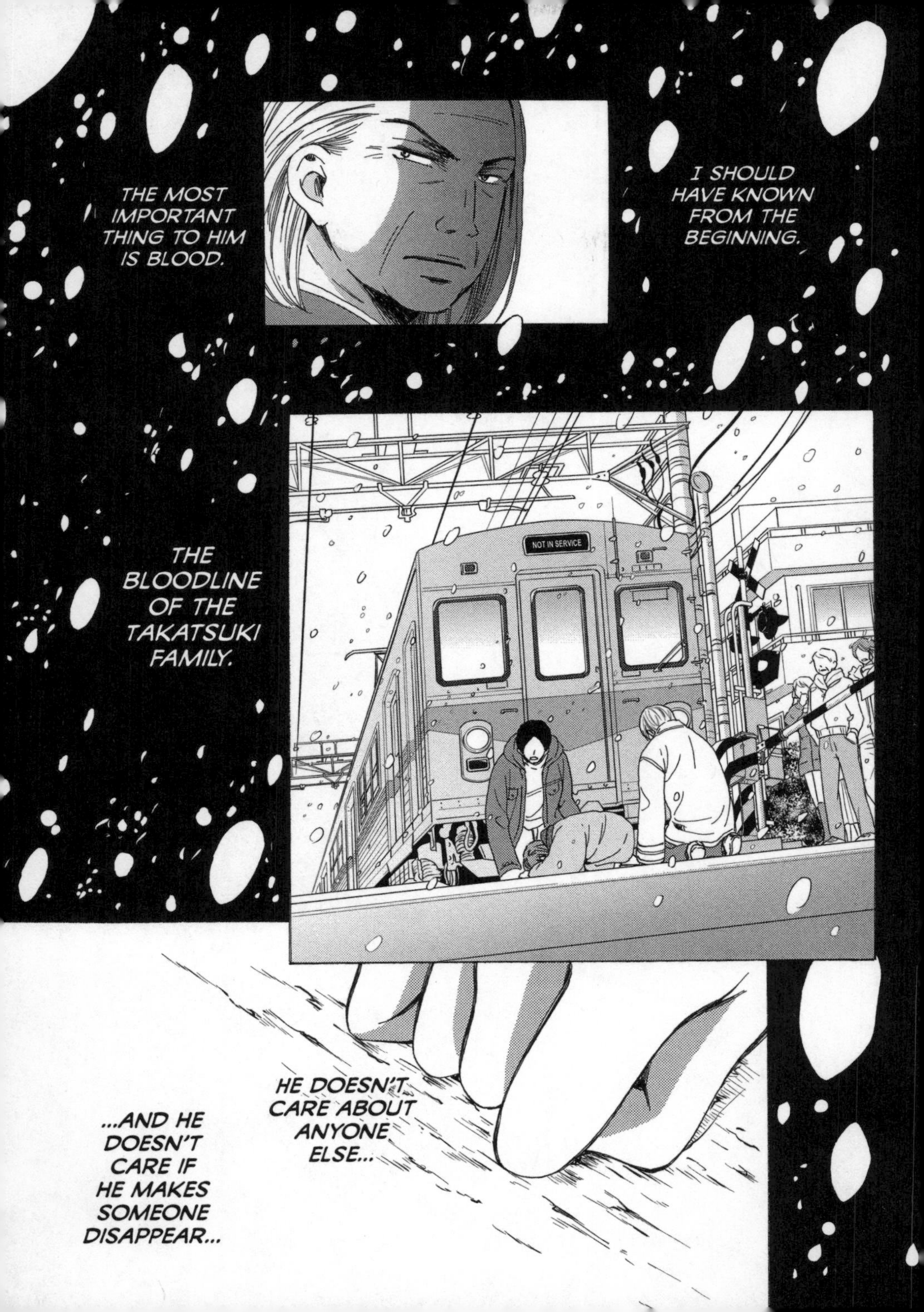
I SHOULD HAVE KNOWN FROM THE BEGINNING.
THE MOST IMPORTANT THING TO HIM IS BLOOD.
THE BLOODLINE OF THE TAKATSUKI FAMILY.
NOT IN SERVICE
HE DOESN'T CARE ABOUT ANYONE ELSE...
...AND HE DOESN'T CARE IF HE MAKES SOMEONE DISAPPEAR...

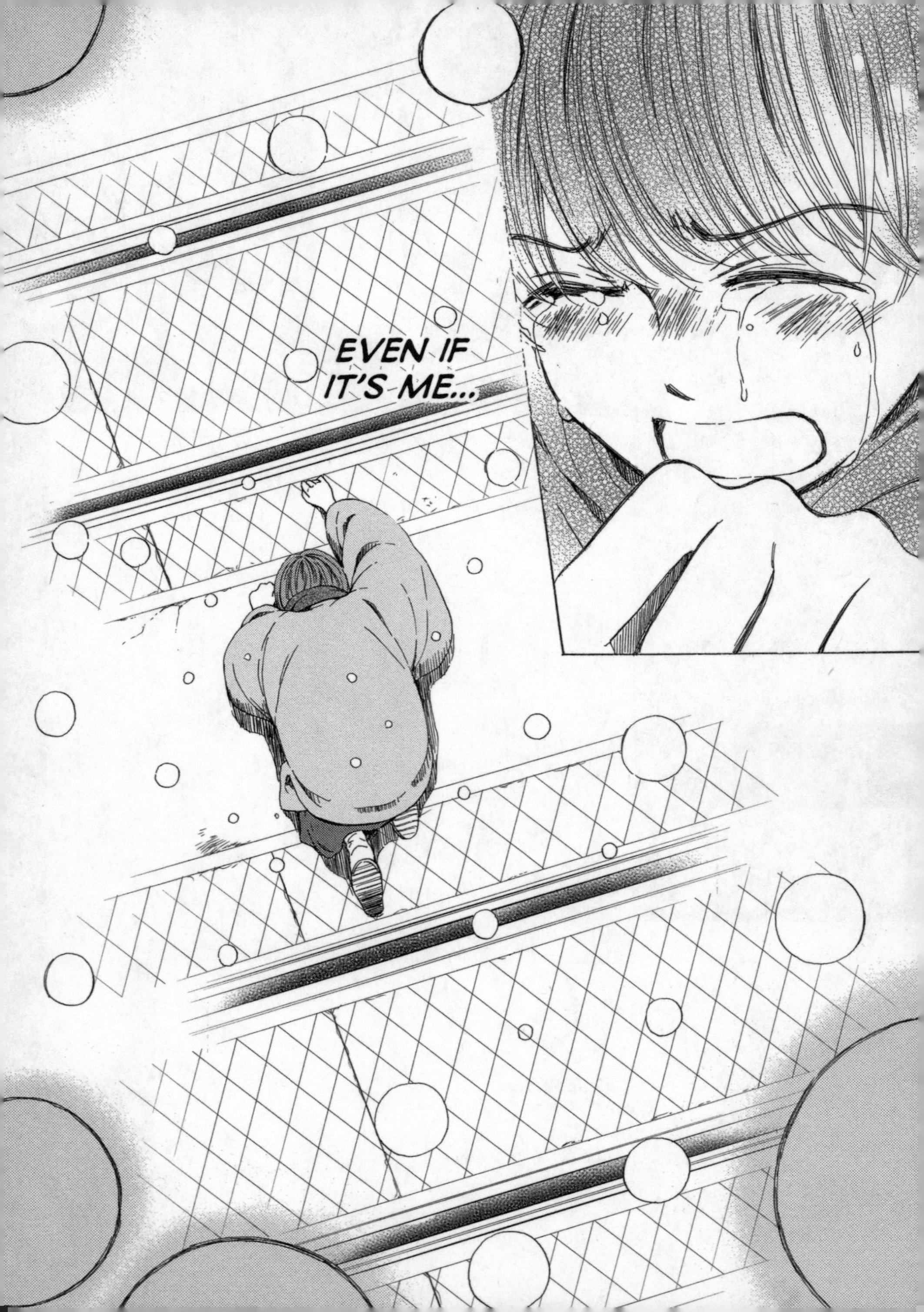
EVEN IF IT'S ME...

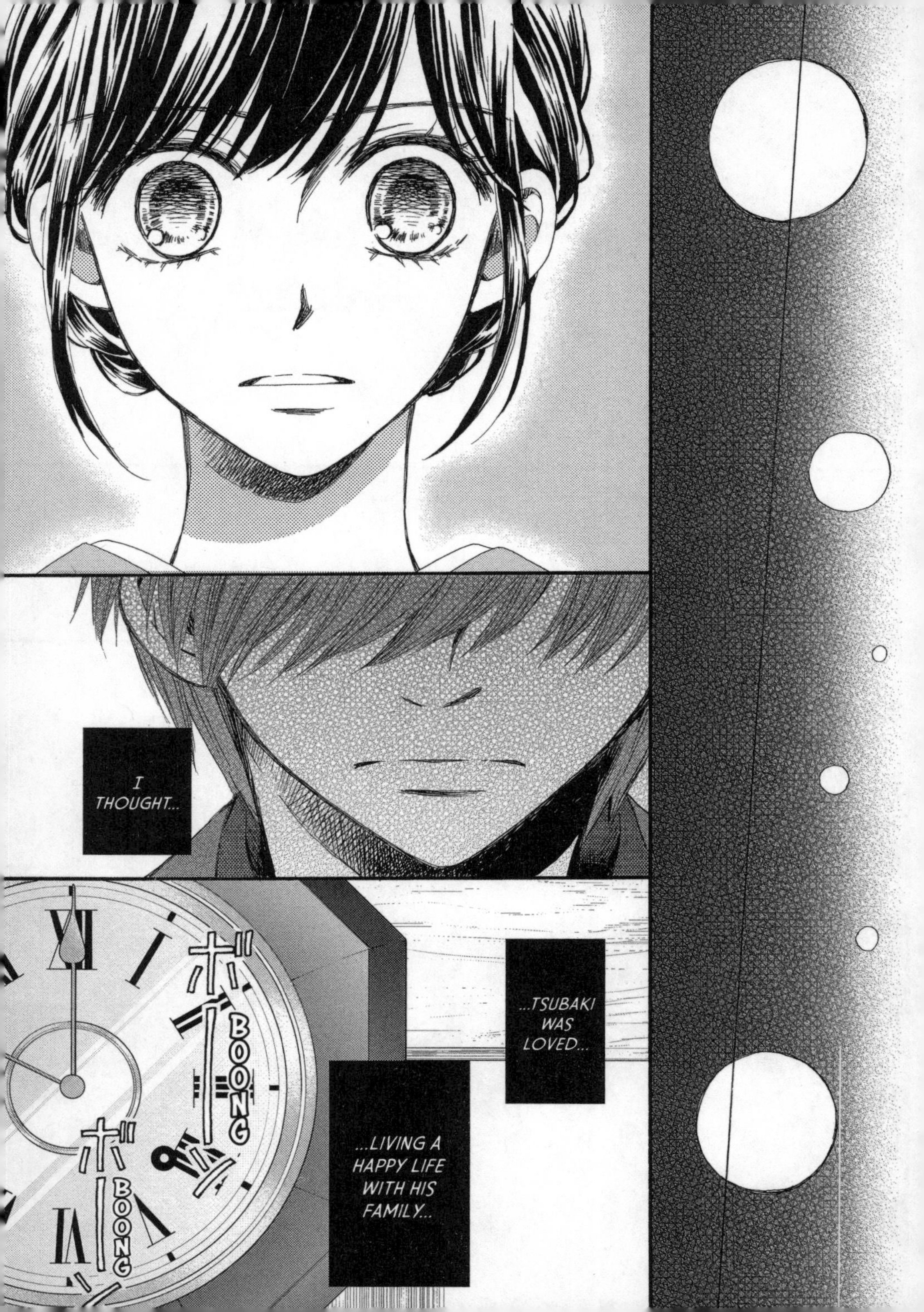
I THOUGHT...
...TSUBAKI WAS LOVED...
...LIVING A HAPPY LIFE WITH HIS FAMILY...
BOONG
BOONG

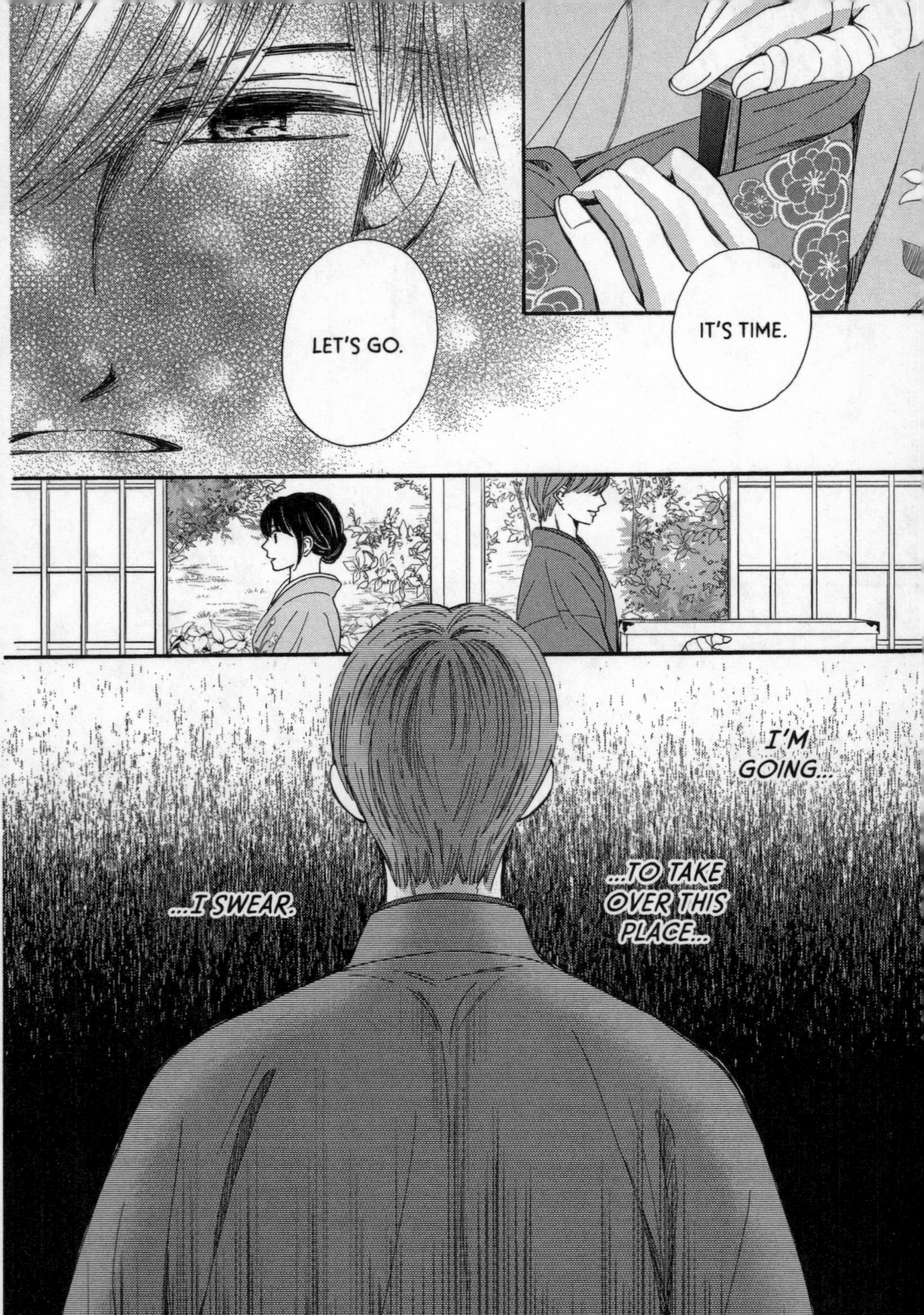
IT'S TIME.
LET'S GO.
I'M GOING...
...TO TAKE OVER THIS PLACE...
...I SWEAR.

Something's
Wrong
With Us

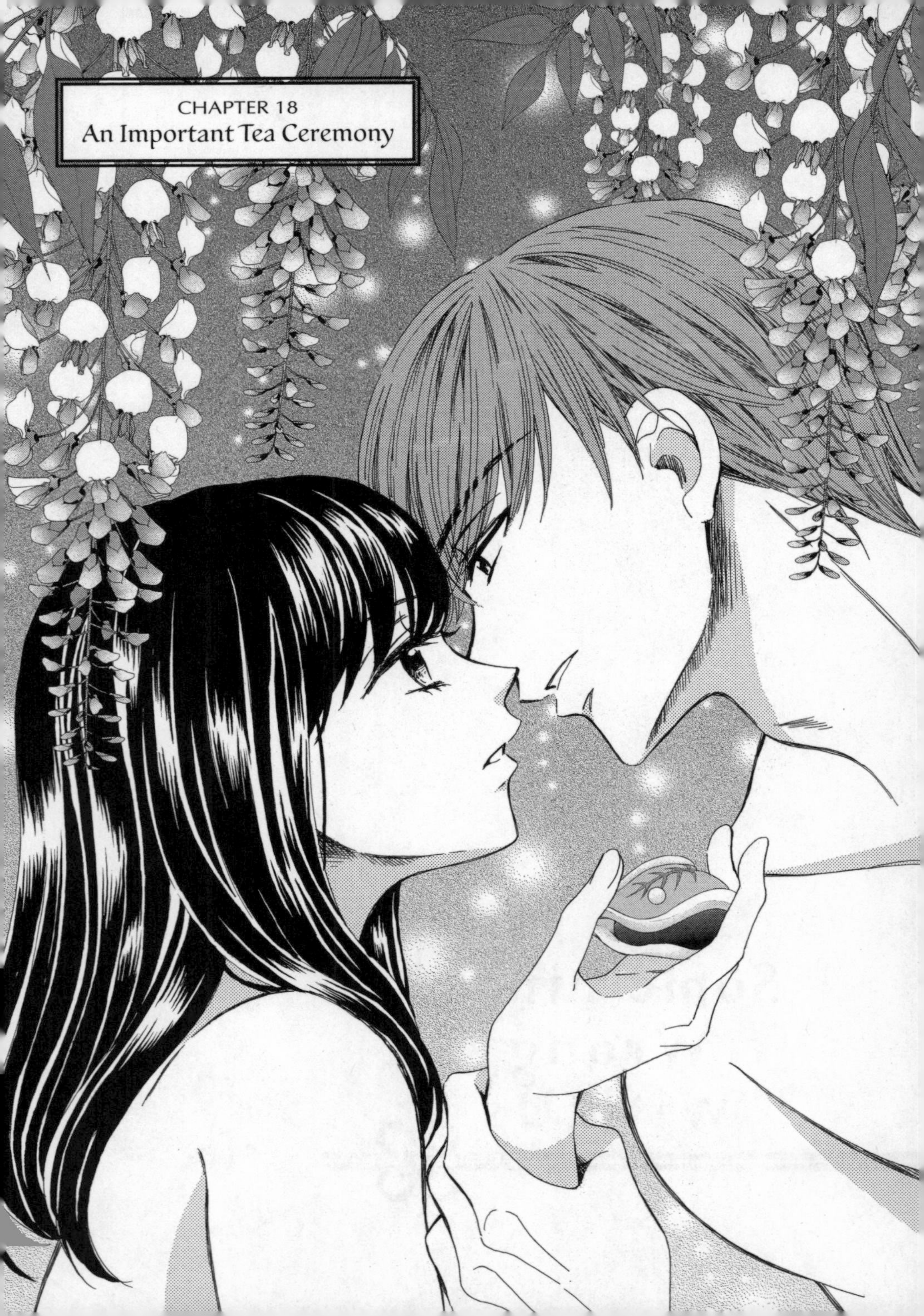
CHAPTER 18
An Important Tea Ceremony

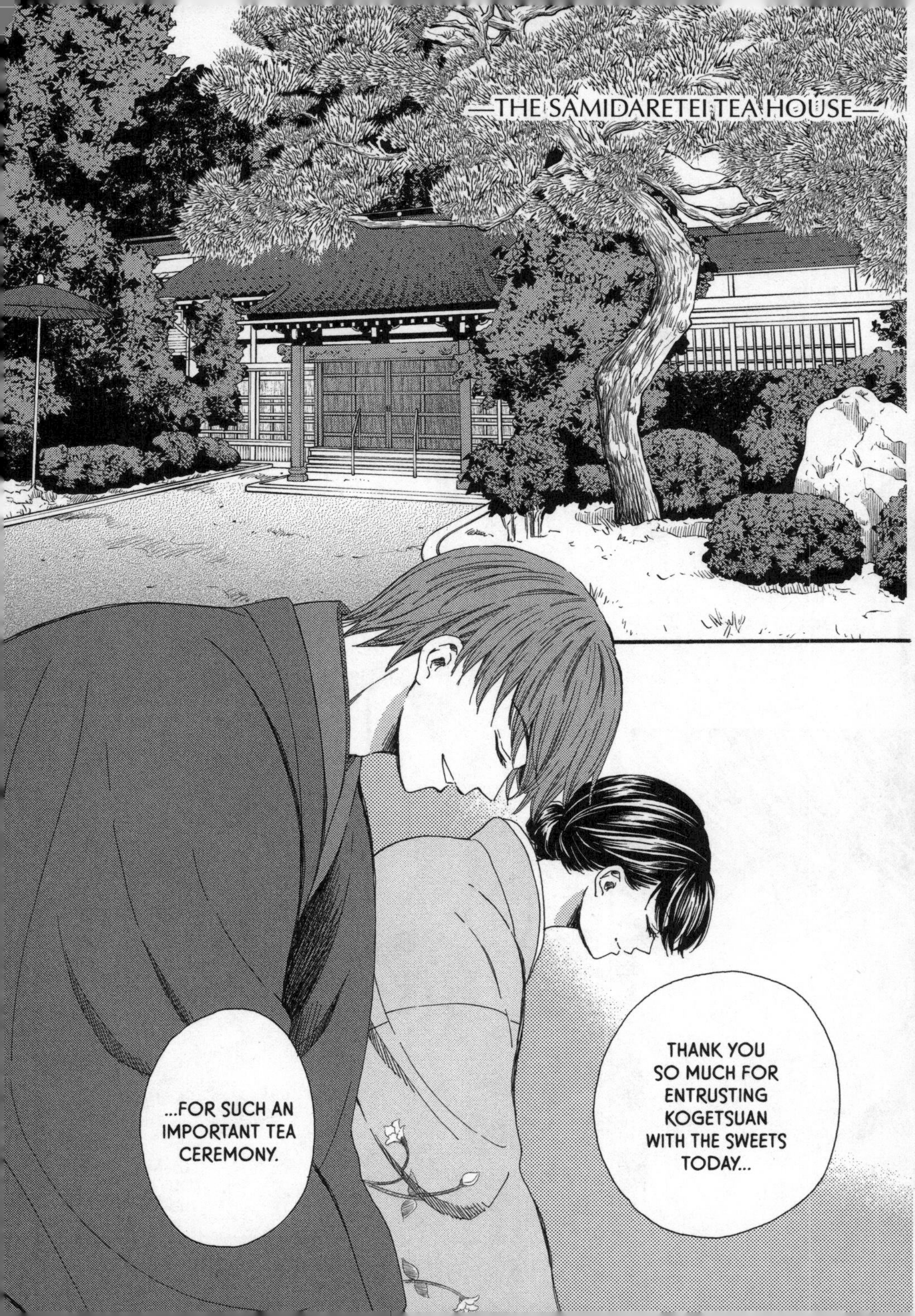
—THE SAMIDARETEI TEA HOUSE—
THANK YOU SO MUCH FOR ENTRUSTING KOGETSUAN WITH THE SWEETS TODAY...
...FOR SUCH AN IMPORTANT TEA CEREMONY.

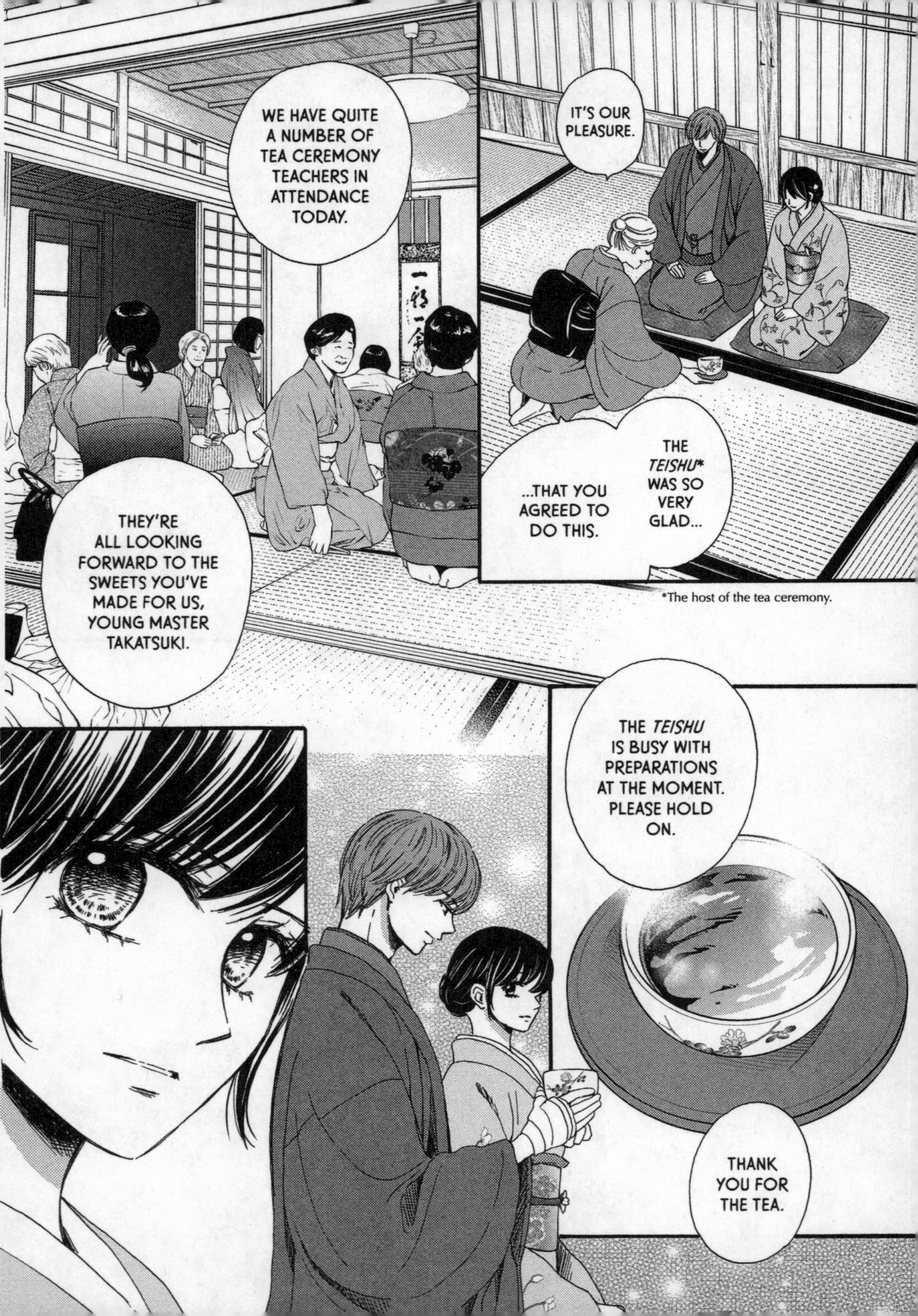
IT'S OUR PLEASURE.
THE *TEISHU** WAS SO VERY GLAD...
...THAT YOU AGREED TO DO THIS.
WE HAVE QUITE A NUMBER OF TEA CEREMONY TEACHERS IN ATTENDANCE TODAY.
THEY'RE ALL LOOKING FORWARD TO THE SWEETS YOU'VE MADE FOR US, YOUNG MASTER TAKATSUKI.
THE *TEISHU* IS BUSY WITH PREPARATIONS AT THE MOMENT. PLEASE HOLD ON.
THANK YOU FOR THE TEA.

*The host of the tea ceremony.

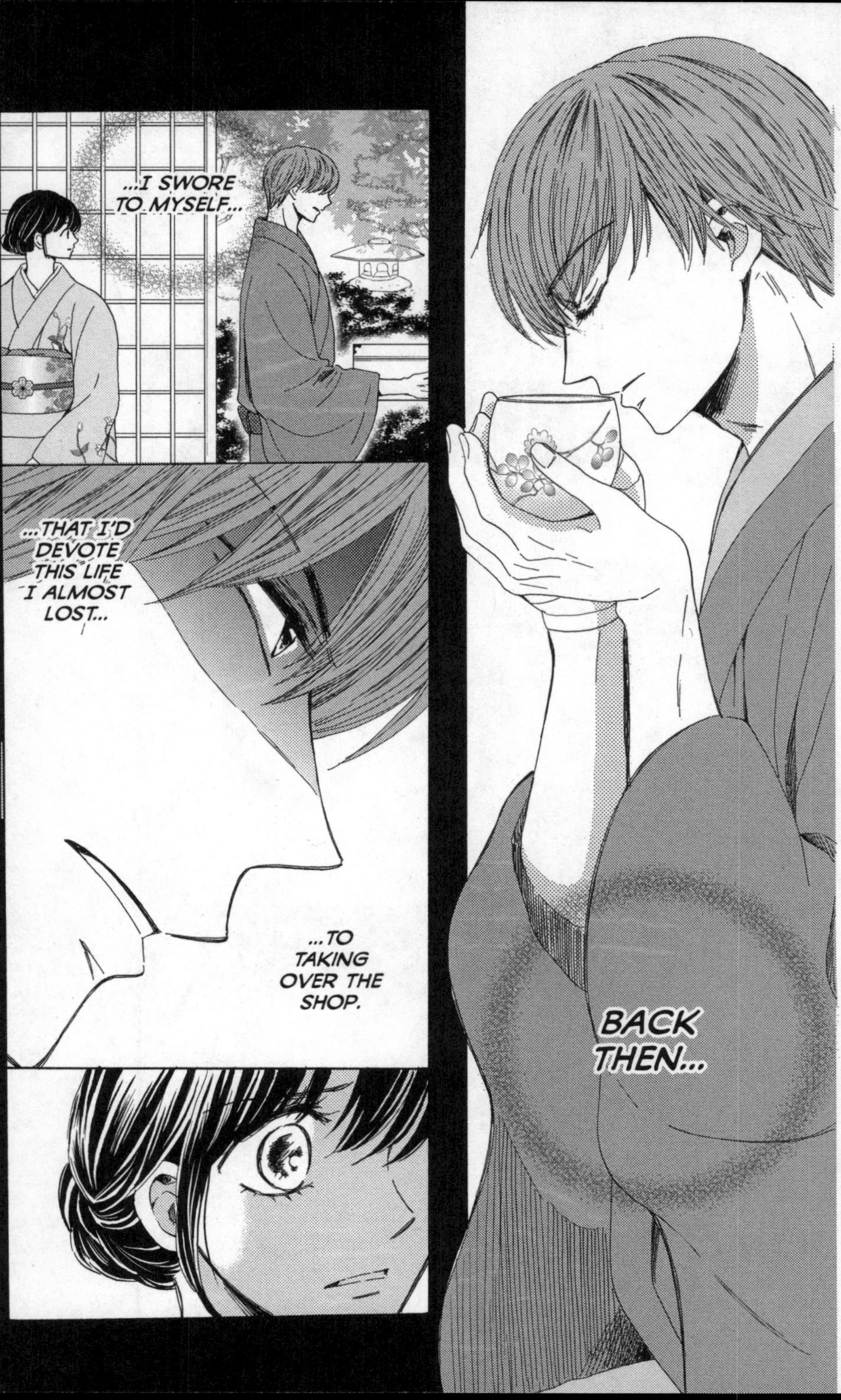
BACK THEN...
...I SWORE TO MYSELF...
...THAT I'D DEVOTE THIS LIFE I ALMOST LOST...
...TO TAKING OVER THE SHOP.

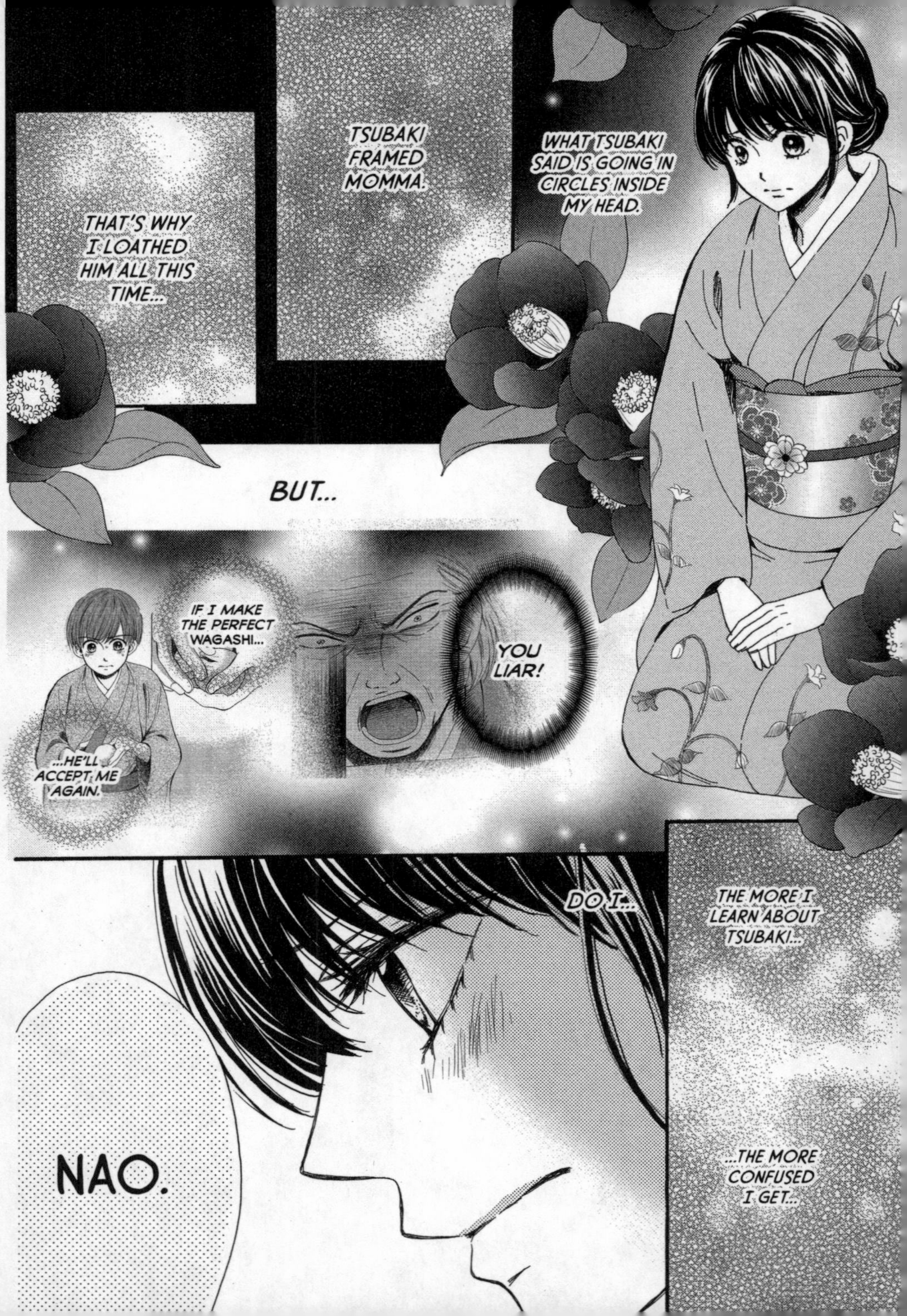
WHAT TSUBAKI SAID IS GOING IN CIRCLES INSIDE MY HEAD.
TSUBAKI FRAMED MOMMA.
THAT'S WHY I LOATHED HIM ALL THIS TIME...
BUT...
YOU LIAR!
IF I MAKE THE PERFECT WAGASHI...
...HE'LL ACCEPT ME AGAIN.
THE MORE I LEARN ABOUT TSUBAKI...
...THE MORE CONFUSED I GET...
DO I...
NAO.

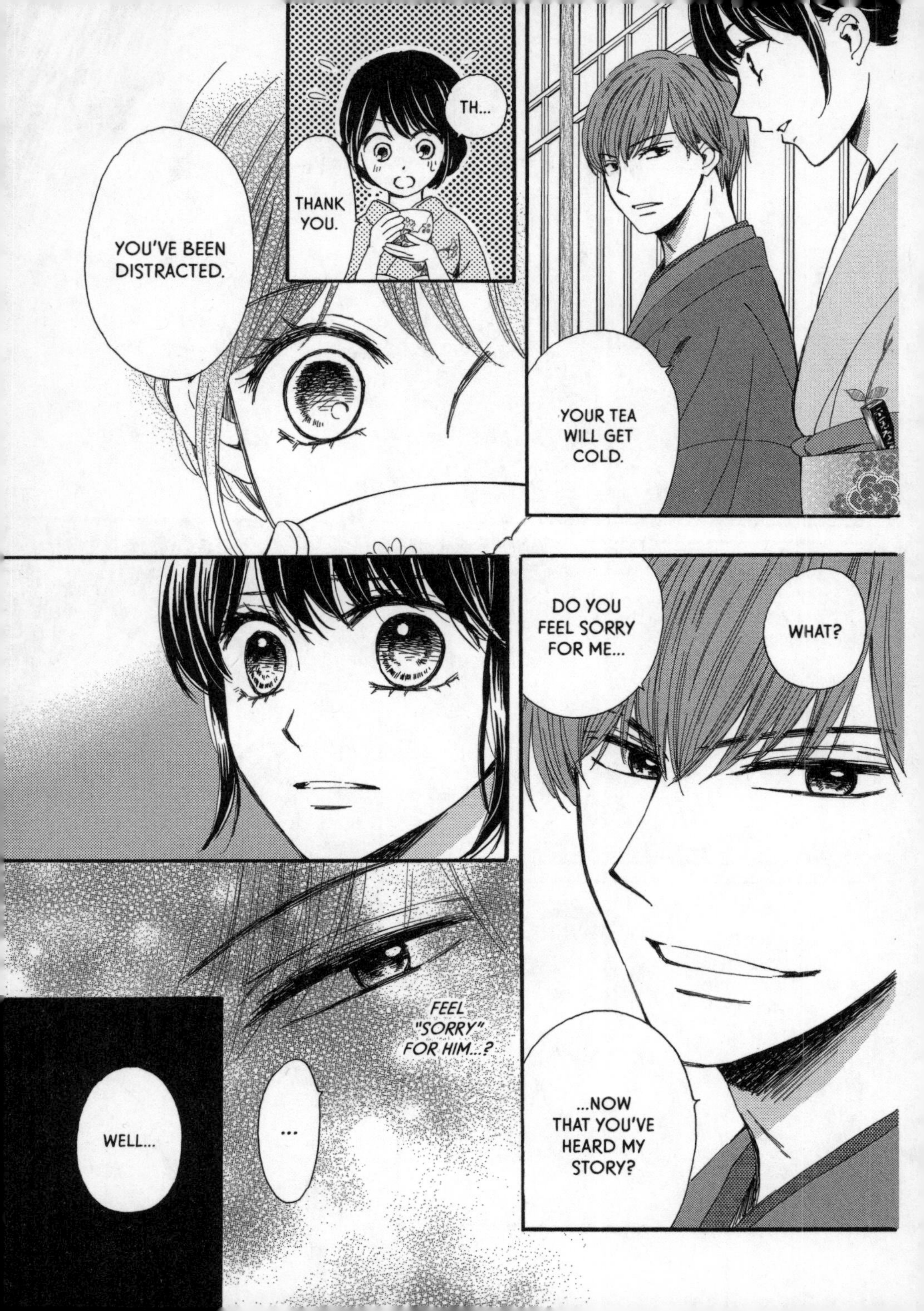
YOUR TEA WILL GET COLD.
YOU'VE BEEN DISTRACTED.
TH...
THANK YOU.
WHAT?
DO YOU FEEL SORRY FOR ME...
...NOW THAT YOU'VE HEARD MY STORY?
FEEL "SORRY" FOR HIM...?
...
WELL...

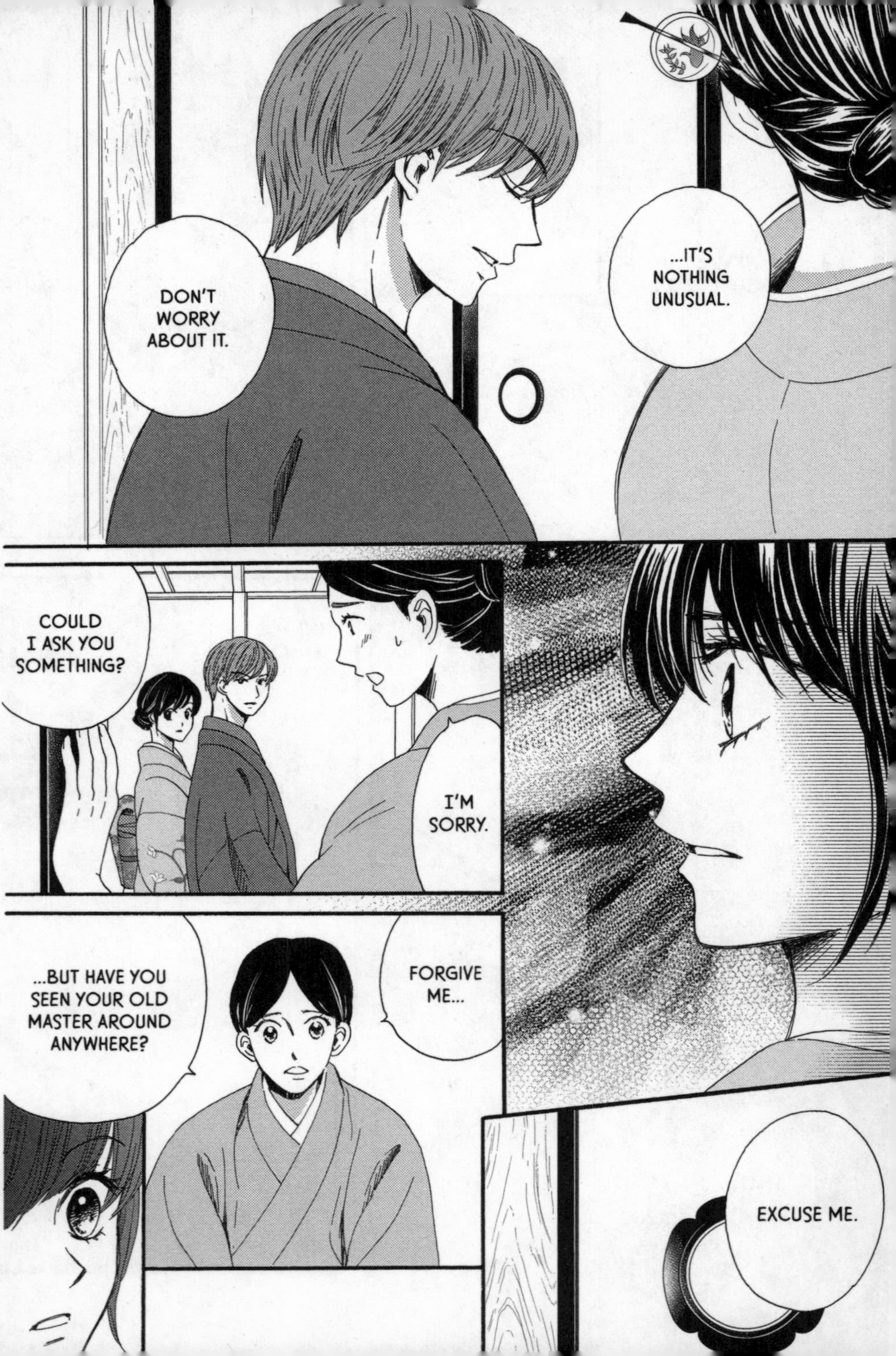
...IT'S NOTHING UNUSUAL.
DON'T WORRY ABOUT IT.
I'M SORRY.
COULD I ASK YOU SOMETHING?
FORGIVE ME...
...BUT HAVE YOU SEEN YOUR OLD MASTER AROUND ANYWHERE?
EXCUSE ME.

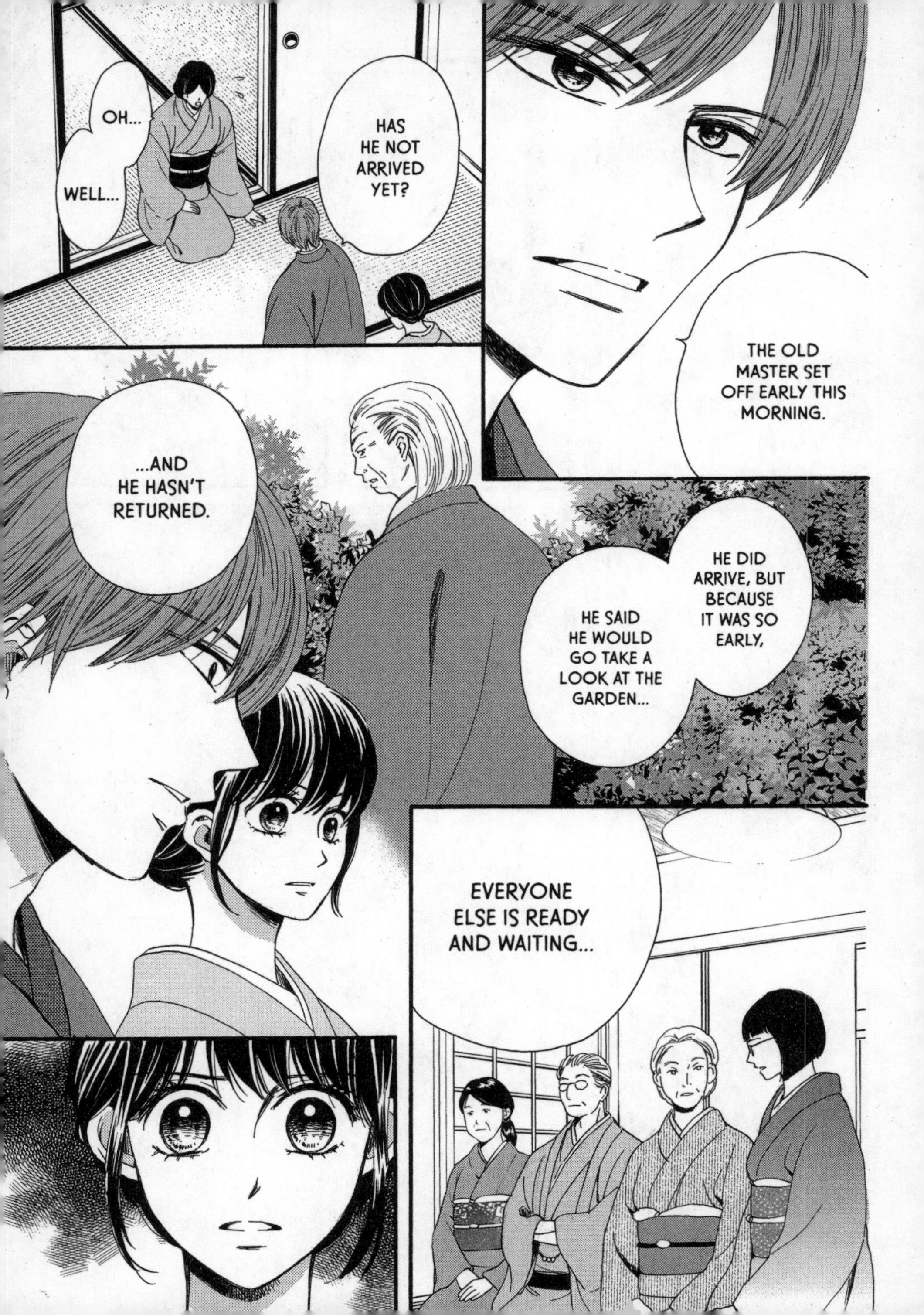
THE OLD MASTER SET OFF EARLY THIS MORNING.
...AND HE HASN'T RETURNED.
HAS HE NOT ARRIVED YET?
OH...
WELL...
HE DID ARRIVE, BUT BECAUSE IT WAS SO EARLY,
HE SAID HE WOULD GO TAKE A LOOK AT THE GARDEN...
EVERYONE ELSE IS READY AND WAITING...

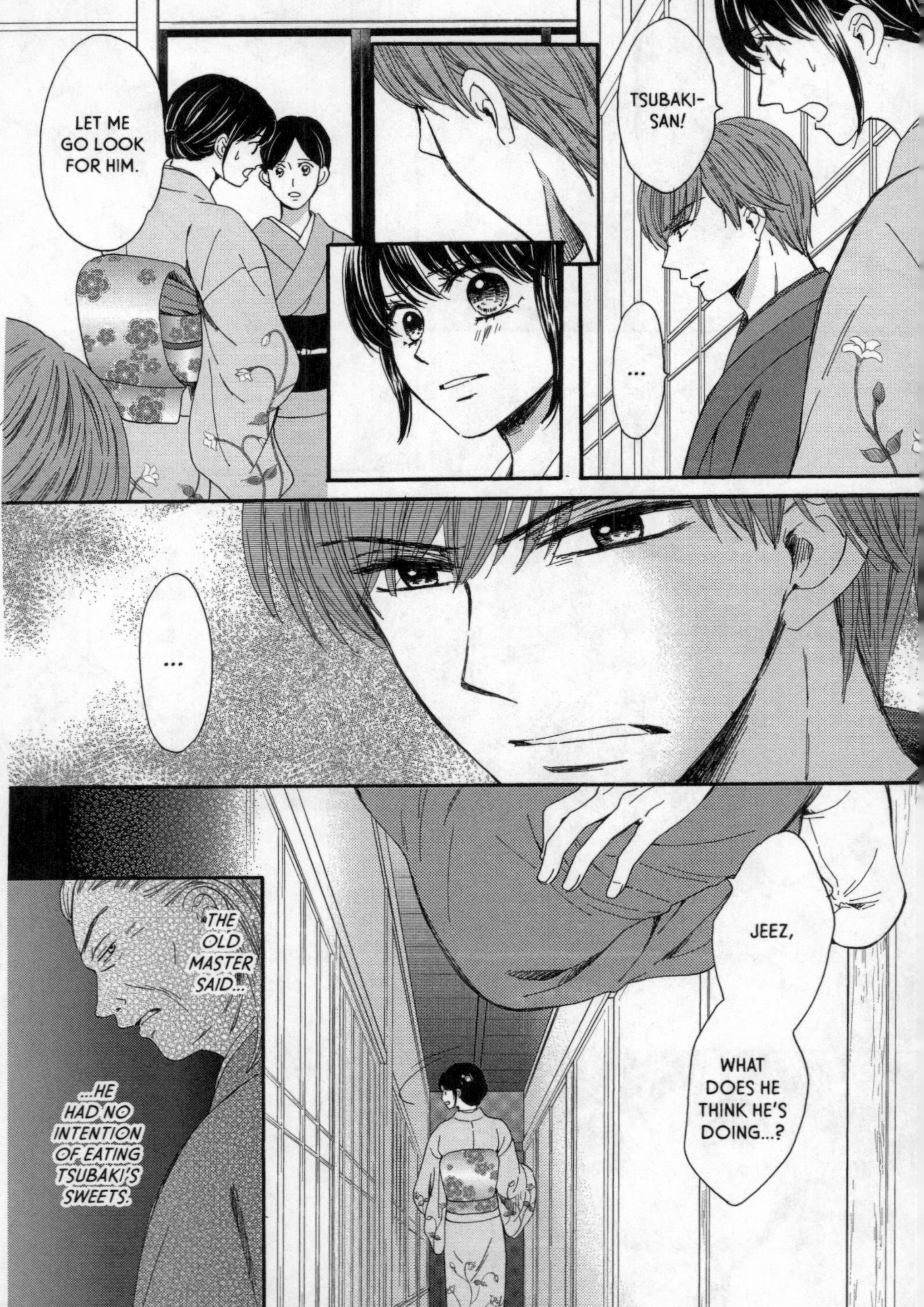
TSUBAKI-SAN!
...
LET ME GO LOOK FOR HIM.
...
JEEZ,
WHAT DOES HE THINK HE'S DOING...?
THE OLD MASTER SAID...
...HE HAD NO INTENTION OF EATING TSUBAKI'S SWEETS.

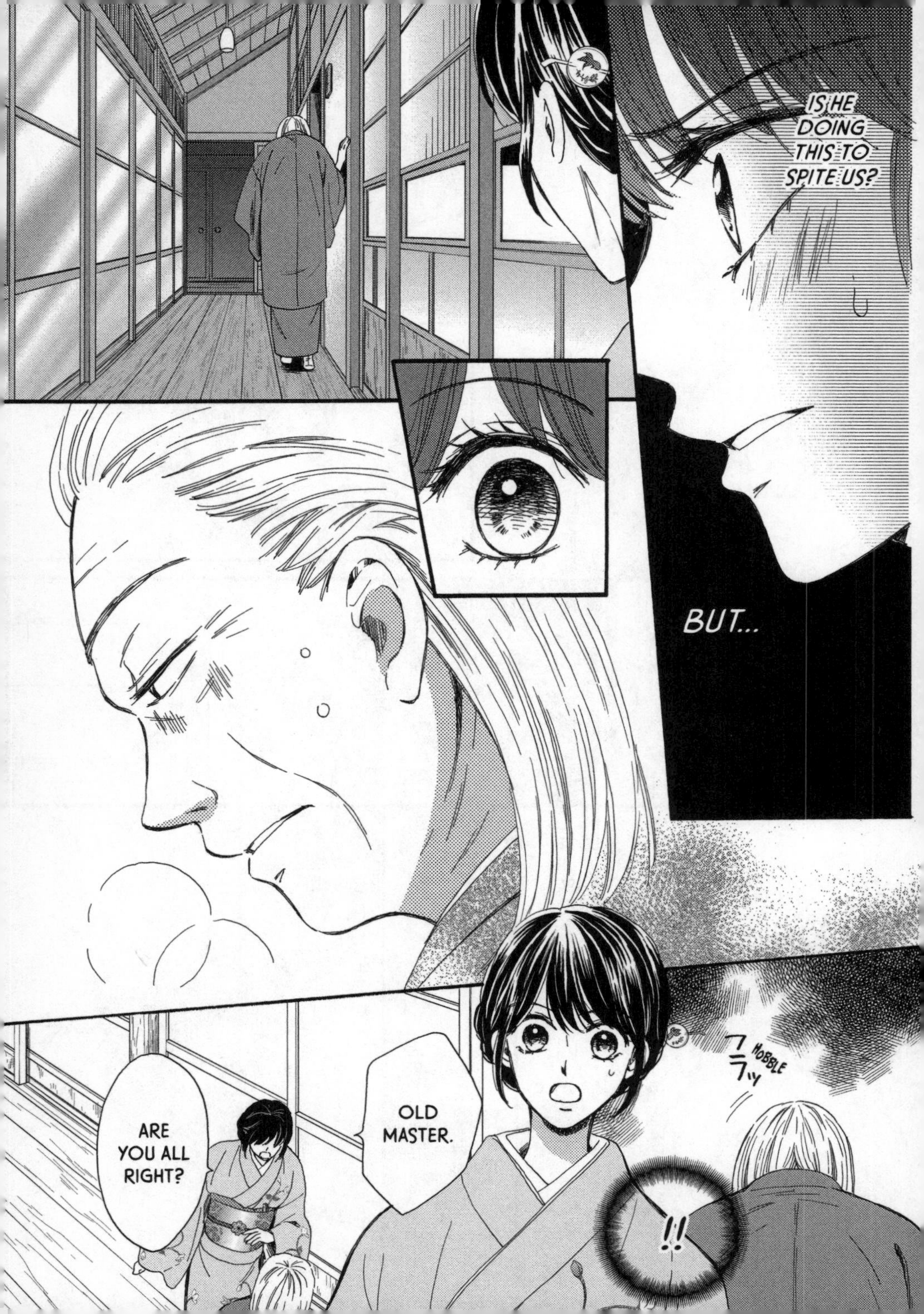
IS HE DOING THIS TO SPITE US?
BUT...
フラッ HOBBLE
OLD MASTER.
ARE YOU ALL RIGHT?
!!

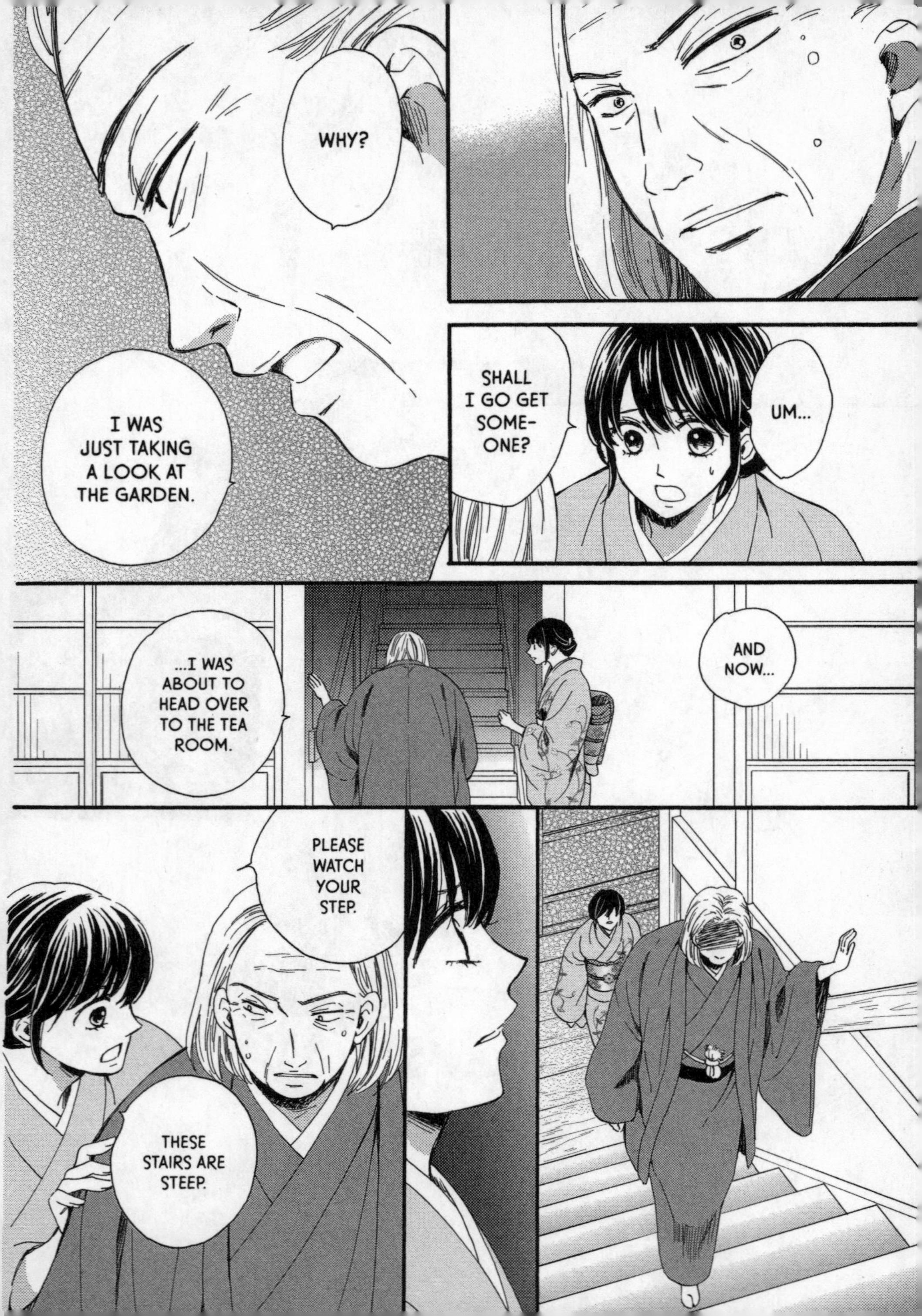
UM...
SHALL I GO GET SOME-ONE?
WHY?
I WAS JUST TAKING A LOOK AT THE GARDEN.
AND NOW...
...I WAS ABOUT TO HEAD OVER TO THE TEA ROOM.
PLEASE WATCH YOUR STEP.
THESE STAIRS ARE STEEP.

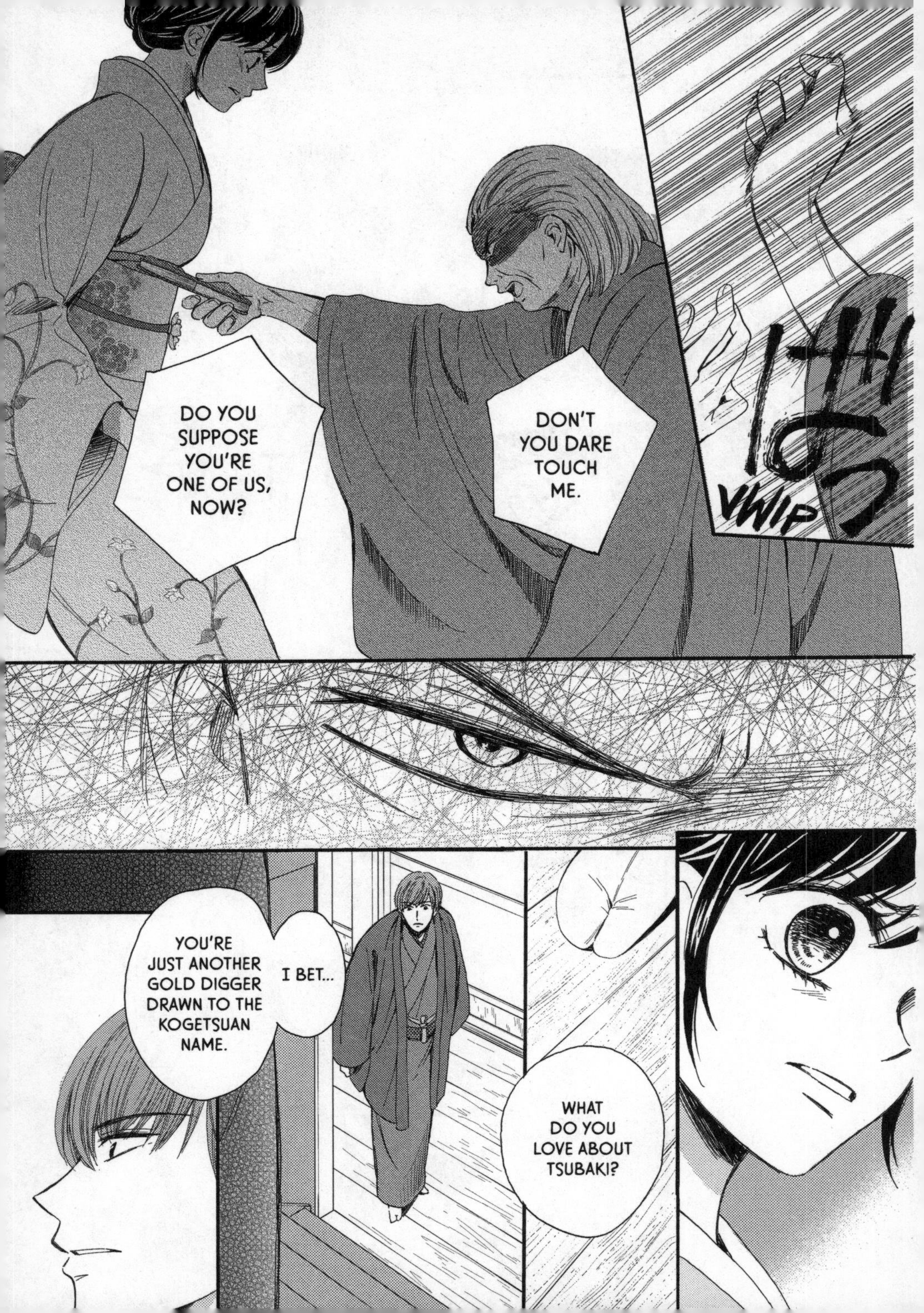
VWIP
DON'T YOU DARE TOUCH ME.
DO YOU SUPPOSE YOU'RE ONE OF US, NOW?
WHAT DO YOU LOVE ABOUT TSUBAKI?
I BET...
YOU'RE JUST ANOTHER GOLD DIGGER DRAWN TO THE KOGETSUAN NAME.

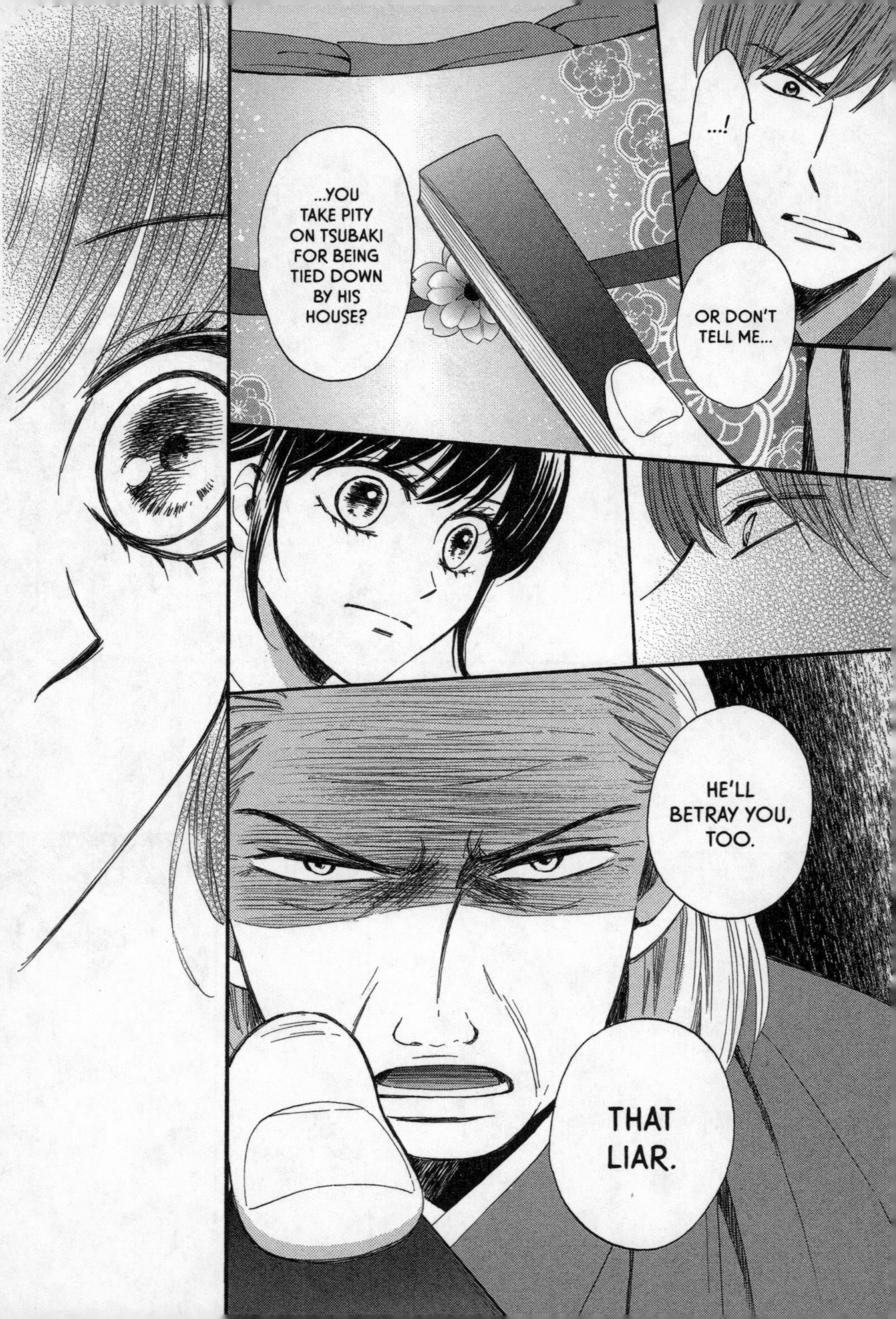
...!
OR DON'T TELL ME...
...YOU TAKE PITY ON TSUBAKI FOR BEING TIED DOWN BY HIS HOUSE?
HE'LL BETRAY YOU, TOO.
THAT LIAR.

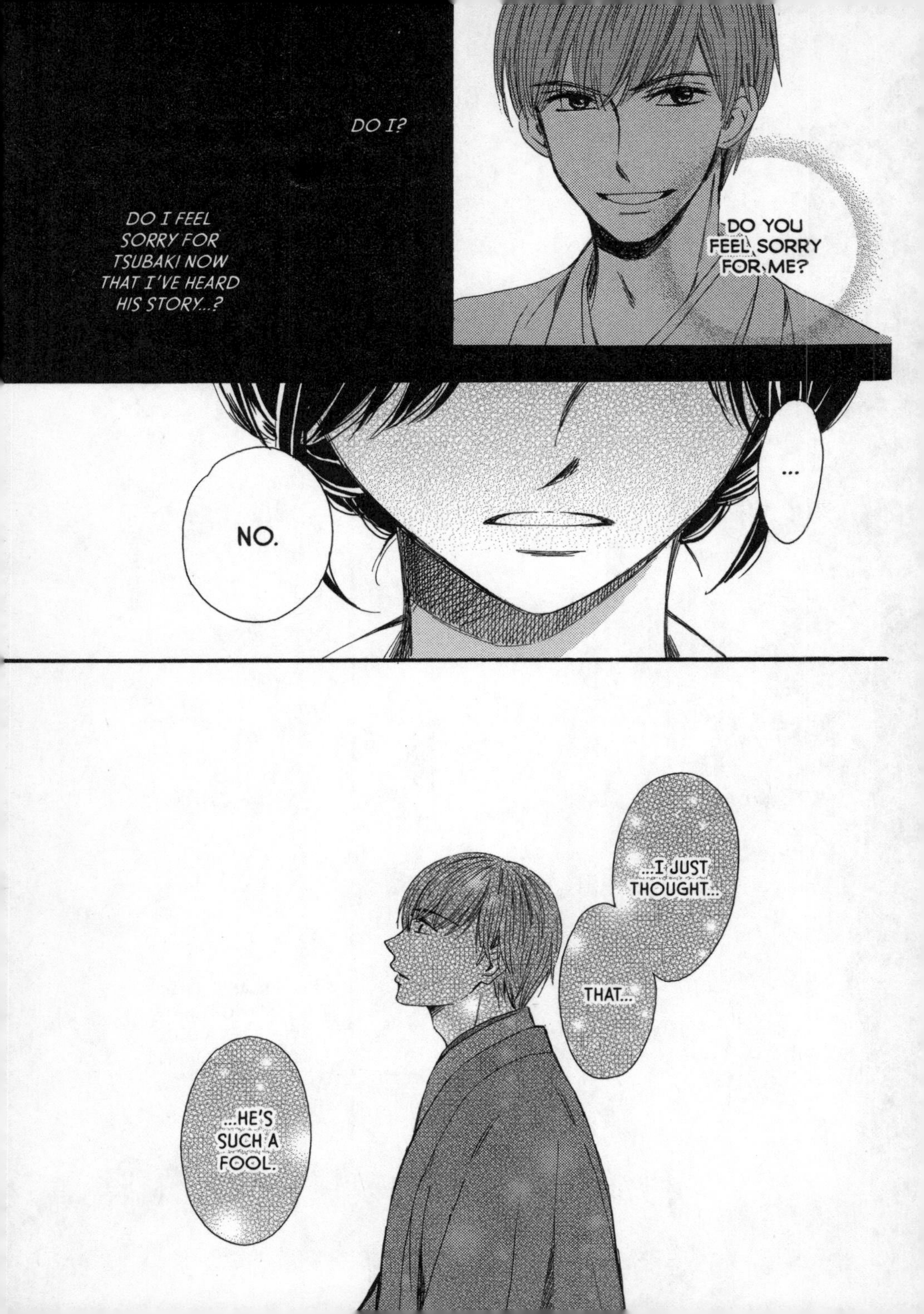
DO YOU FEEL SORRY FOR ME?
DO I?
DO I FEEL SORRY FOR TSUBAKI NOW THAT I'VE HEARD HIS STORY...?
...
NO.
...I JUST THOUGHT...
THAT...
...HE'S SUCH A FOOL.

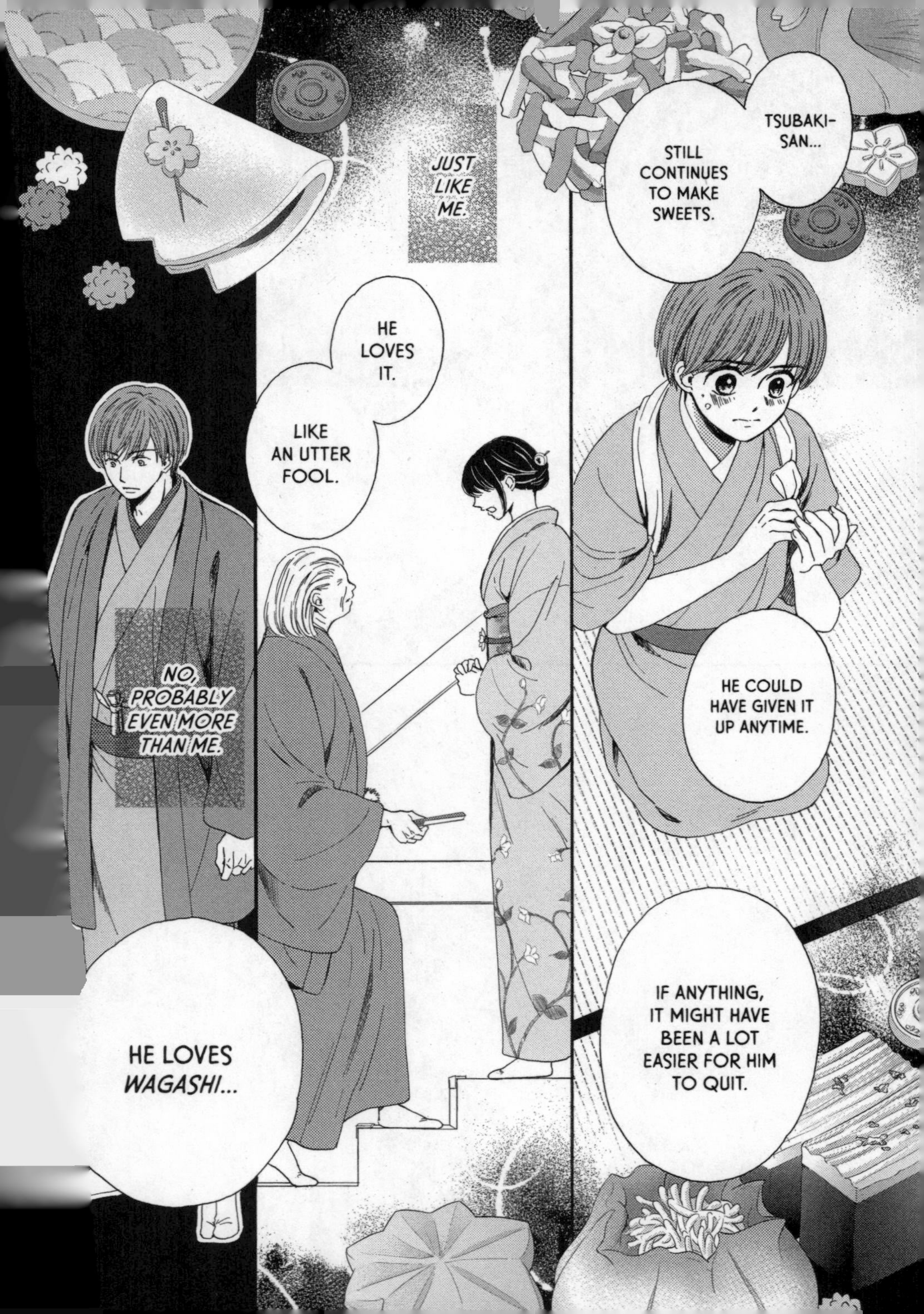
TSUBAKI-SAN...
STILL CONTINUES TO MAKE SWEETS.
HE COULD HAVE GIVEN IT UP ANYTIME.
IF ANYTHING, IT MIGHT HAVE BEEN A LOT EASIER FOR HIM TO QUIT.
JUST LIKE ME.
HE LOVES IT.
LIKE AN UTTER FOOL.
NO, PROBABLY EVEN MORE THAN ME.
HE LOVES *WAGASHI*...

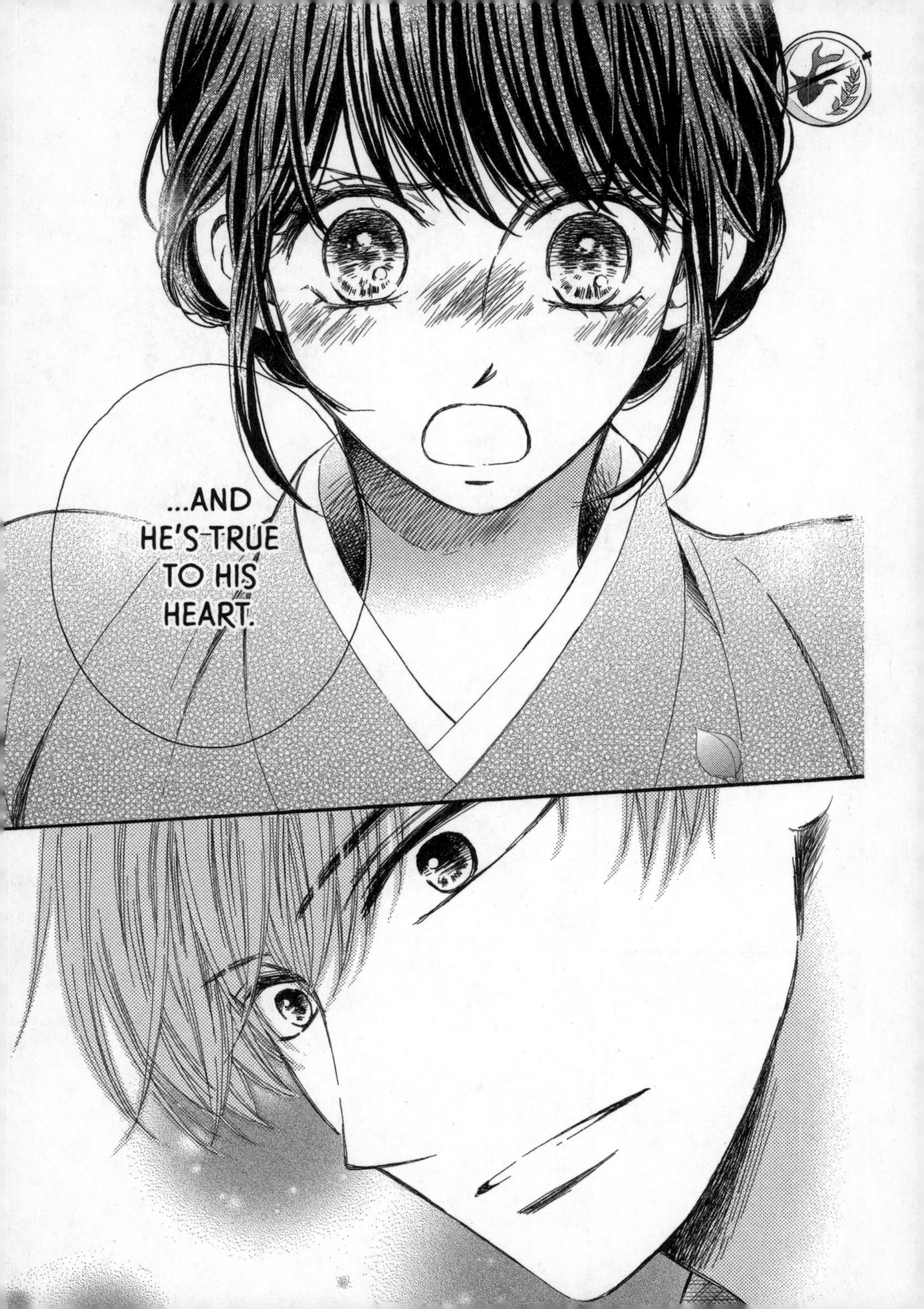
...AND HE'S TRUE TO HIS HEART.

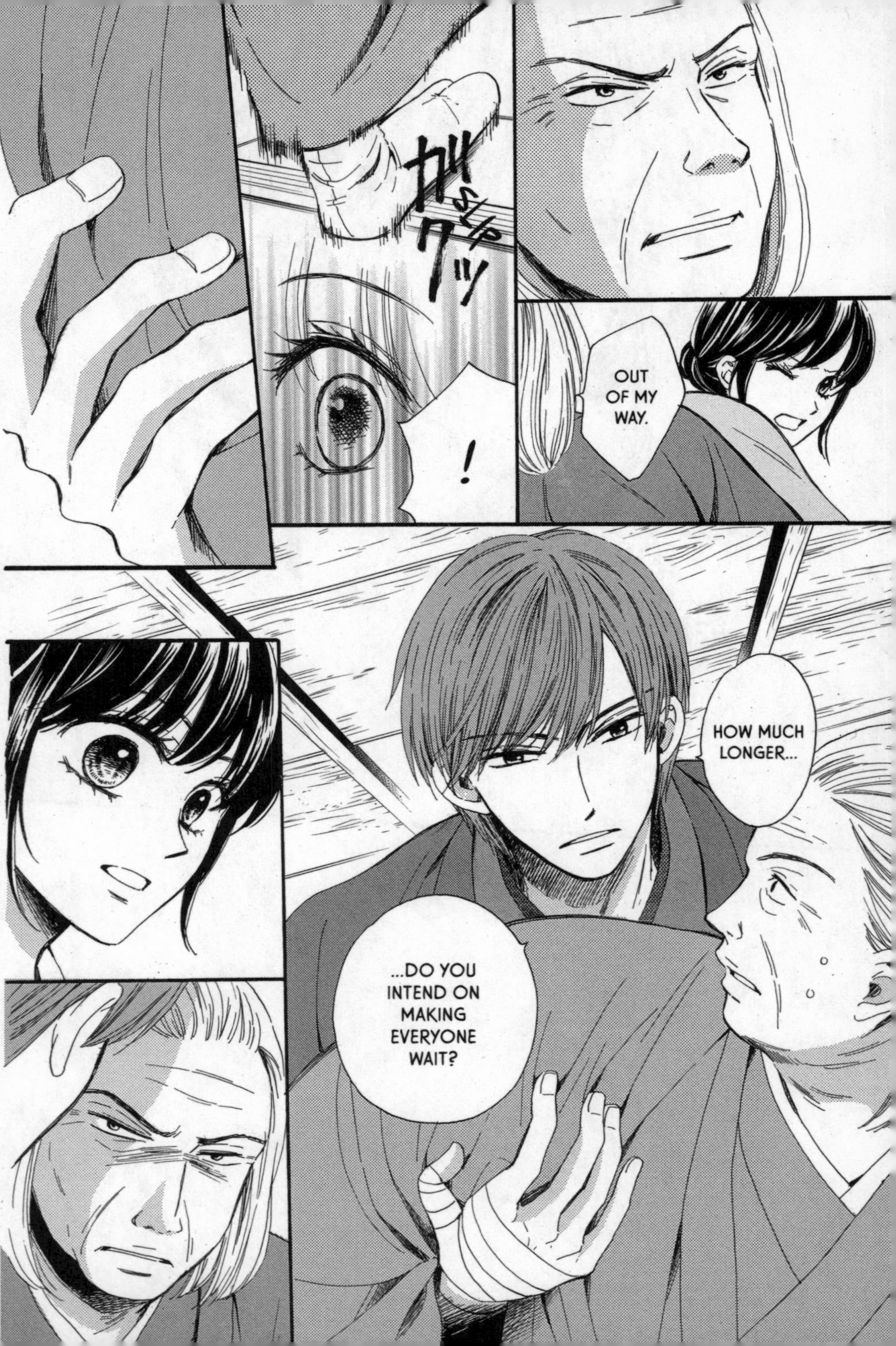
OUT OF MY WAY.
ガクッ
SLIP
!
HOW MUCH LONGER...
...DO YOU INTEND ON MAKING EVERYONE WAIT?

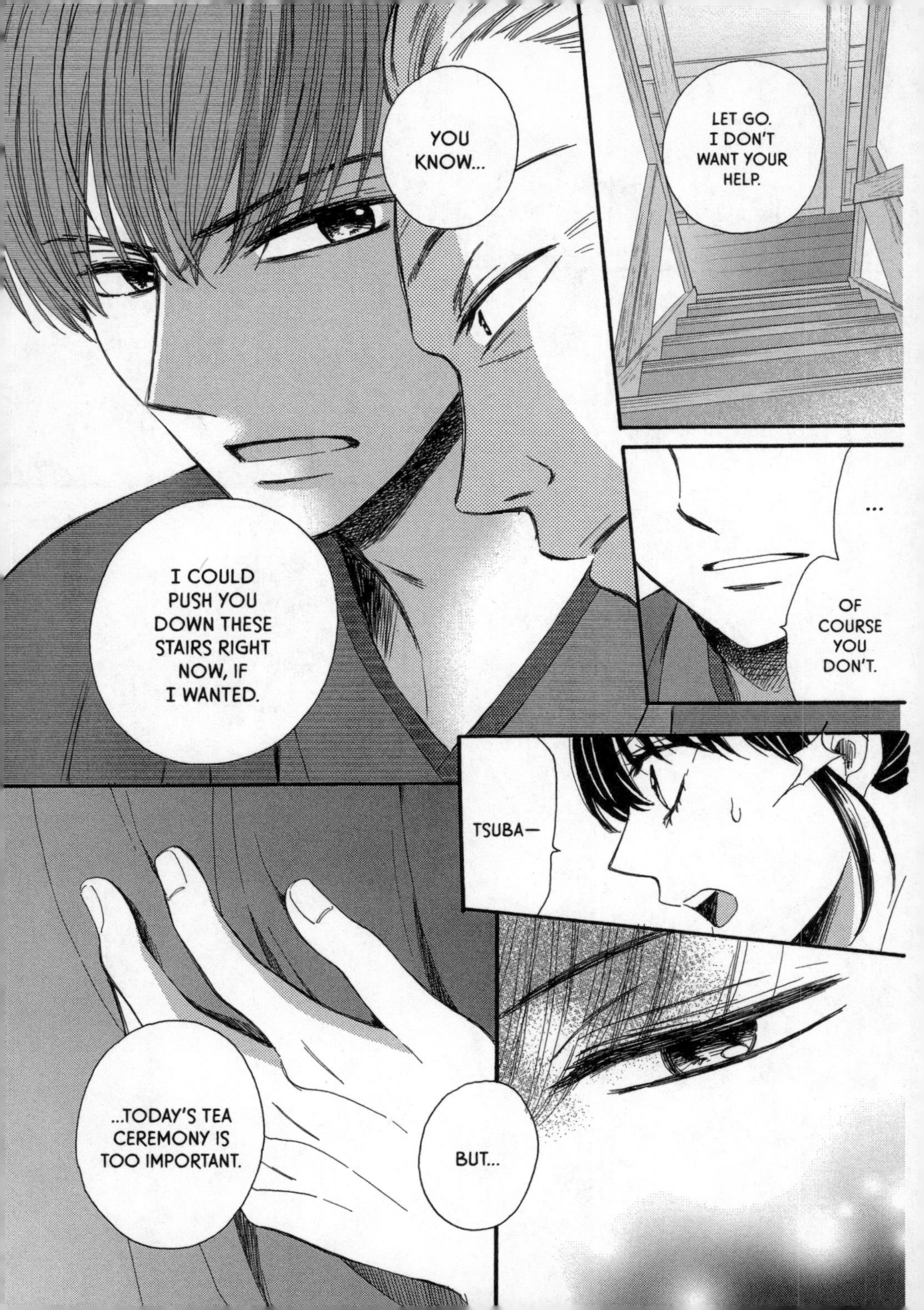
LET GO. I DON'T WANT YOUR HELP.
...
OF COURSE YOU DON'T.
TSUBA—
YOU KNOW...
I COULD PUSH YOU DOWN THESE STAIRS RIGHT NOW, IF I WANTED.
BUT...
...TODAY'S TEA CEREMONY IS TOO IMPORTANT.

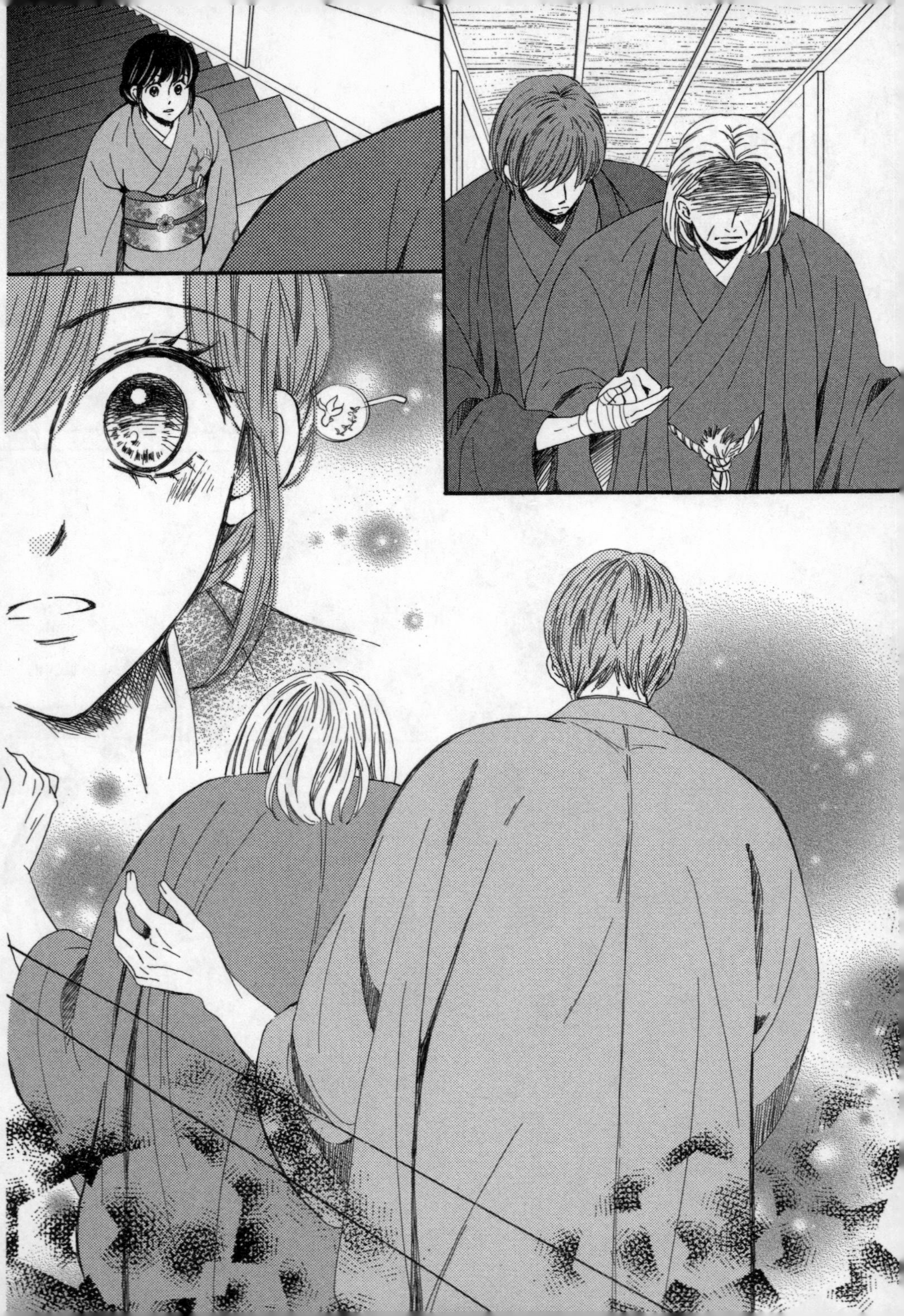

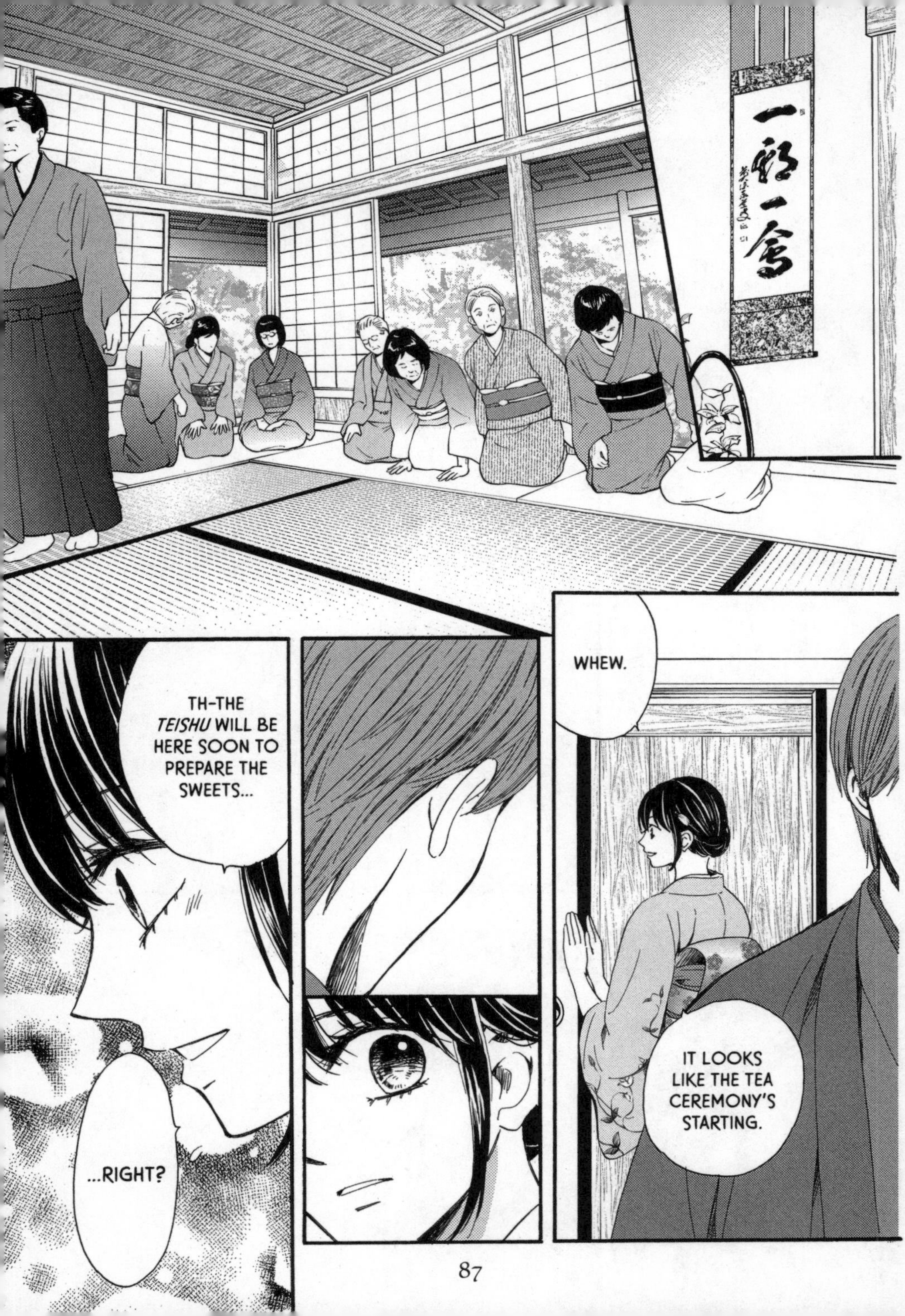
WHEW.
IT LOOKS LIKE THE TEA CEREMONY'S STARTING.
TH-THE *TEISHU* WILL BE HERE SOON TO PREPARE THE SWEETS...
...RIGHT?

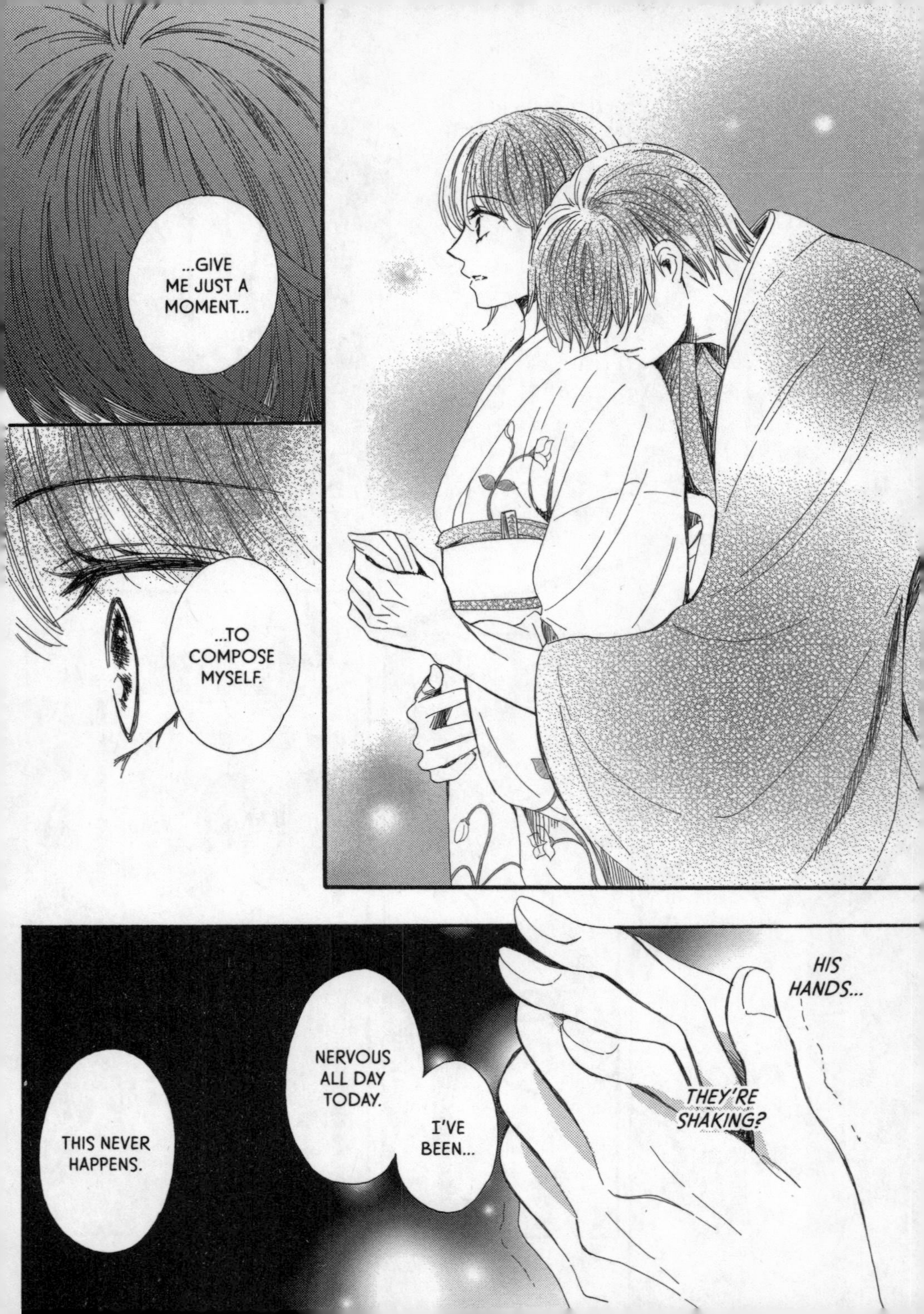
...GIVE ME JUST A MOMENT...
...TO COMPOSE MYSELF.
HIS HANDS...
THEY'RE SHAKING?
I'VE BEEN...
NERVOUS ALL DAY TODAY.
THIS NEVER HAPPENS.

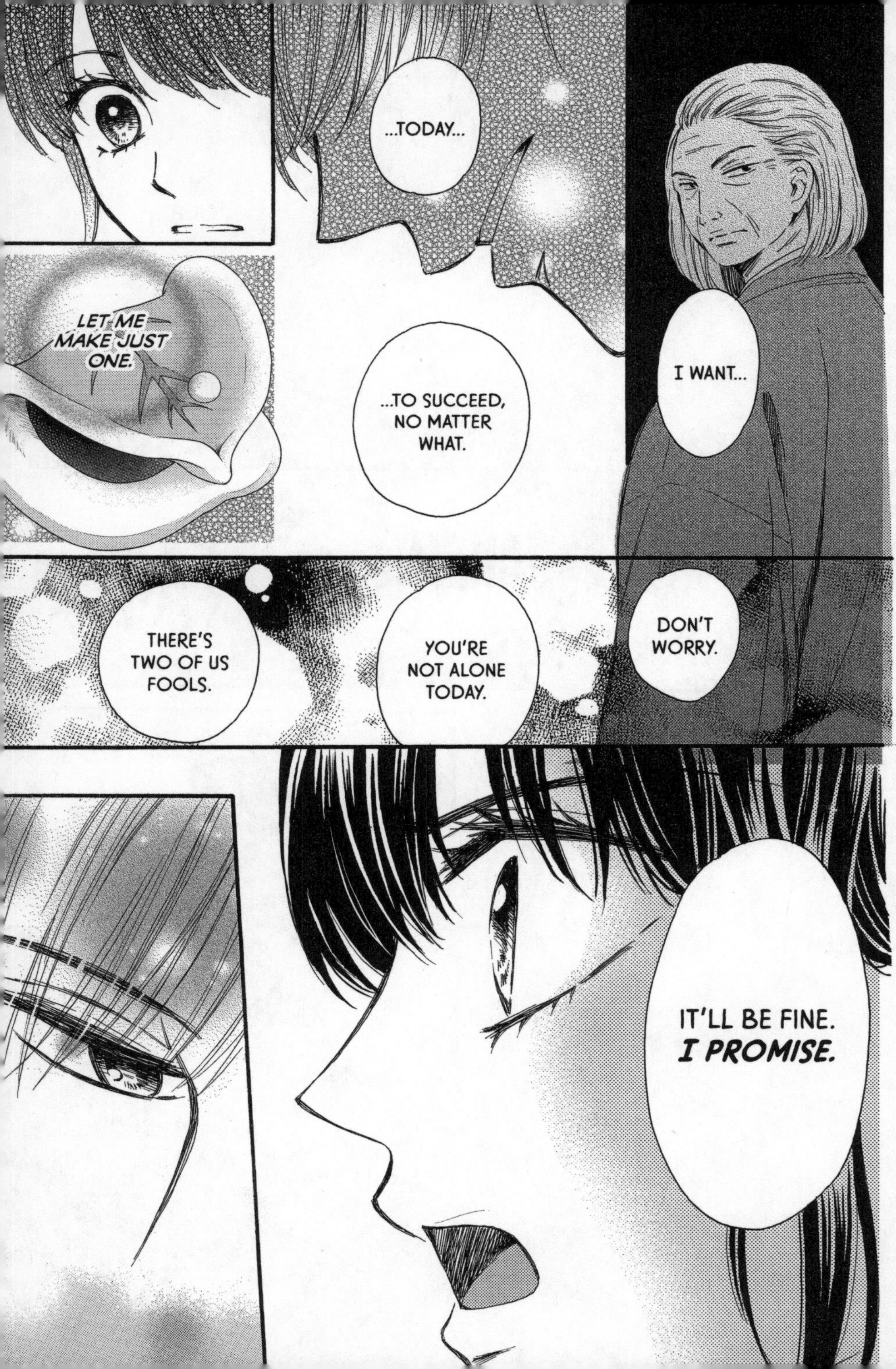
I WANT...
...TODAY...
...TO SUCCEED, NO MATTER WHAT.
LET ME MAKE JUST ONE.
DON'T WORRY.
YOU'RE NOT ALONE TODAY.
THERE'S TWO OF US FOOLS.
IT'LL BE FINE. **I PROMISE.**

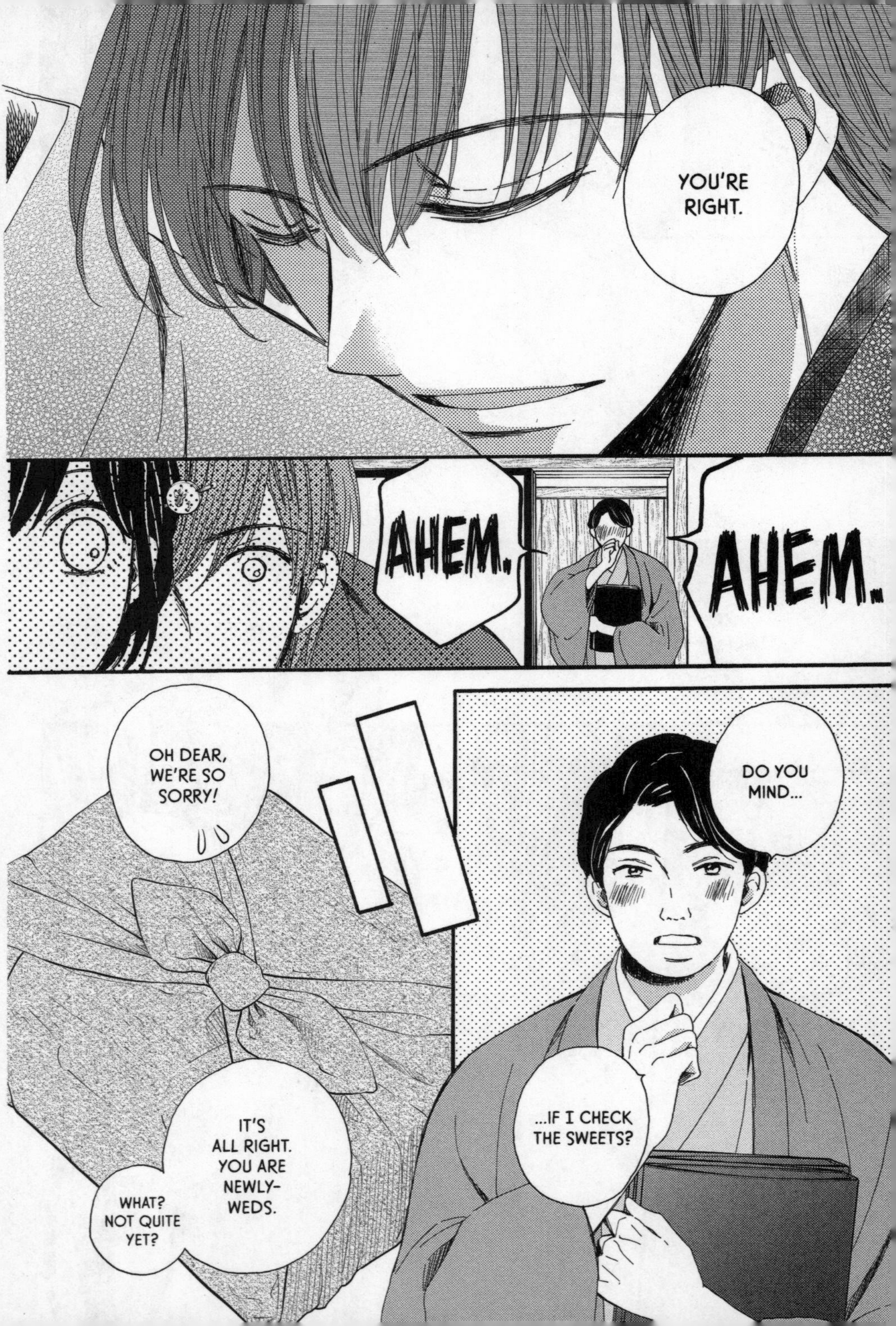
YOU'RE RIGHT.
AHEM..
AHEM.
DO YOU MIND...
...IF I CHECK THE SWEETS?
OH DEAR, WE'RE SO SORRY!
IT'S ALL RIGHT. YOU ARE NEWLY-WEDS.
WHAT? NOT QUITE YET?

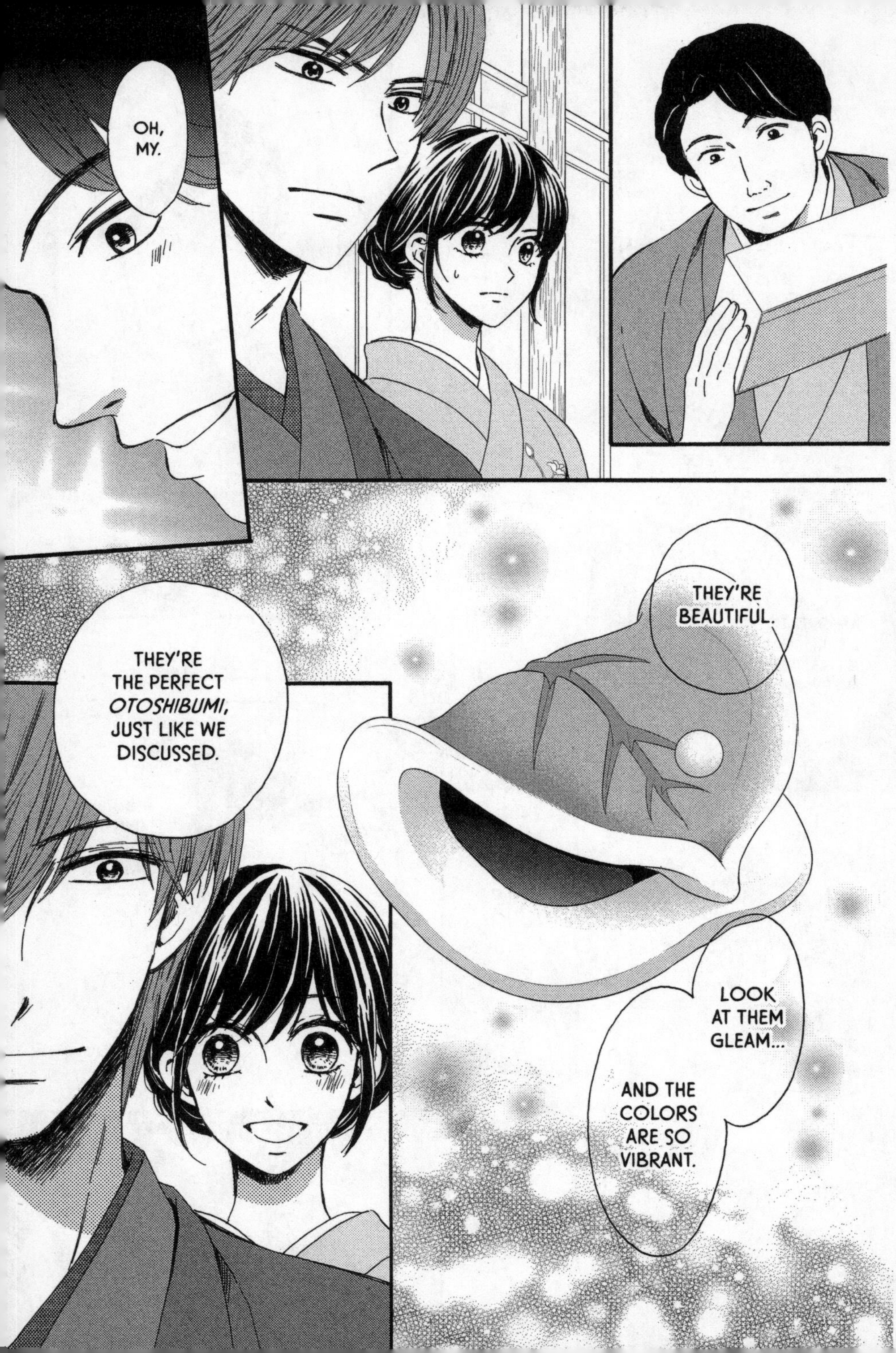

OH, MY.
THEY'RE BEAUTIFUL.
THEY'RE THE PERFECT *OTOSHIBUMI*, JUST LIKE WE DISCUSSED.
LOOK AT THEM GLEAM...
AND THE COLORS ARE SO VIBRANT.

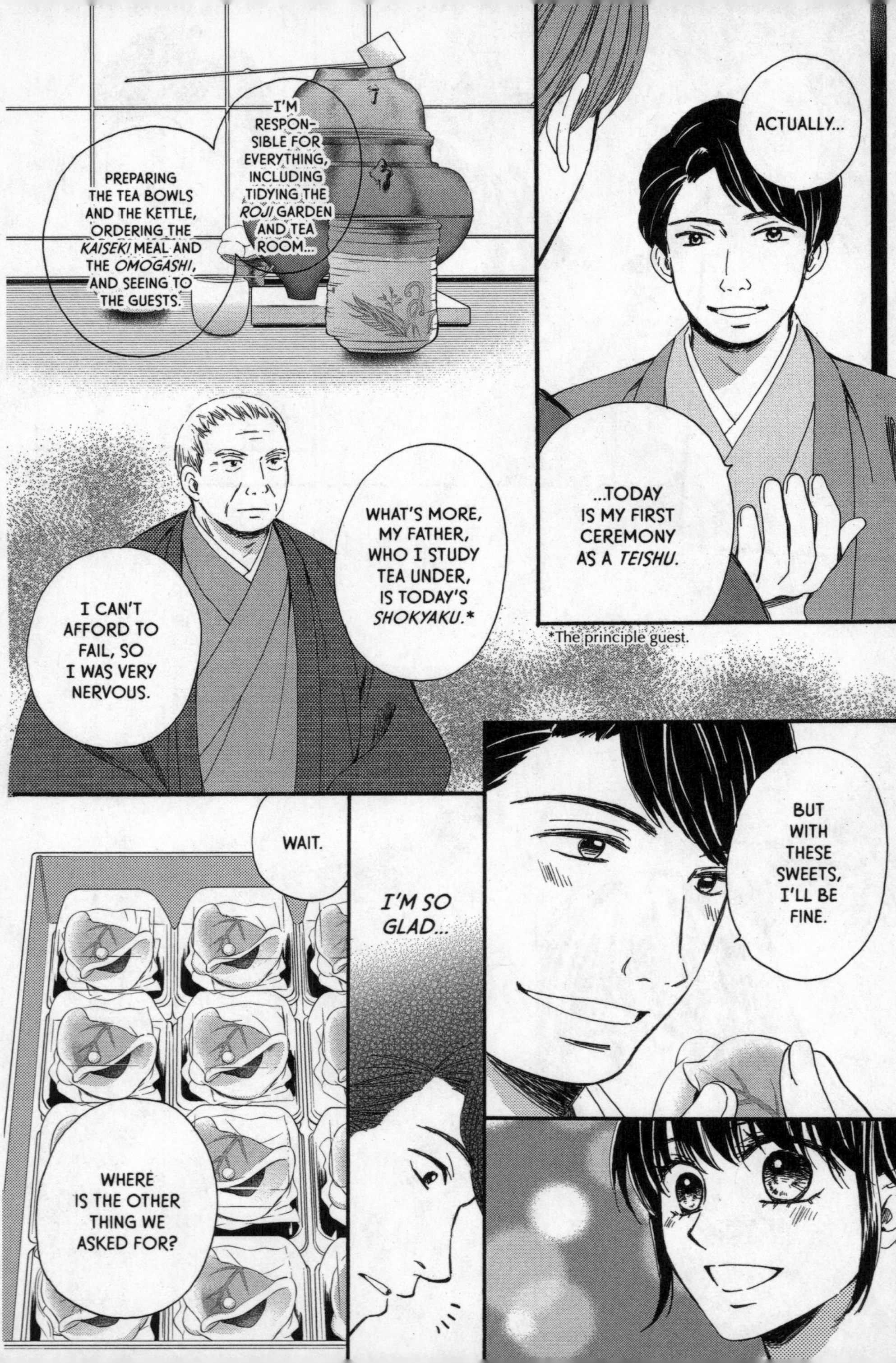

ACTUALLY...
...TODAY IS MY FIRST CEREMONY AS A TEISHU.
I'M RESPONSIBLE FOR EVERYTHING, INCLUDING TIDYING THE ROJI GARDEN AND TEA ROOM...
PREPARING THE TEA BOWLS AND THE KETTLE, ORDERING THE KAISEKI MEAL AND THE OMOGASHI, AND SEEING TO THE GUESTS.
WHAT'S MORE, MY FATHER, WHO I STUDY TEA UNDER, IS TODAY'S SHOKYAKU.*
I CAN'T AFFORD TO FAIL, SO I WAS VERY NERVOUS.
*The principle guest.
BUT WITH THESE SWEETS, I'LL BE FINE.
I'M SO GLAD...
WAIT.
WHERE IS THE OTHER THING WE ASKED FOR?

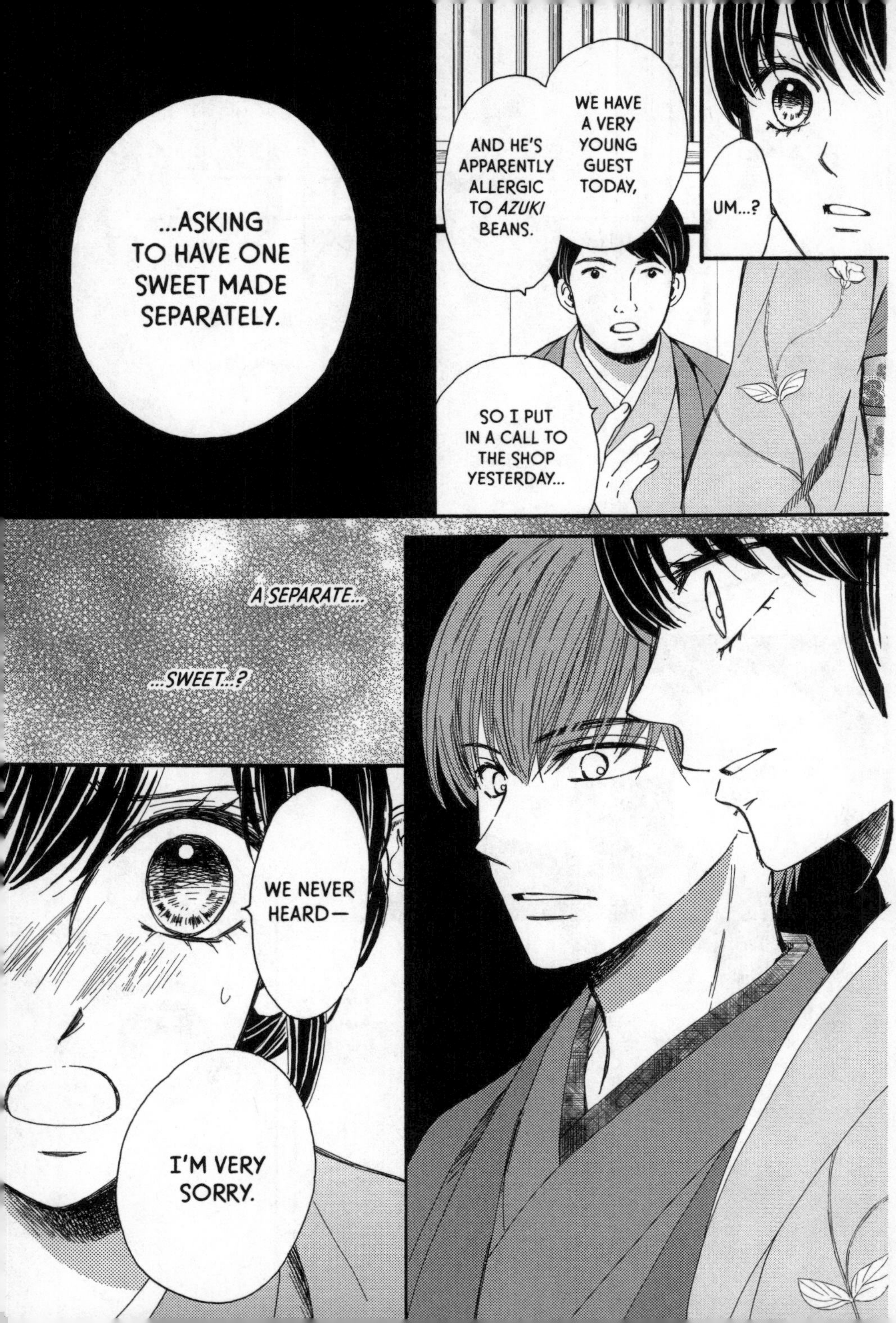
UM...?
WE HAVE A VERY YOUNG GUEST TODAY,
AND HE'S APPARENTLY ALLERGIC TO *AZUKI* BEANS.
SO I PUT IN A CALL TO THE SHOP YESTERDAY...
...ASKING TO HAVE ONE SWEET MADE SEPARATELY.
A SEPARATE...
...SWEET...?
WE NEVER HEARD—
I'M VERY SORRY.

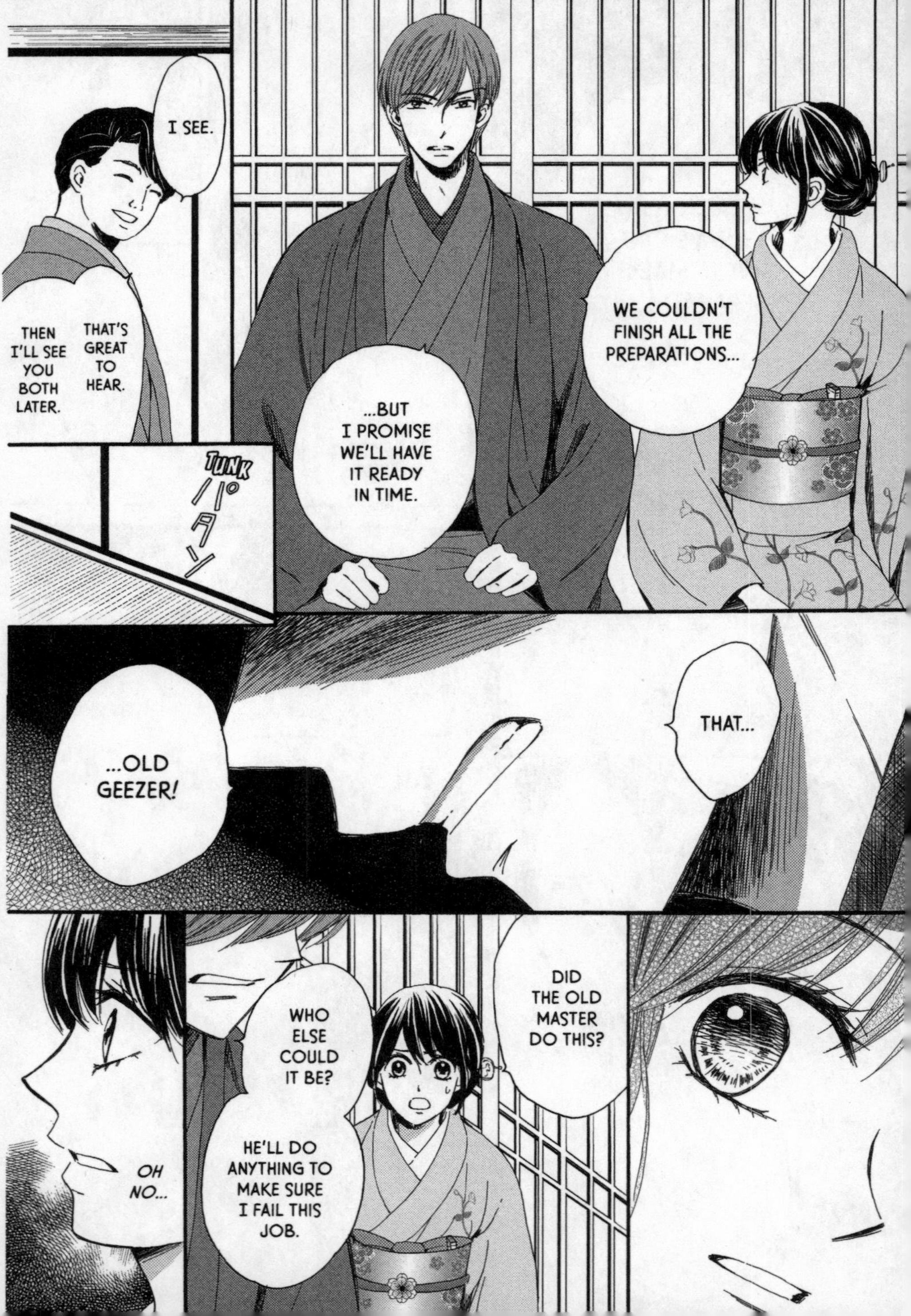
WE COULDN'T FINISH ALL THE PREPARATIONS...
...BUT I PROMISE WE'LL HAVE IT READY IN TIME.
I SEE.
THAT'S GREAT TO HEAR.
THEN I'LL SEE YOU BOTH LATER.
TUNK
パタン
THAT...
...OLD GEEZER!
DID THE OLD MASTER DO THIS?
WHO ELSE COULD IT BE?
HE'LL DO ANYTHING TO MAKE SURE I FAIL THIS JOB.
OH NO...

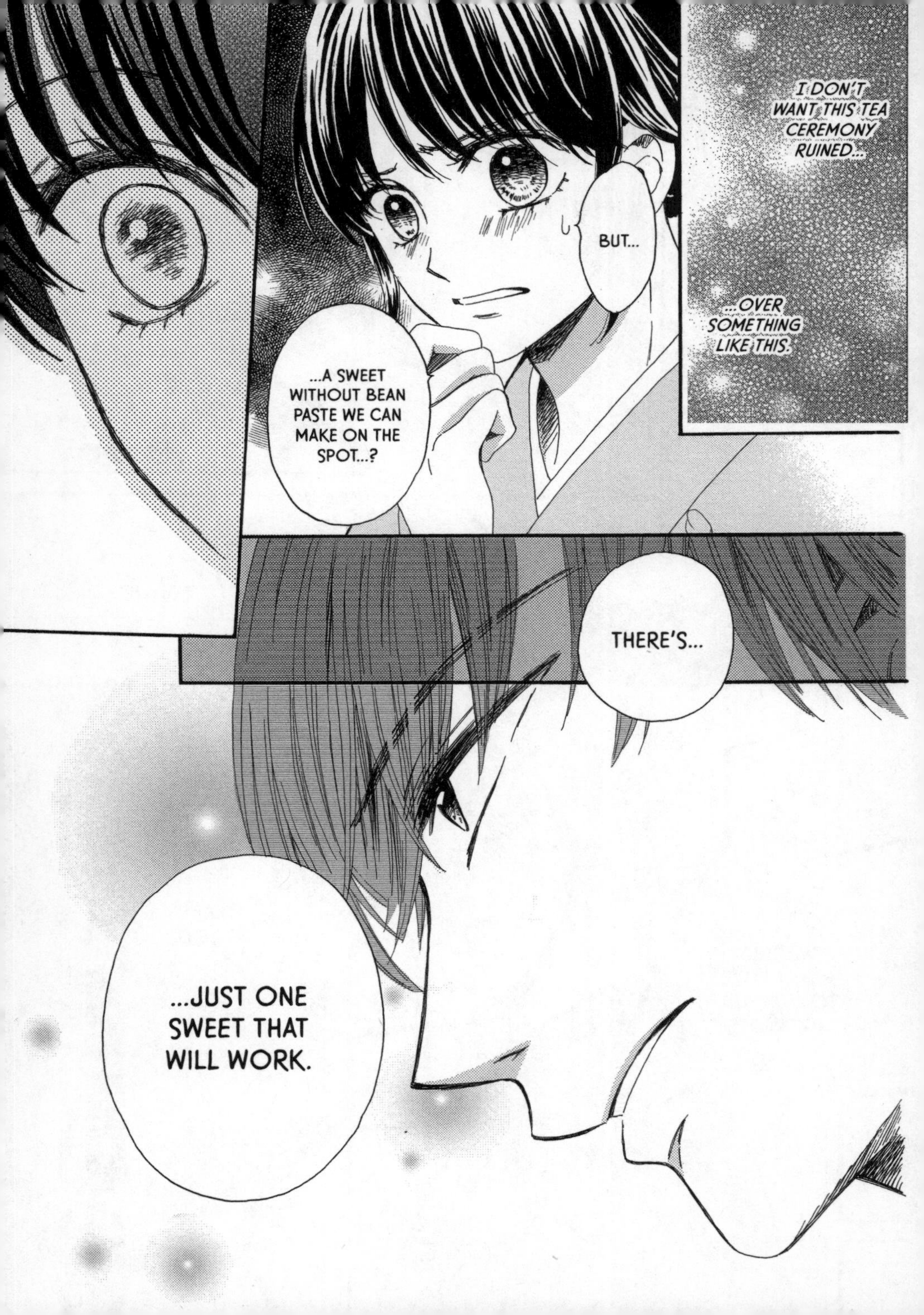
I DON'T WANT THIS TEA CEREMONY RUINED...
...OVER SOMETHING LIKE THIS.
BUT...
...A SWEET WITHOUT BEAN PASTE WE CAN MAKE ON THE SPOT...?
THERE'S...
...JUST ONE SWEET THAT WILL WORK.

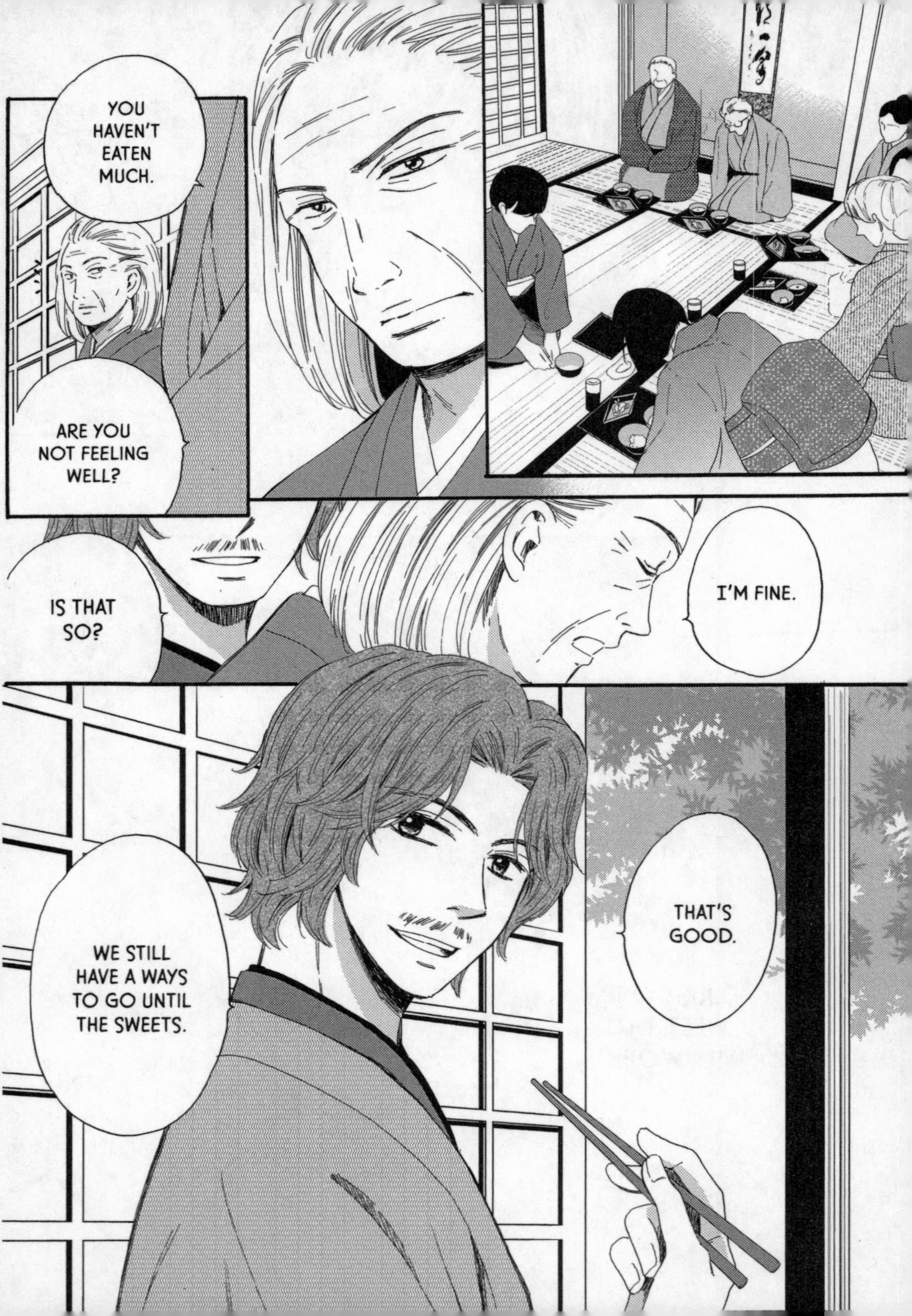
YOU HAVEN'T EATEN MUCH.
ARE YOU NOT FEELING WELL?
I'M FINE.
IS THAT SO?
THAT'S GOOD.
WE STILL HAVE A WAYS TO GO UNTIL THE SWEETS.

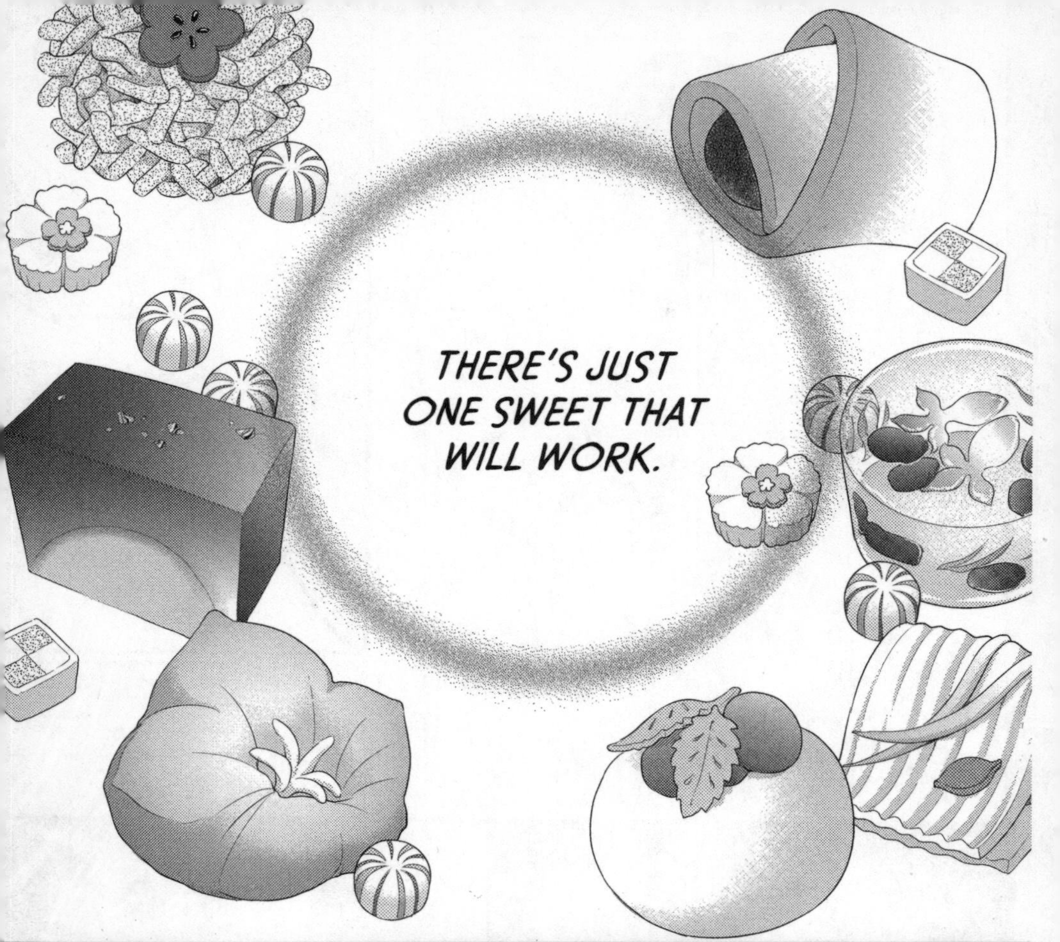
THERE'S JUST ONE SWEET THAT WILL WORK.

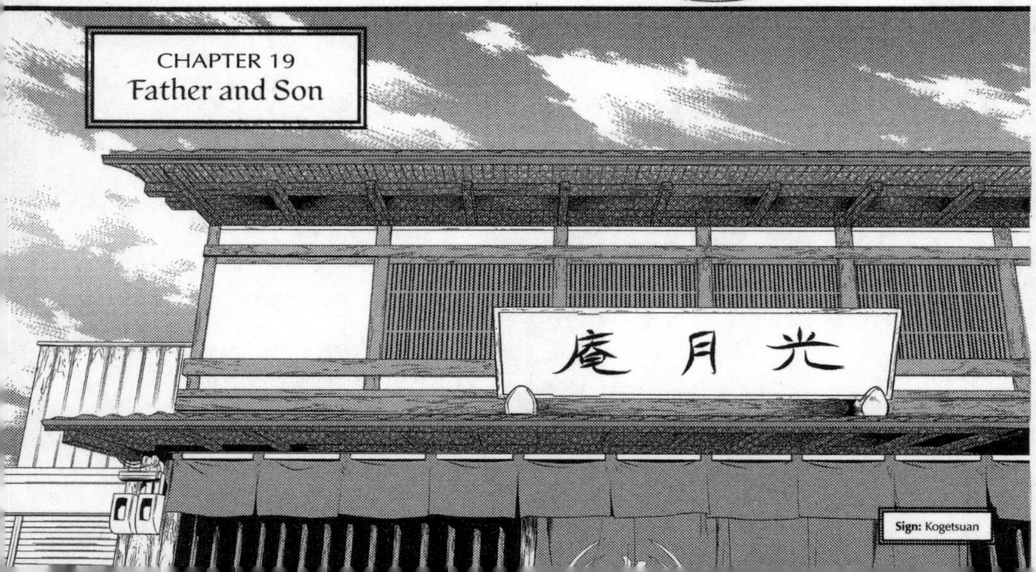
CHAPTER 19
Father and Son
光月庵
Sign: Kogetsuan

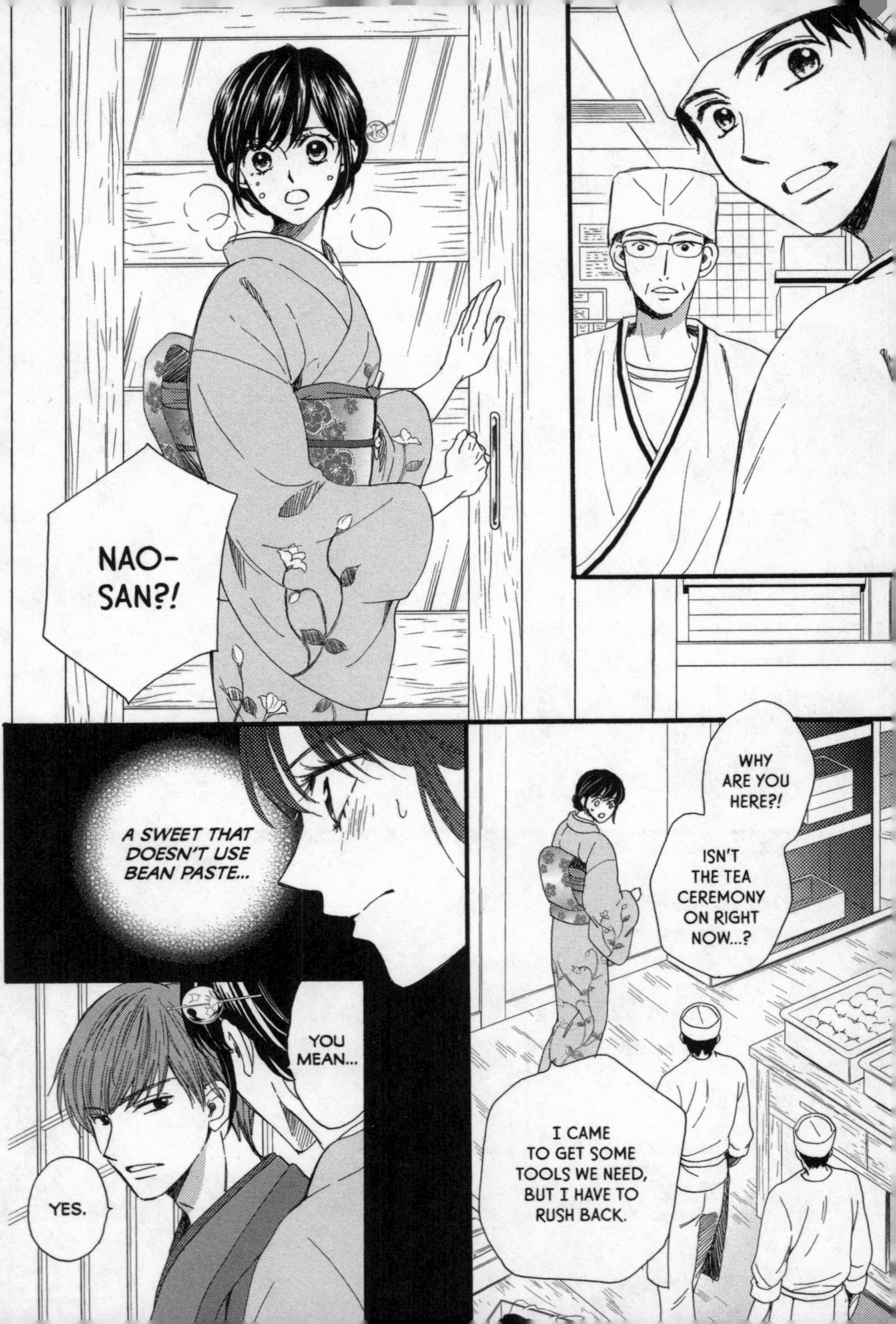
NAO-SAN?!
WHY ARE YOU HERE?!
ISN'T THE TEA CEREMONY ON RIGHT NOW...?
I CAME TO GET SOME TOOLS WE NEED, BUT I HAVE TO RUSH BACK.
A SWEET THAT DOESN'T USE BEAN PASTE...
YOU MEAN...
YES.

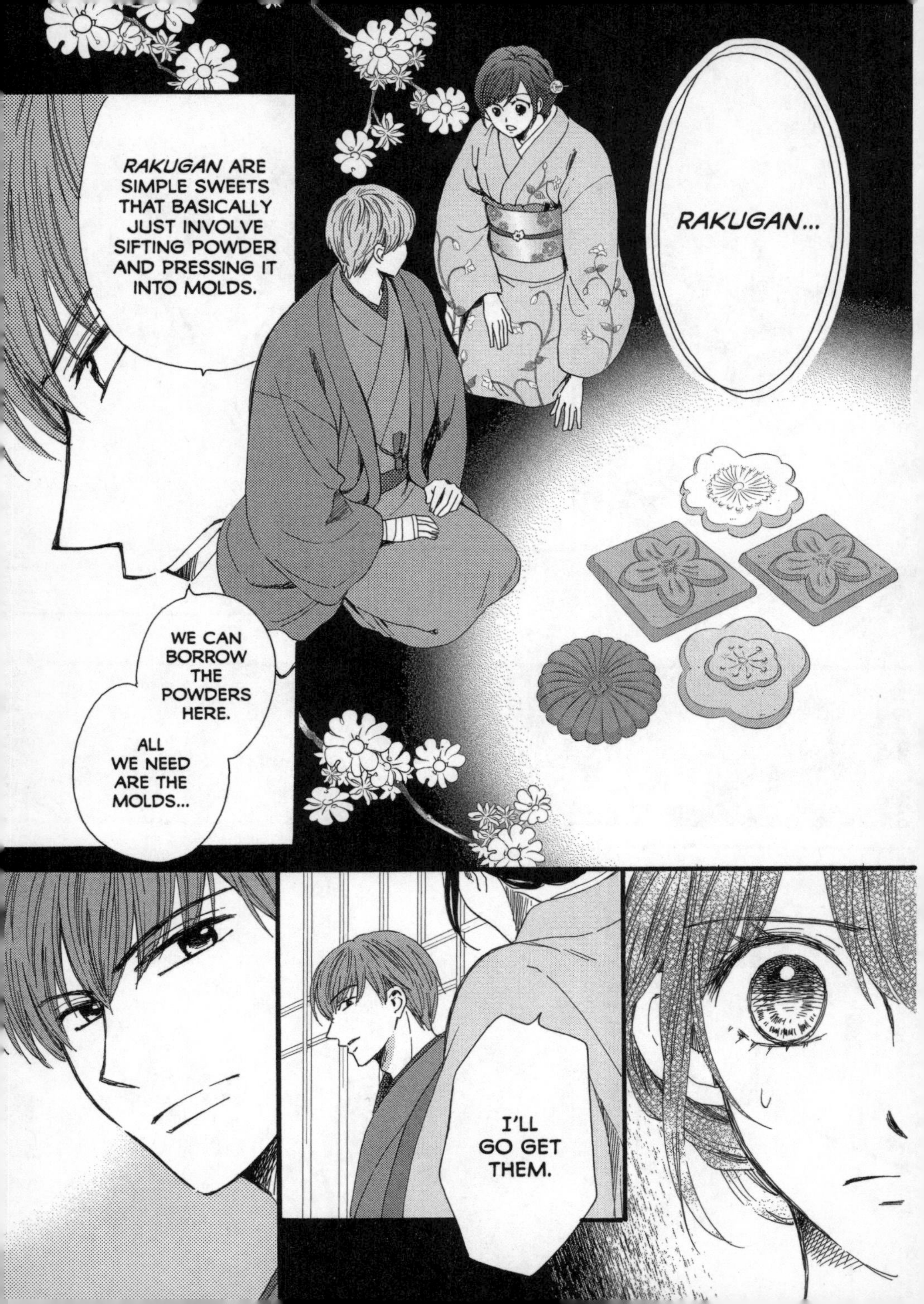
RAKUGAN...
RAKUGAN ARE SIMPLE SWEETS THAT BASICALLY JUST INVOLVE SIFTING POWDER AND PRESSING IT INTO MOLDS.
WE CAN BORROW THE POWDERS HERE.
ALL WE NEED ARE THE MOLDS...
I'LL GO GET THEM.

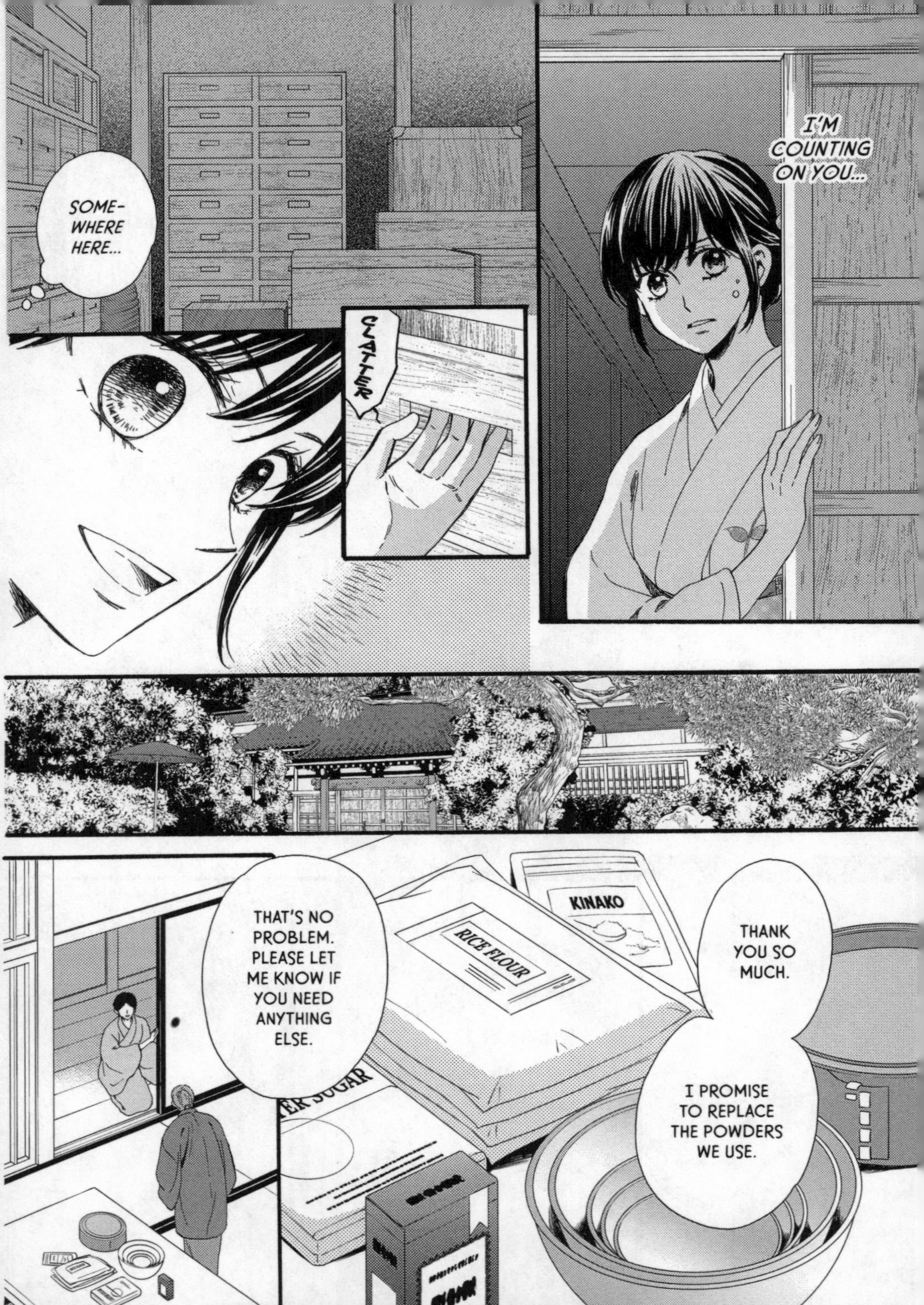
I'M COUNTING ON YOU...
SOME-WHERE HERE...
CLATTER
KINAKO
RICE FLOUR
THAT'S NO PROBLEM. PLEASE LET ME KNOW IF YOU NEED ANYTHING ELSE.
THANK YOU SO MUCH.
I PROMISE TO REPLACE THE POWDERS WE USE.

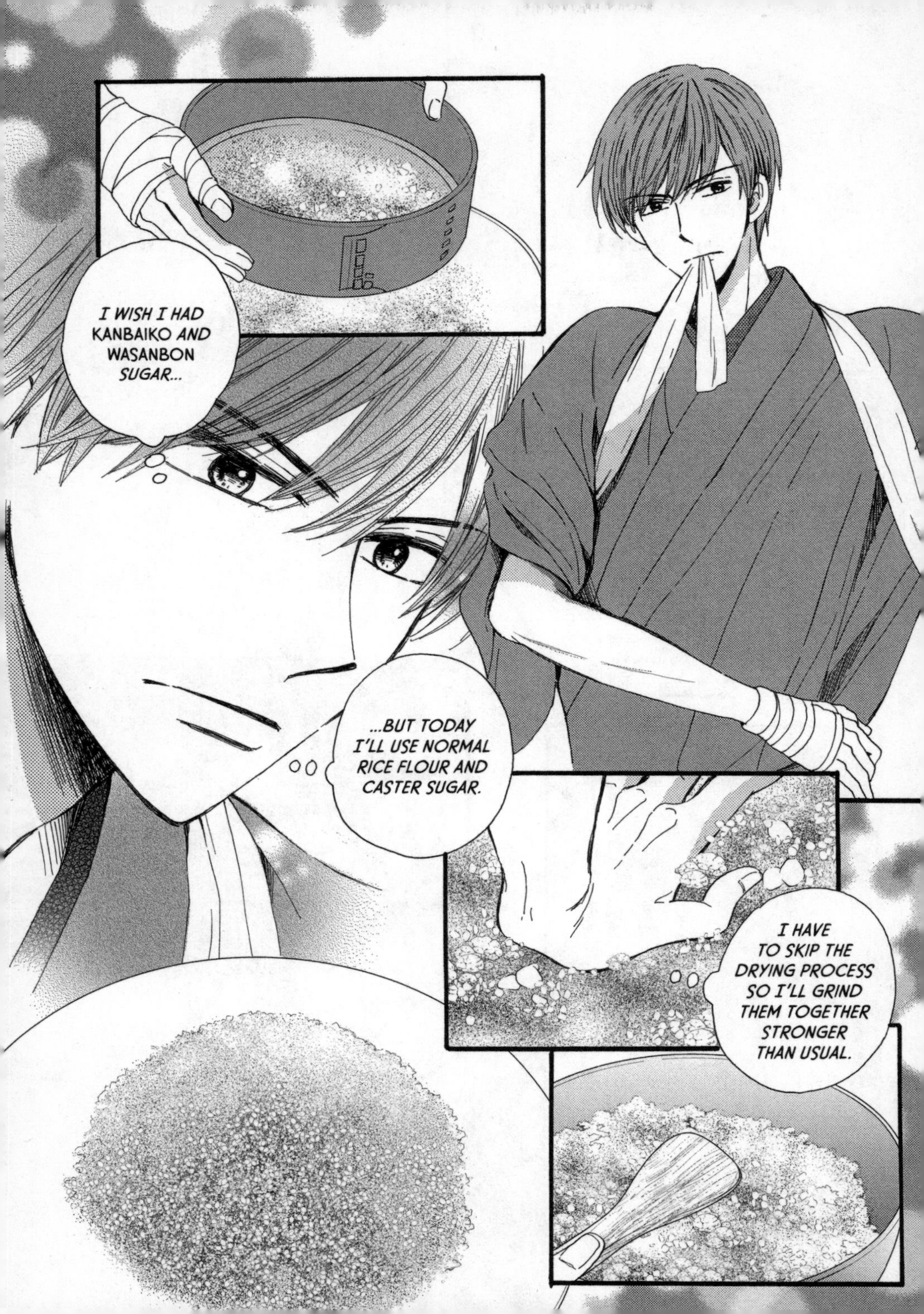
I WISH I HAD KANBAIKO AND WASANBON SUGAR...
...BUT TODAY I'LL USE NORMAL RICE FLOUR AND CASTER SUGAR.
I HAVE TO SKIP THE DRYING PROCESS SO I'LL GRIND THEM TOGETHER STRONGER THAN USUAL.

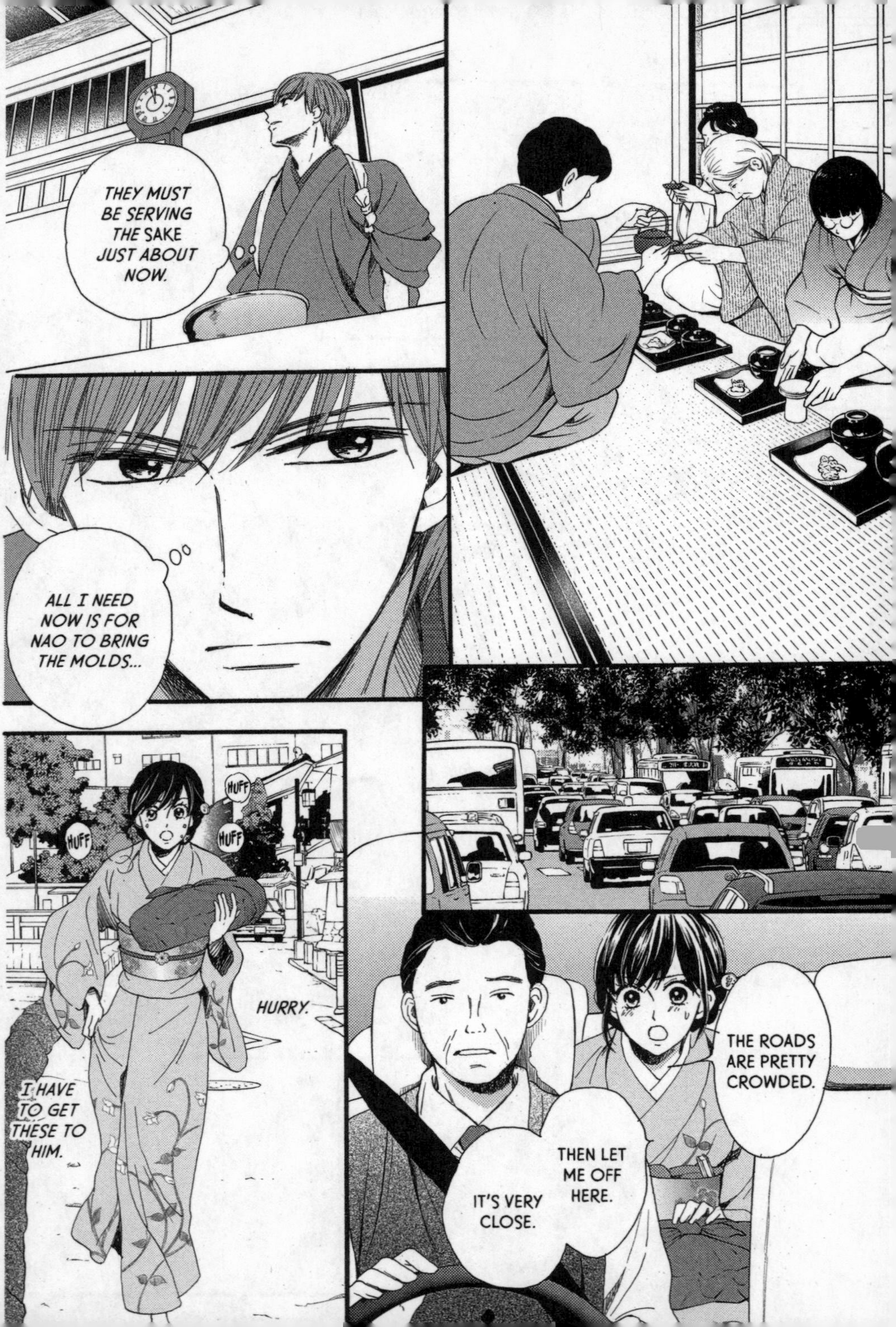
THEY MUST BE SERVING THE SAKE JUST ABOUT NOW.
ALL I NEED NOW IS FOR NAO TO BRING THE MOLDS...
THE ROADS ARE PRETTY CROWDED.
THEN LET ME OFF HERE.
IT'S VERY CLOSE.
HUFF
HUFF
HUFF
HURRY.
I HAVE TO GET THESE TO HIM.

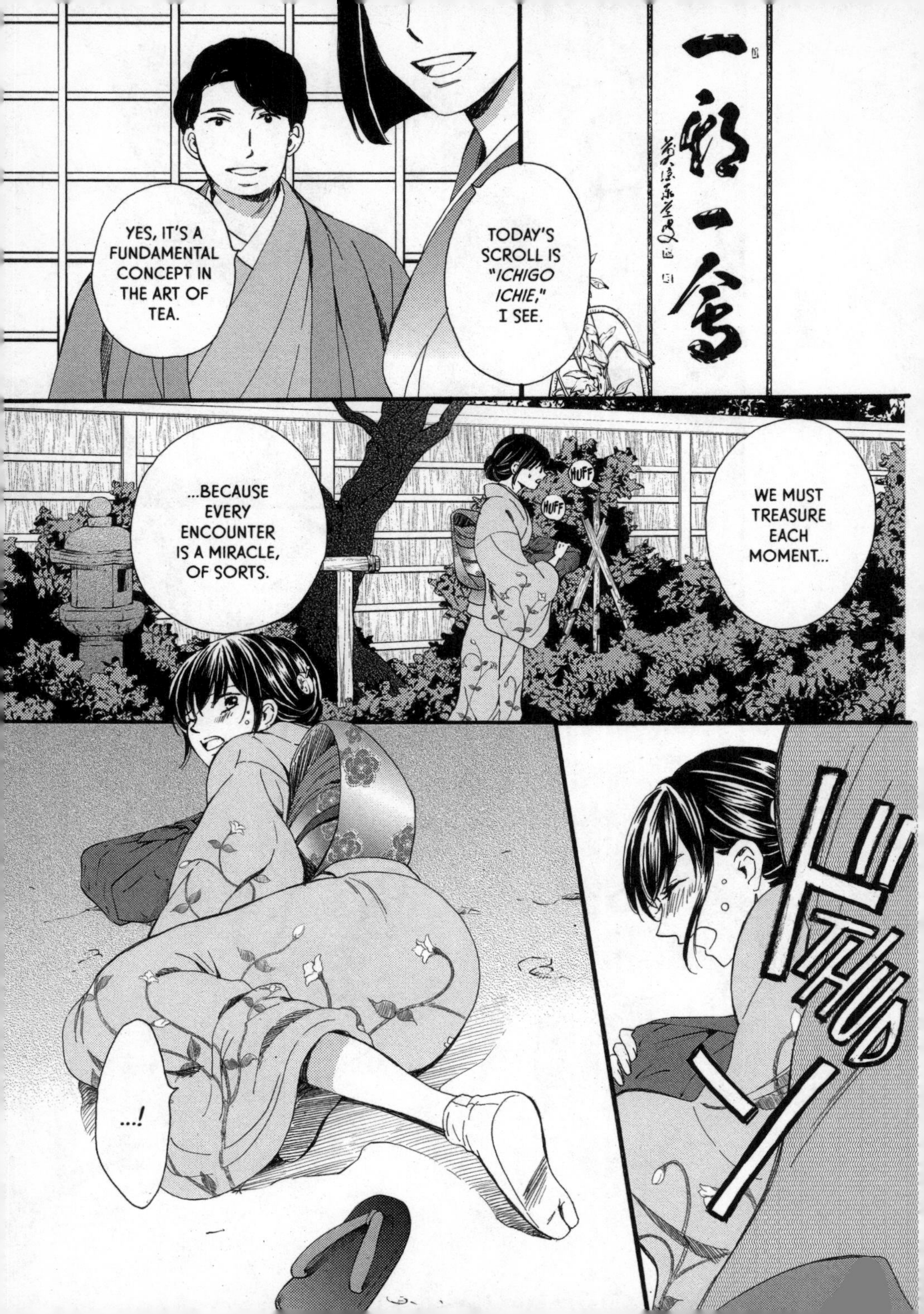
TODAY'S SCROLL IS "ICHIGO ICHIE," I SEE.
YES, IT'S A FUNDAMENTAL CONCEPT IN THE ART OF TEA.
WE MUST TREASURE EACH MOMENT...
HUFF
HUFF
...BECAUSE EVERY ENCOUNTER IS A MIRACLE, OF SORTS.
THUD
...!

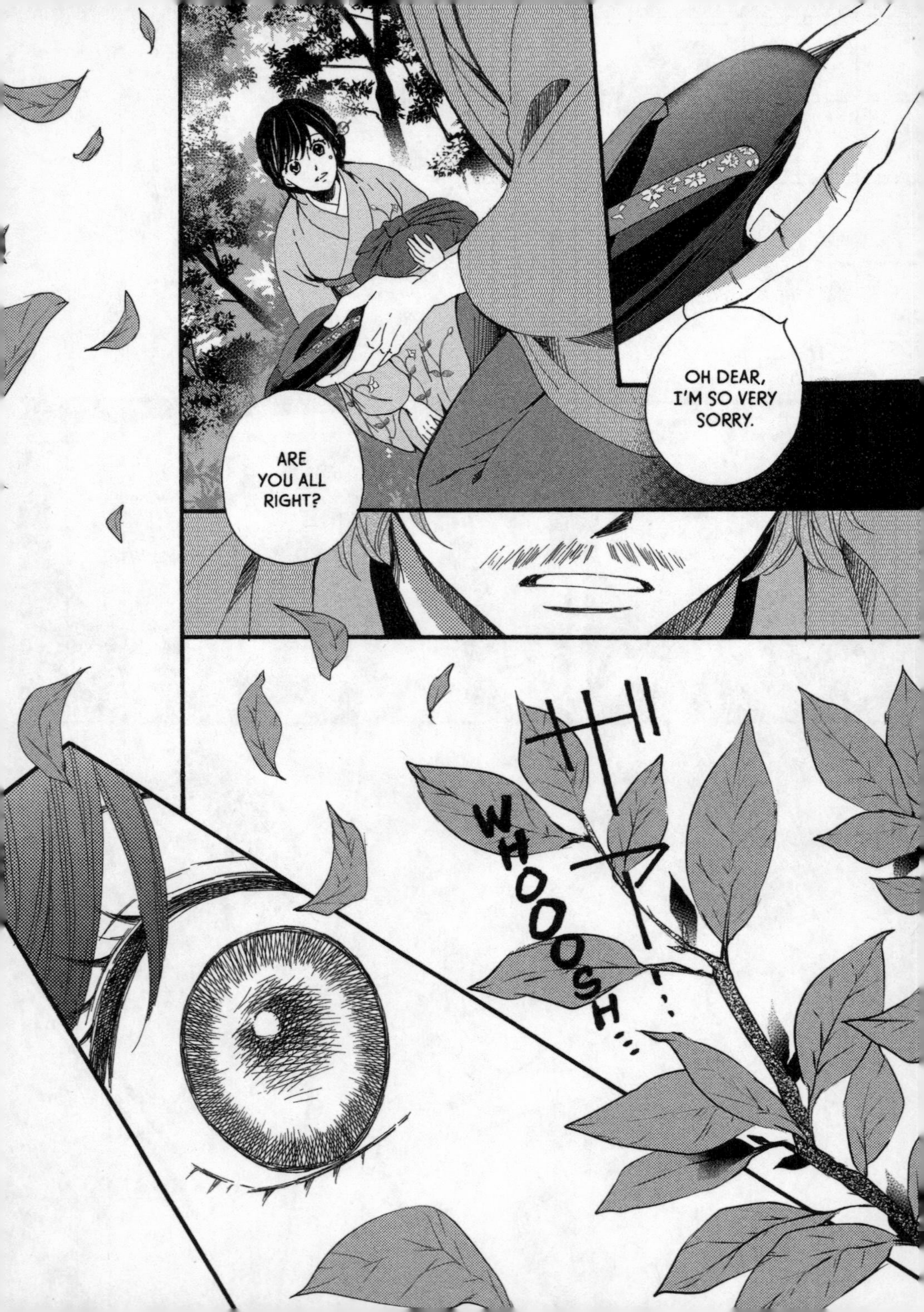
OH DEAR, I'M SO VERY SORRY.
ARE YOU ALL RIGHT?
WHOOOSH...

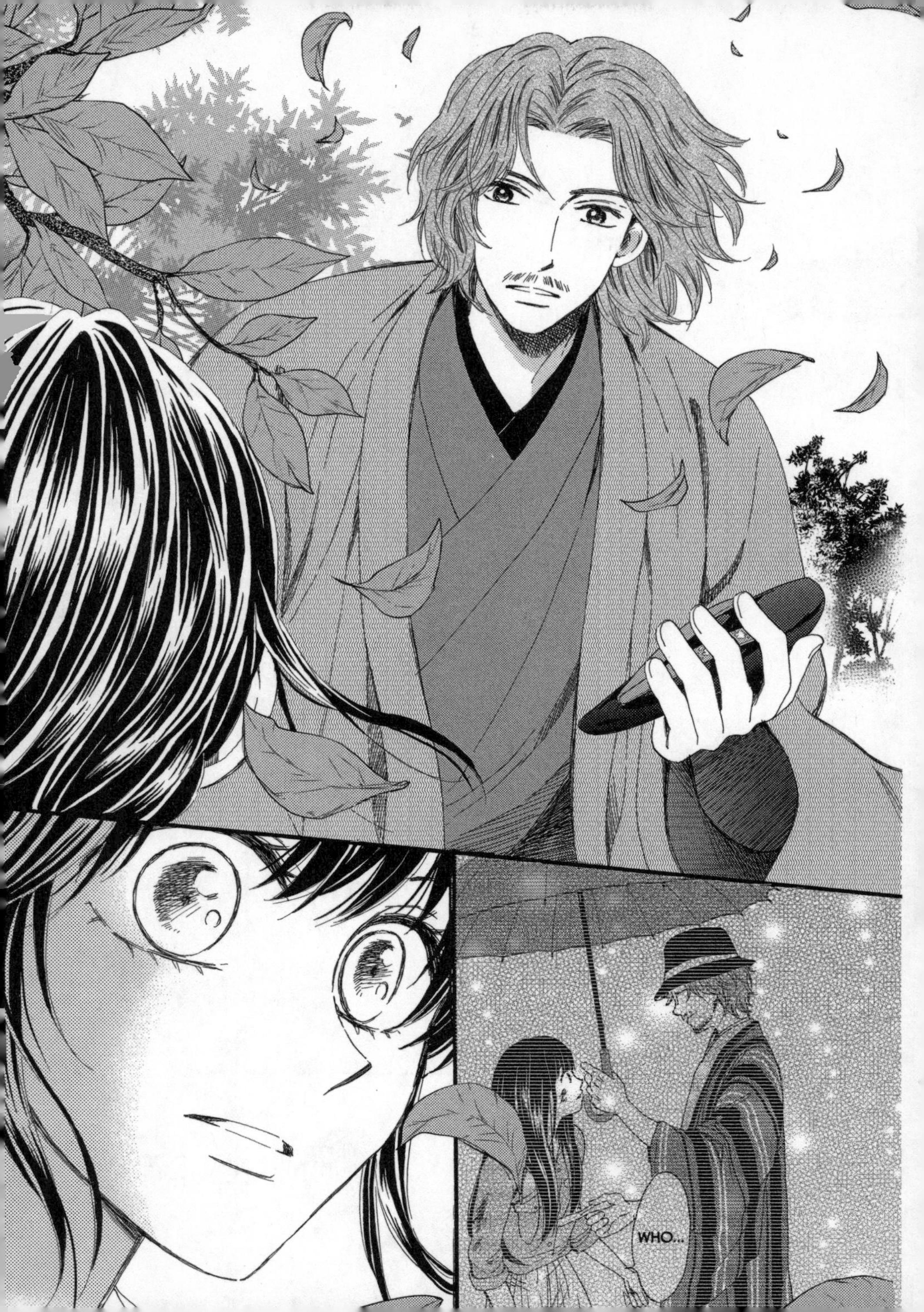
WHO...

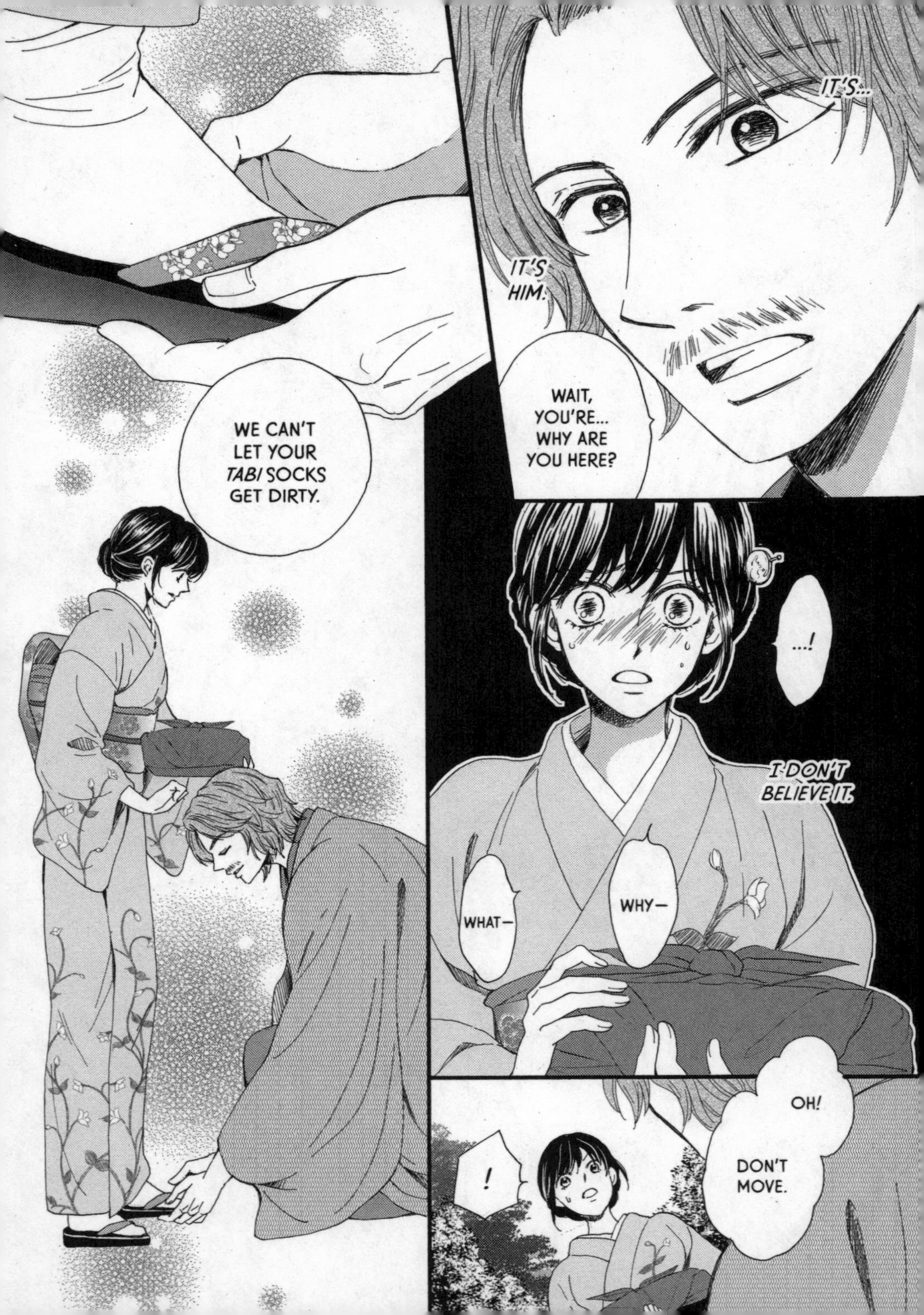
IT'S...
IT'S HIM.
WAIT, YOU'RE... WHY ARE YOU HERE?
...!
I DON'T BELIEVE IT.
WHY—
WHAT—
OH!
DON'T MOVE.
!
WE CAN'T LET YOUR *TABI* SOCKS GET DIRTY.

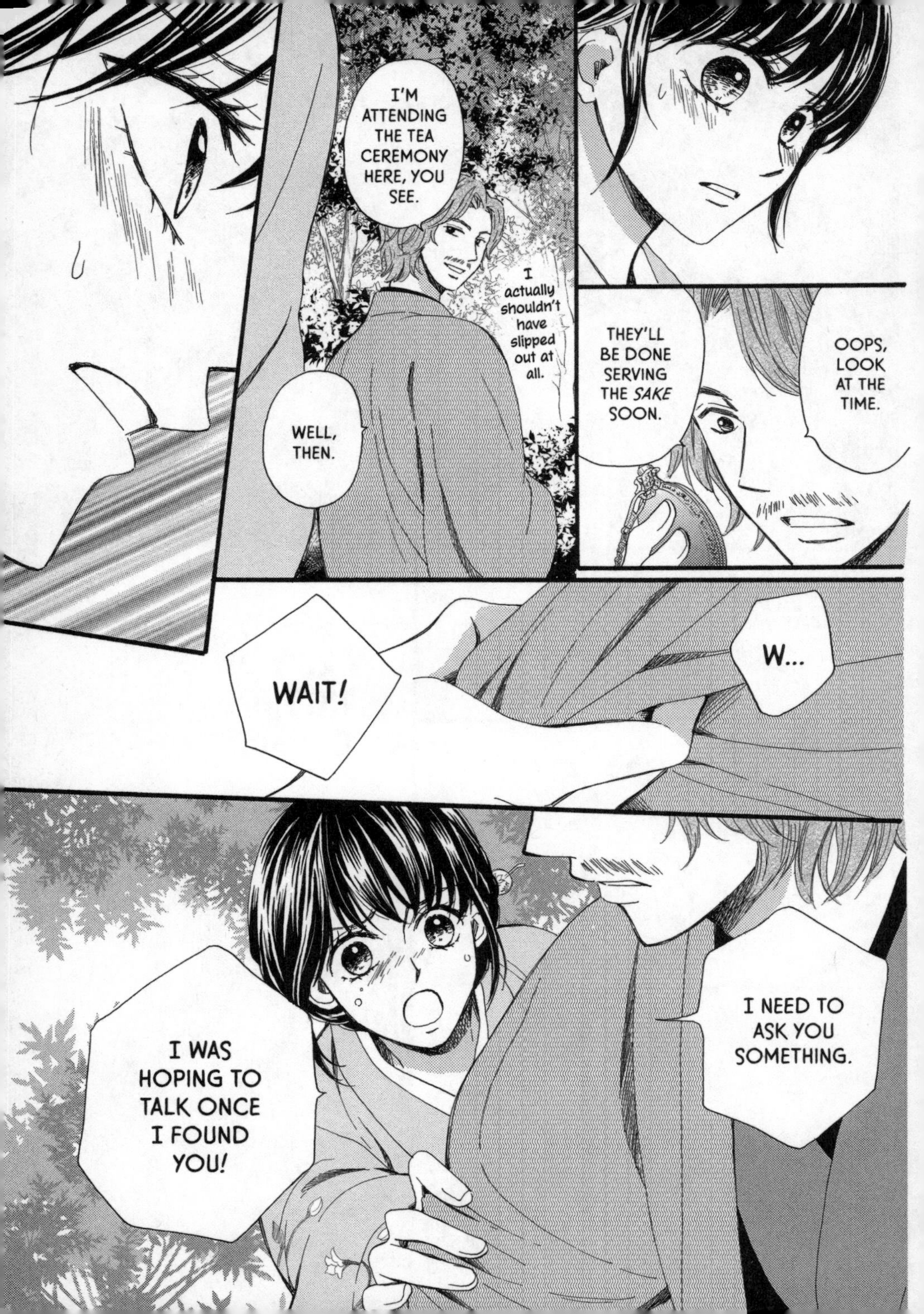
OOPS, LOOK AT THE TIME.
THEY'LL BE DONE SERVING THE *SAKE* SOON.
I'M ATTENDING THE TEA CEREMONY HERE, YOU SEE.
I actually shouldn't have slipped out at all.
WELL, THEN.
W...
WAIT!
I NEED TO ASK YOU SOMETHING.
I WAS HOPING TO TALK ONCE I FOUND YOU!

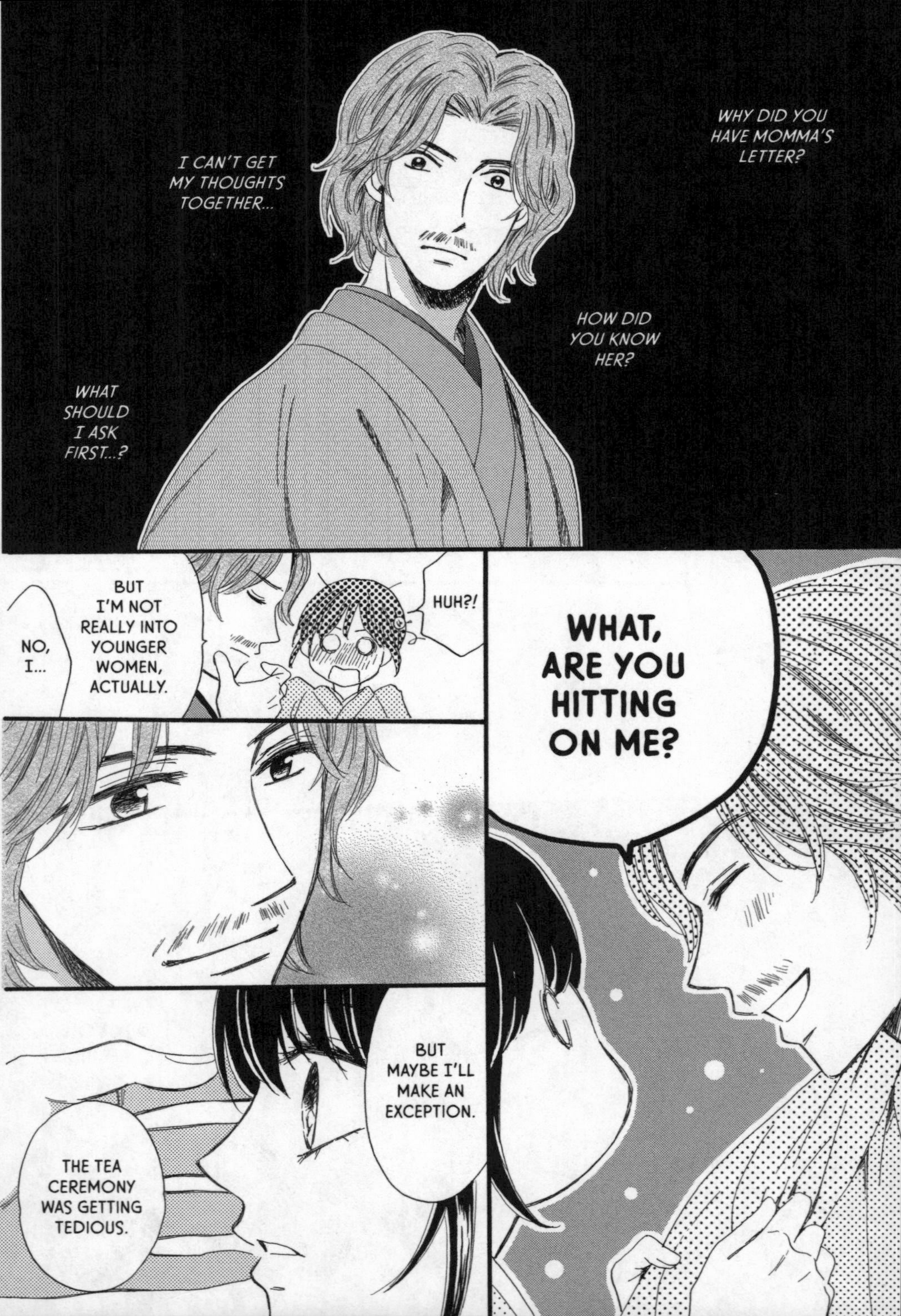
WHY DID YOU HAVE MOMMA'S LETTER?
HOW DID YOU KNOW HER?
I CAN'T GET MY THOUGHTS TOGETHER...
WHAT SHOULD I ASK FIRST...?
WHAT, ARE YOU HITTING ON ME?
HUH?!
BUT I'M NOT REALLY INTO YOUNGER WOMEN, ACTUALLY.
NO, I...
BUT MAYBE I'LL MAKE AN EXCEPTION.
THE TEA CEREMONY WAS GETTING TEDIOUS.

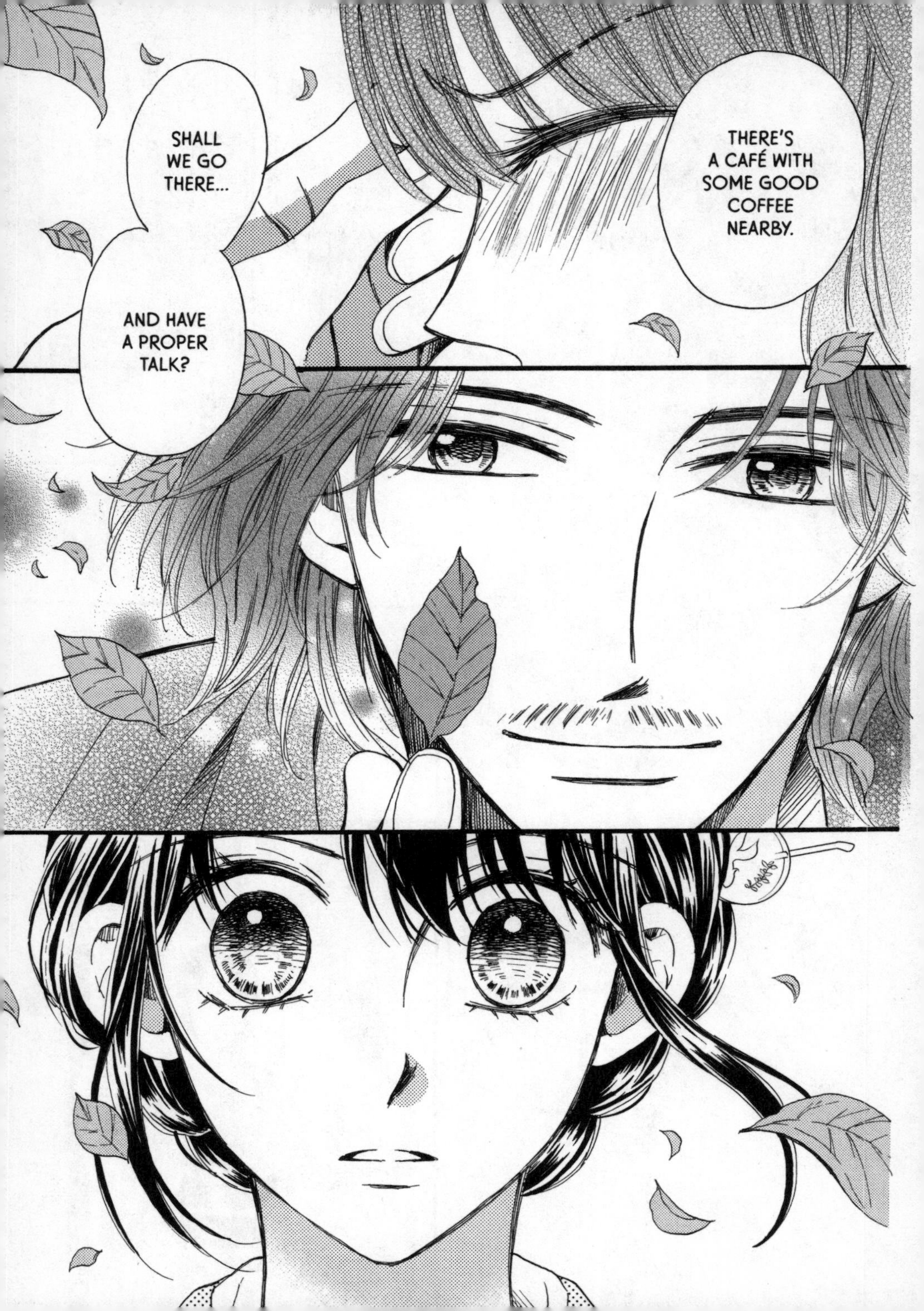
THERE'S A CAFÉ WITH SOME GOOD COFFEE NEARBY.
SHALL WE GO THERE...
AND HAVE A PROPER TALK?

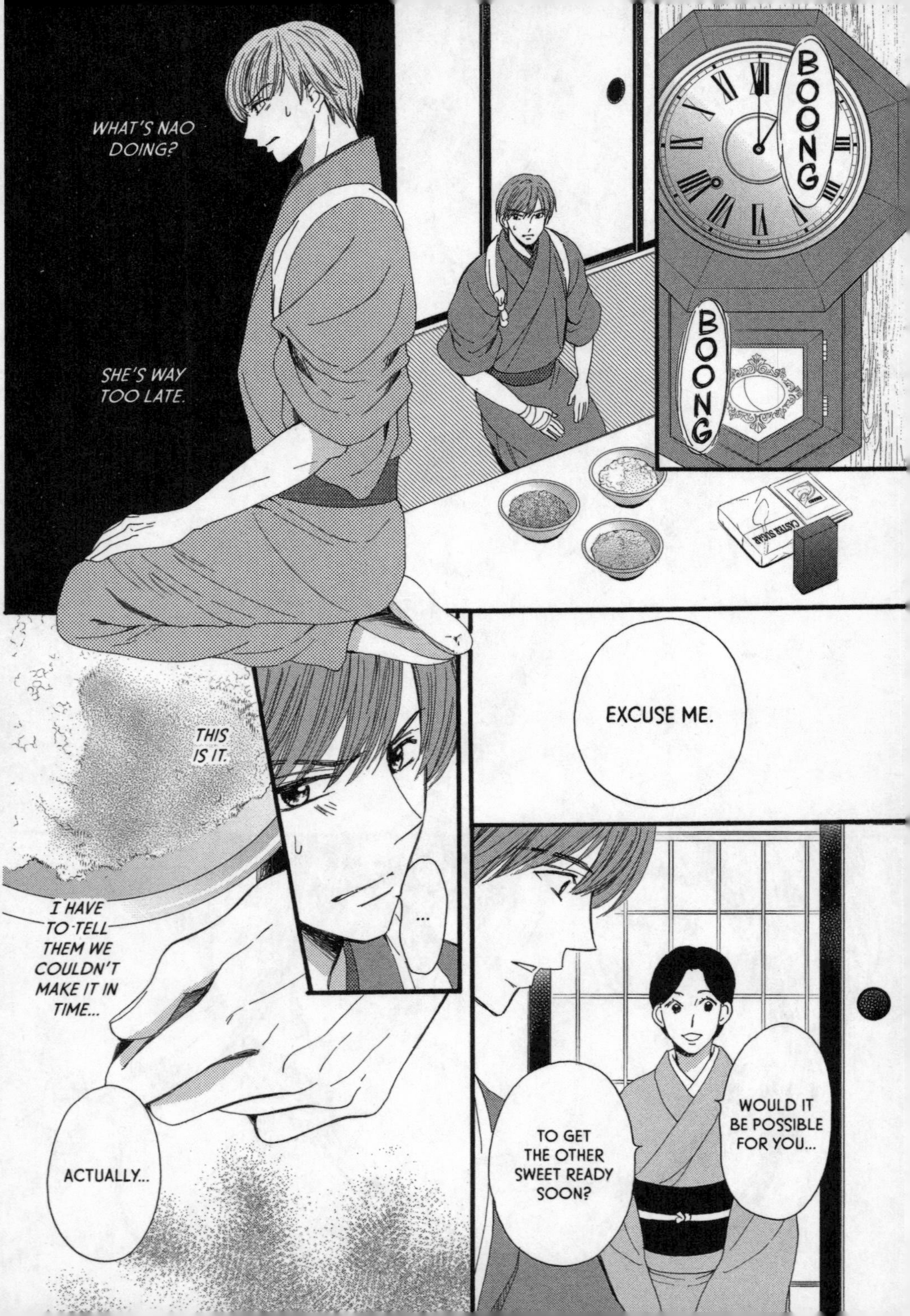
BOONG
BOONG
WHAT'S NAO DOING?
SHE'S WAY TOO LATE.
EXCUSE ME.
WOULD IT BE POSSIBLE FOR YOU...
TO GET THE OTHER SWEET READY SOON?
THIS IS IT.
...
I HAVE TO TELL THEM WE COULDN'T MAKE IT IN TIME...
ACTUALLY...

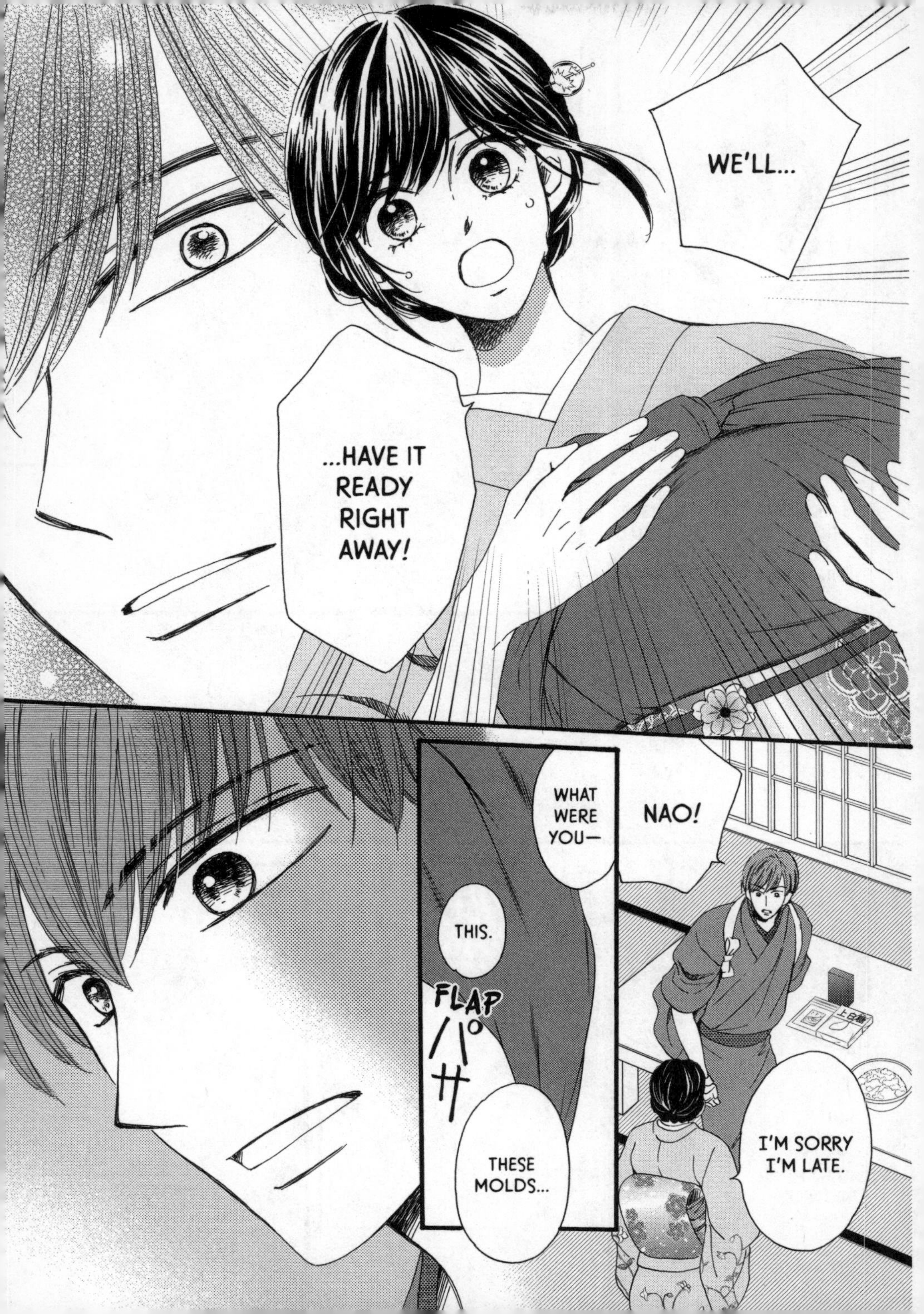
WE'LL...
...HAVE IT READY RIGHT AWAY!
NAO!
I'M SORRY I'M LATE.
WHAT WERE YOU—
THIS.
FLAP
パサ
THESE MOLDS...

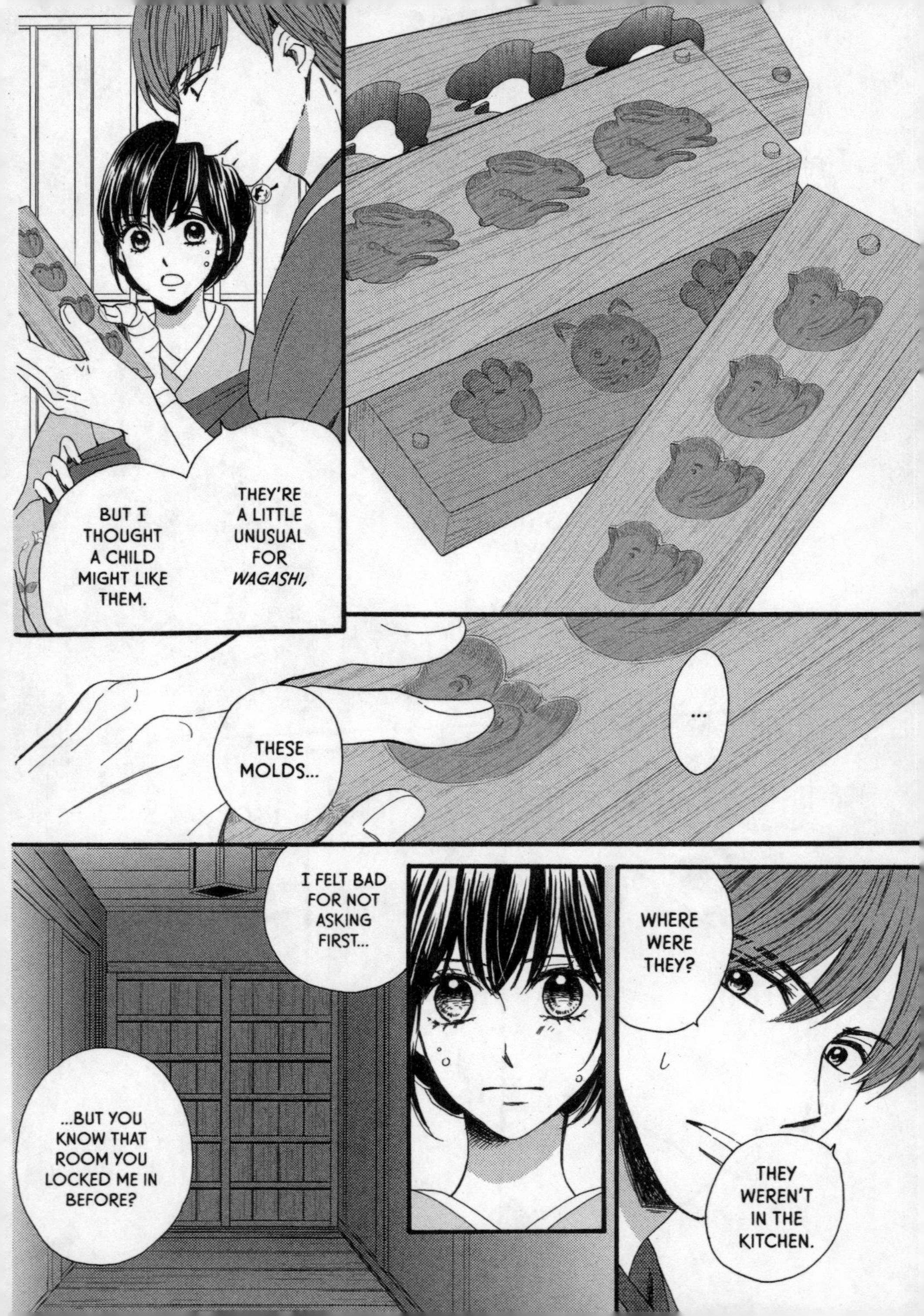
THEY'RE A LITTLE UNUSUAL FOR *WAGASHI,*
BUT I THOUGHT A CHILD MIGHT LIKE THEM.
...
THESE MOLDS...
WHERE WERE THEY?
THEY WEREN'T IN THE KITCHEN.
I FELT BAD FOR NOT ASKING FIRST...
...BUT YOU KNOW THAT ROOM YOU LOCKED ME IN BEFORE?

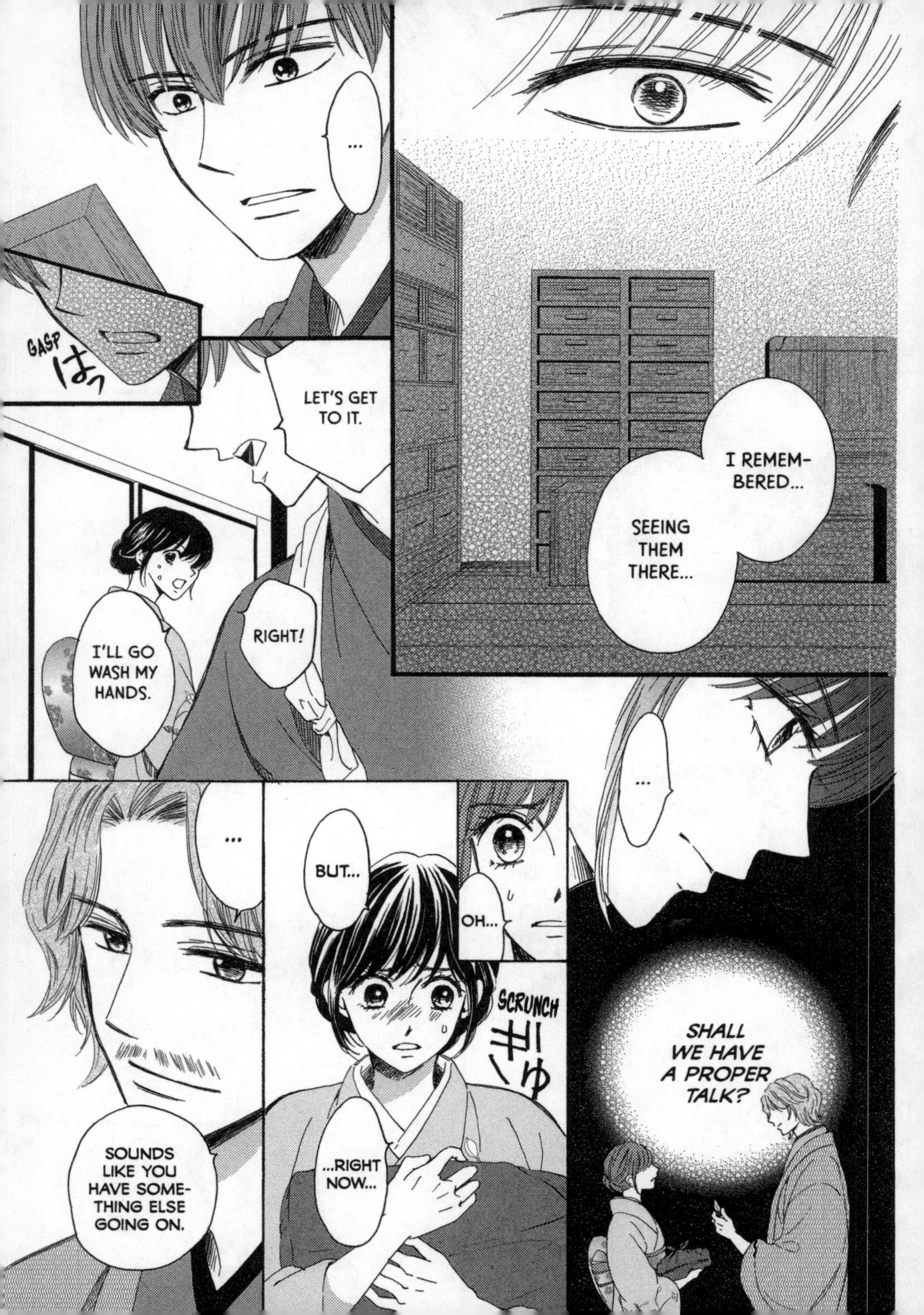
I REMEMBERED...
SEEING THEM THERE...
...
GASP
はっ
LET'S GET TO IT.
RIGHT!
I'LL GO WASH MY HANDS.
...
SHALL WE HAVE A PROPER TALK?
OH...
BUT...
SCRUNCH
きゅ
...RIGHT NOW...
...
SOUNDS LIKE YOU HAVE SOMETHING ELSE GOING ON.

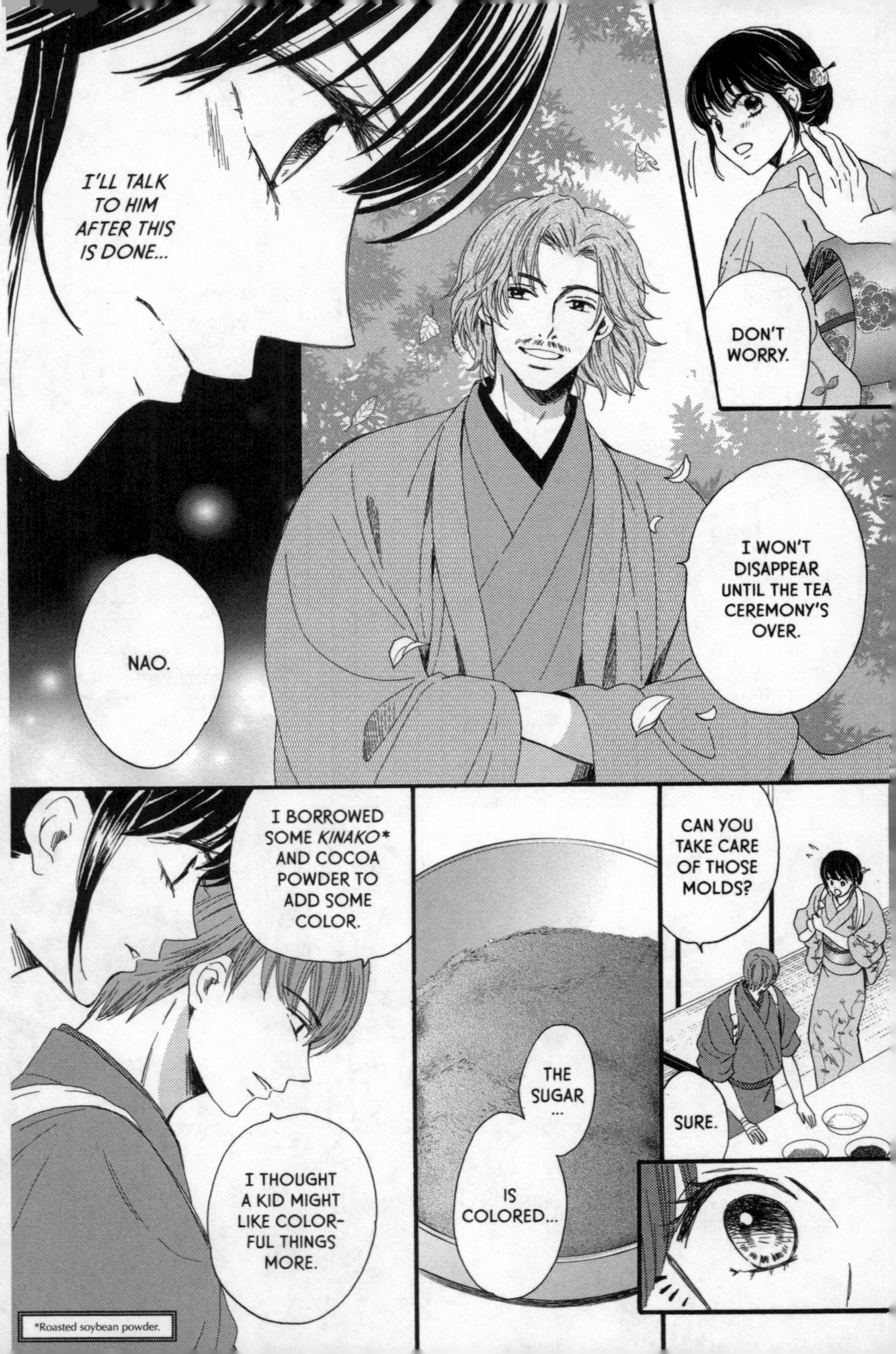
DON'T WORRY.
I WON'T DISAPPEAR UNTIL THE TEA CEREMONY'S OVER.
I'LL TALK TO HIM AFTER THIS IS DONE...
NAO.
CAN YOU TAKE CARE OF THOSE MOLDS?
SURE.
THE SUGAR ...
IS COLORED...
I BORROWED SOME *KINAKO** AND COCOA POWDER TO ADD SOME COLOR.
I THOUGHT A KID MIGHT LIKE COLOR-FUL THINGS MORE.

*Roasted soybean powder.

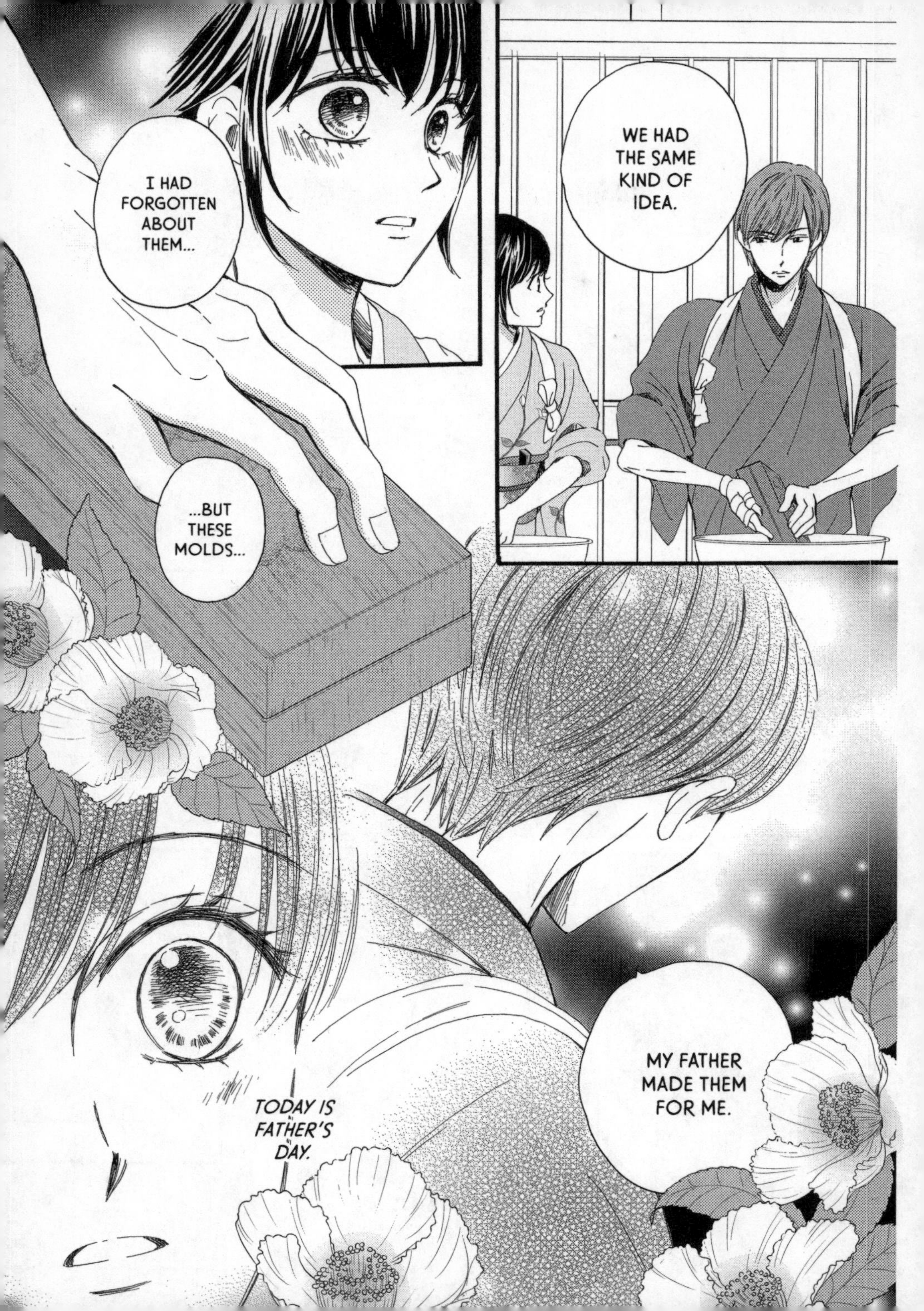
WE HAD THE SAME KIND OF IDEA.
I HAD FORGOTTEN ABOUT THEM...
...BUT THESE MOLDS...
MY FATHER MADE THEM FOR ME.
TODAY IS FATHER'S DAY.

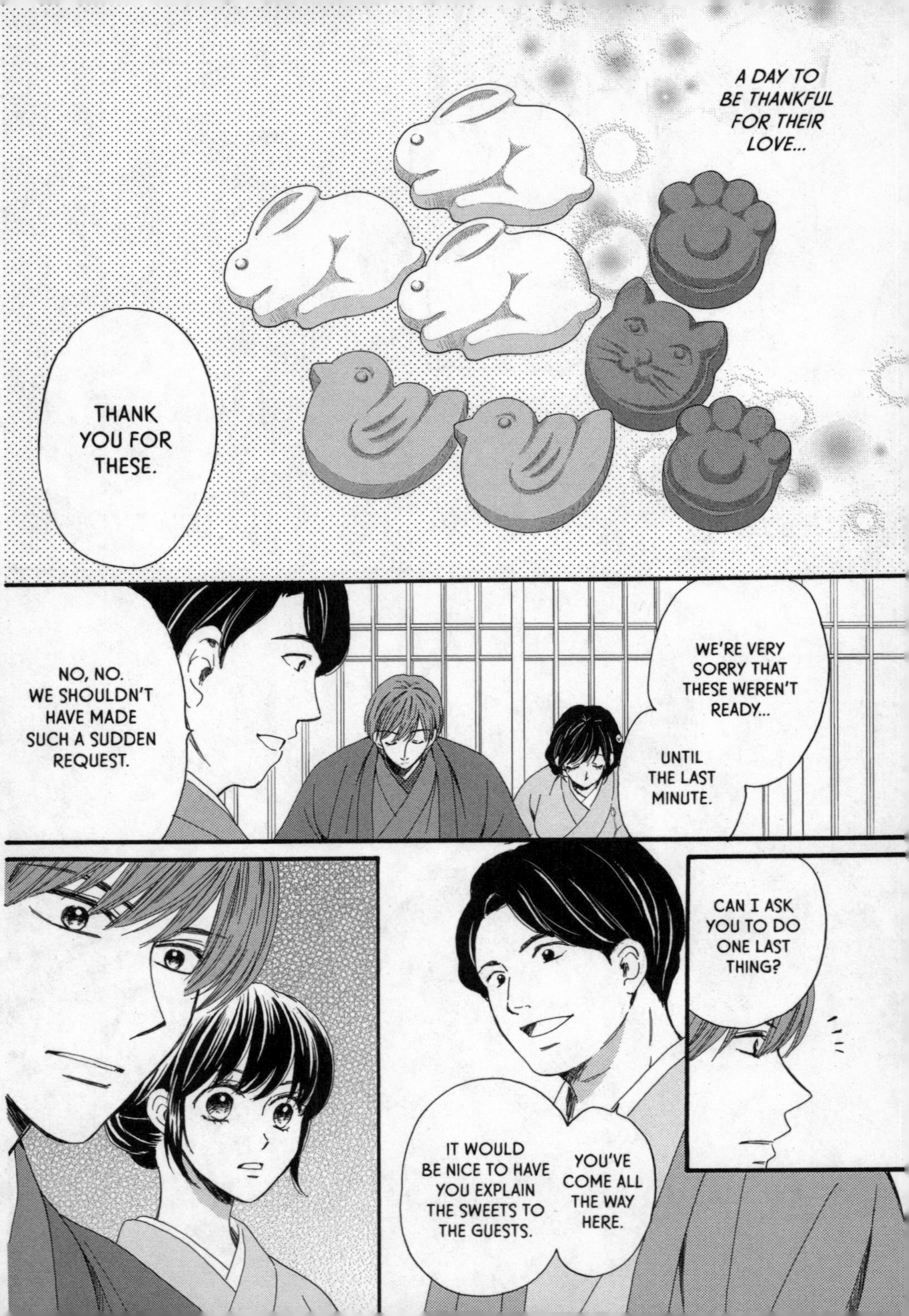
A DAY TO BE THANKFUL FOR THEIR LOVE...
THANK YOU FOR THESE.
WE'RE VERY SORRY THAT THESE WEREN'T READY...
UNTIL THE LAST MINUTE.
NO, NO. WE SHOULDN'T HAVE MADE SUCH A SUDDEN REQUEST.
CAN I ASK YOU TO DO ONE LAST THING?
YOU'VE COME ALL THE WAY HERE.
IT WOULD BE NICE TO HAVE YOU EXPLAIN THE SWEETS TO THE GUESTS.

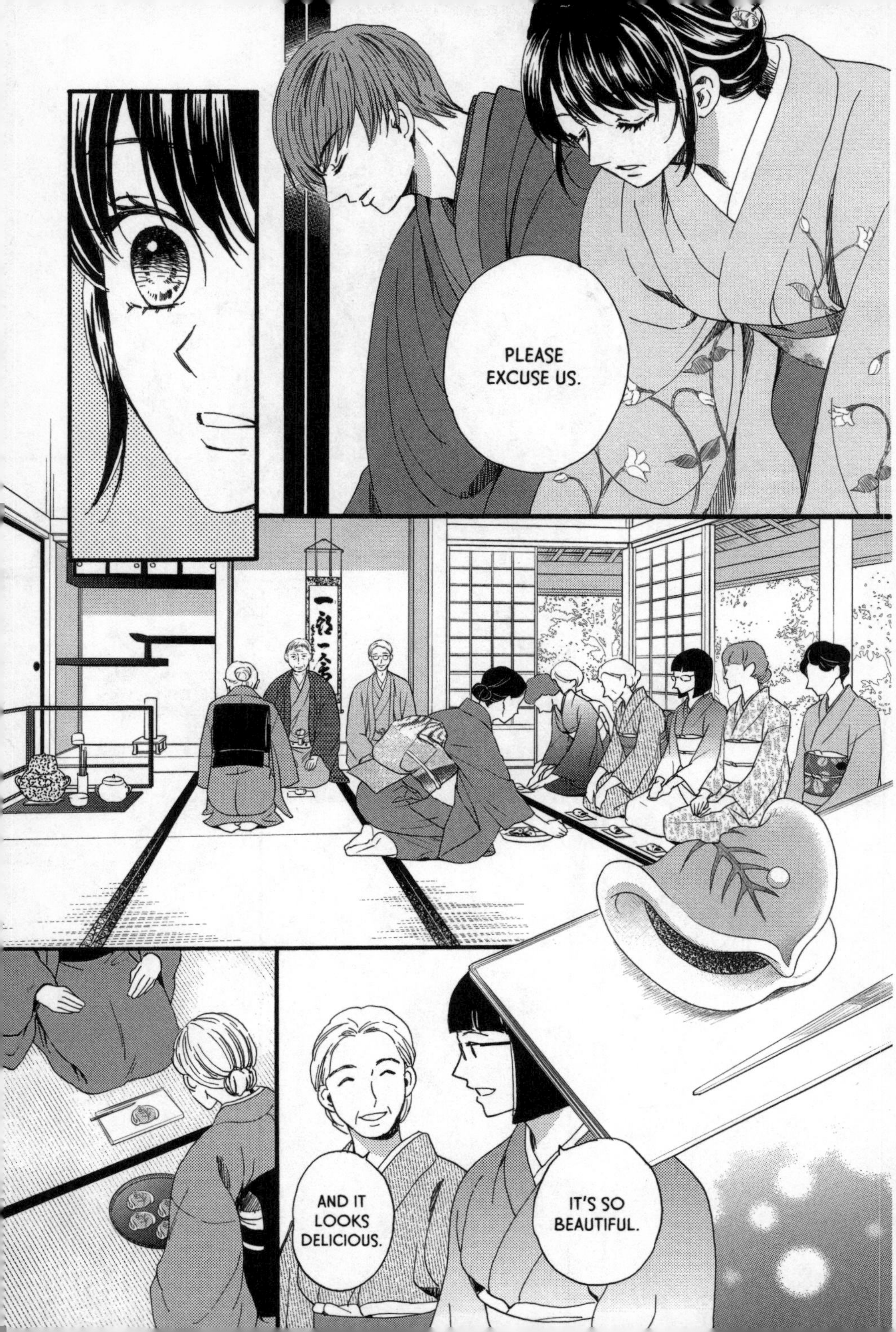
PLEASE EXCUSE US.
IT'S SO BEAUTIFUL.
AND IT LOOKS DELICIOUS.

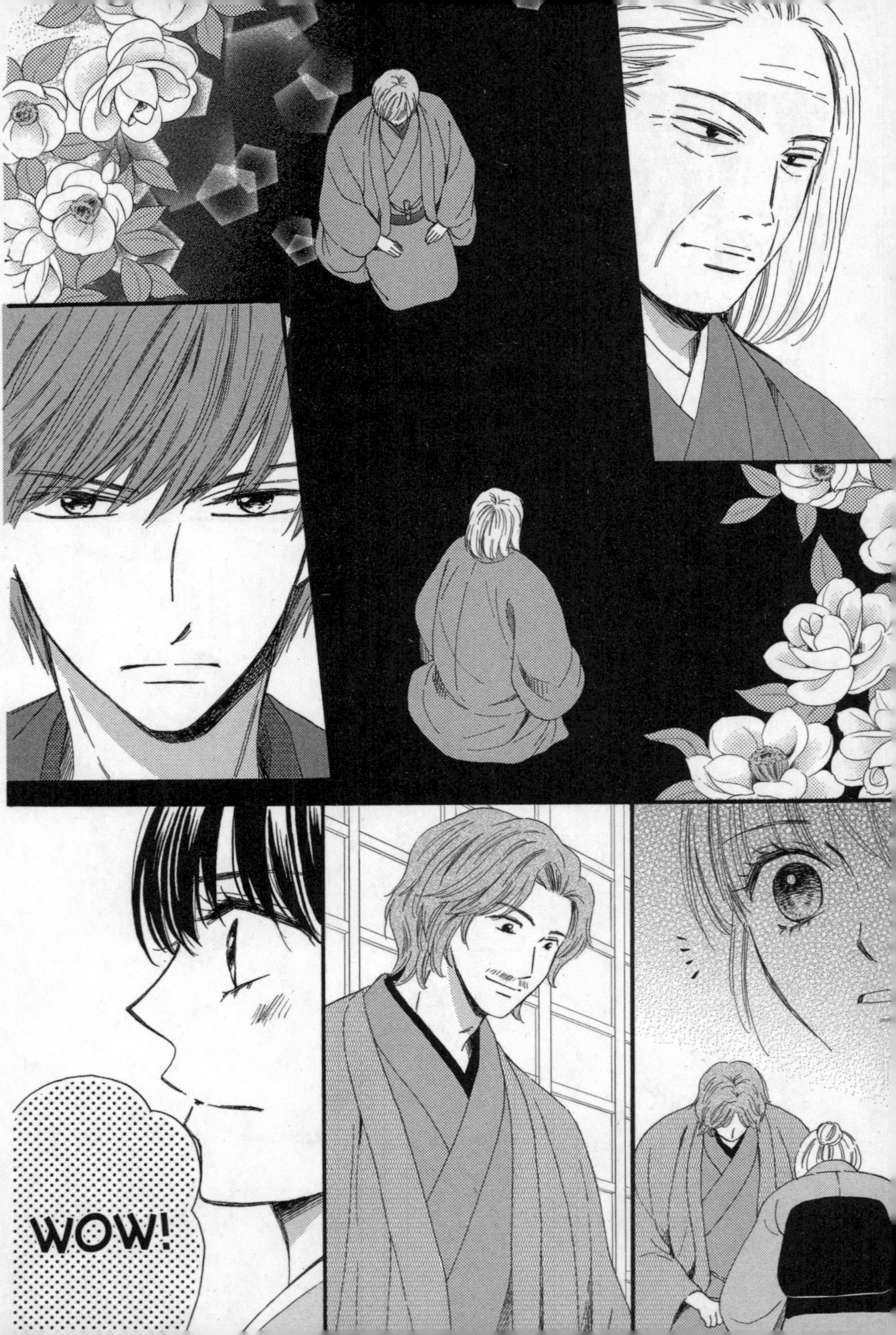
WOW!

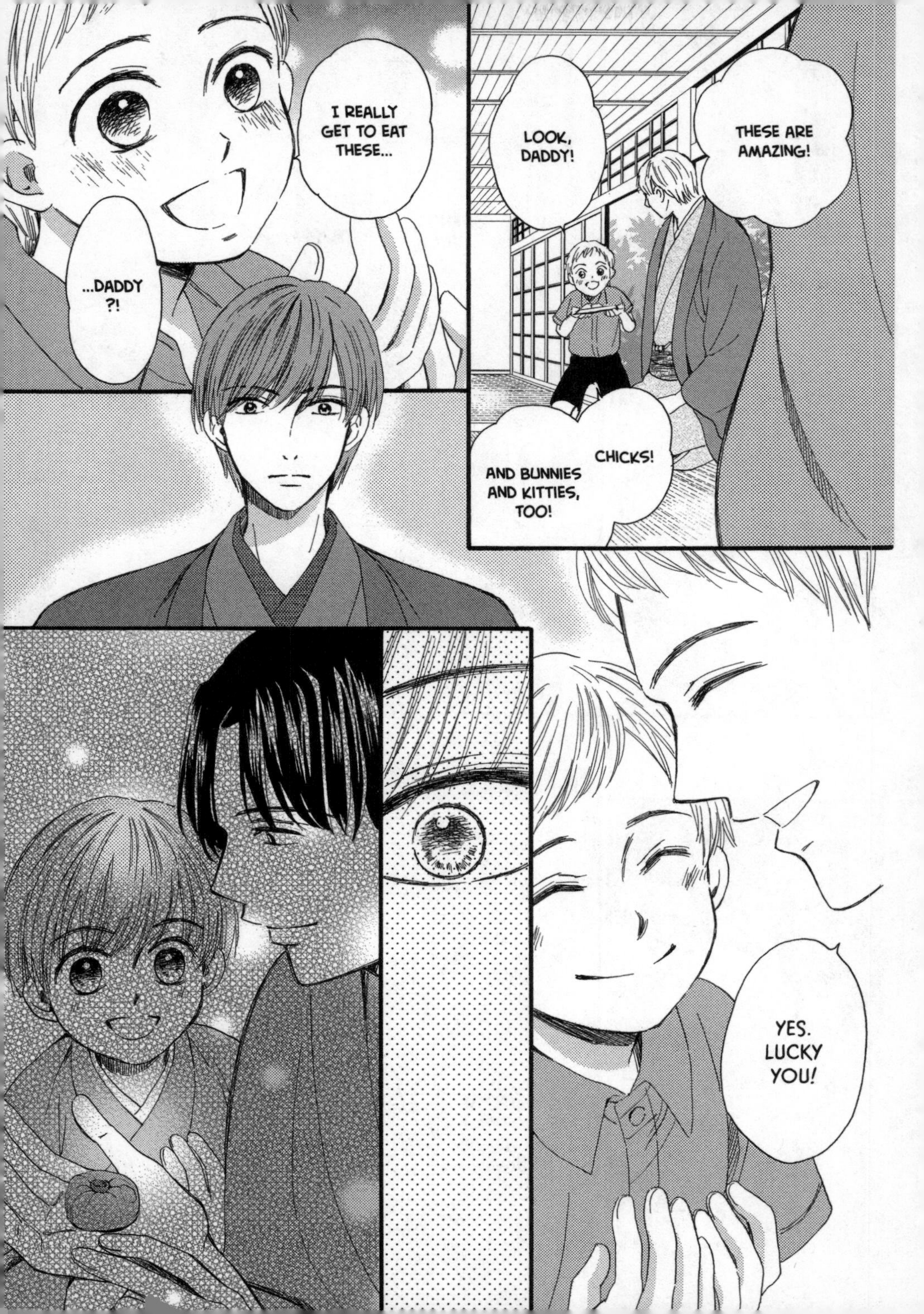
THESE ARE AMAZING!
LOOK, DADDY!
CHICKS!
AND BUNNIES AND KITTIES, TOO!
I REALLY GET TO EAT THESE...
...DADDY ?!
YES. LUCKY YOU!

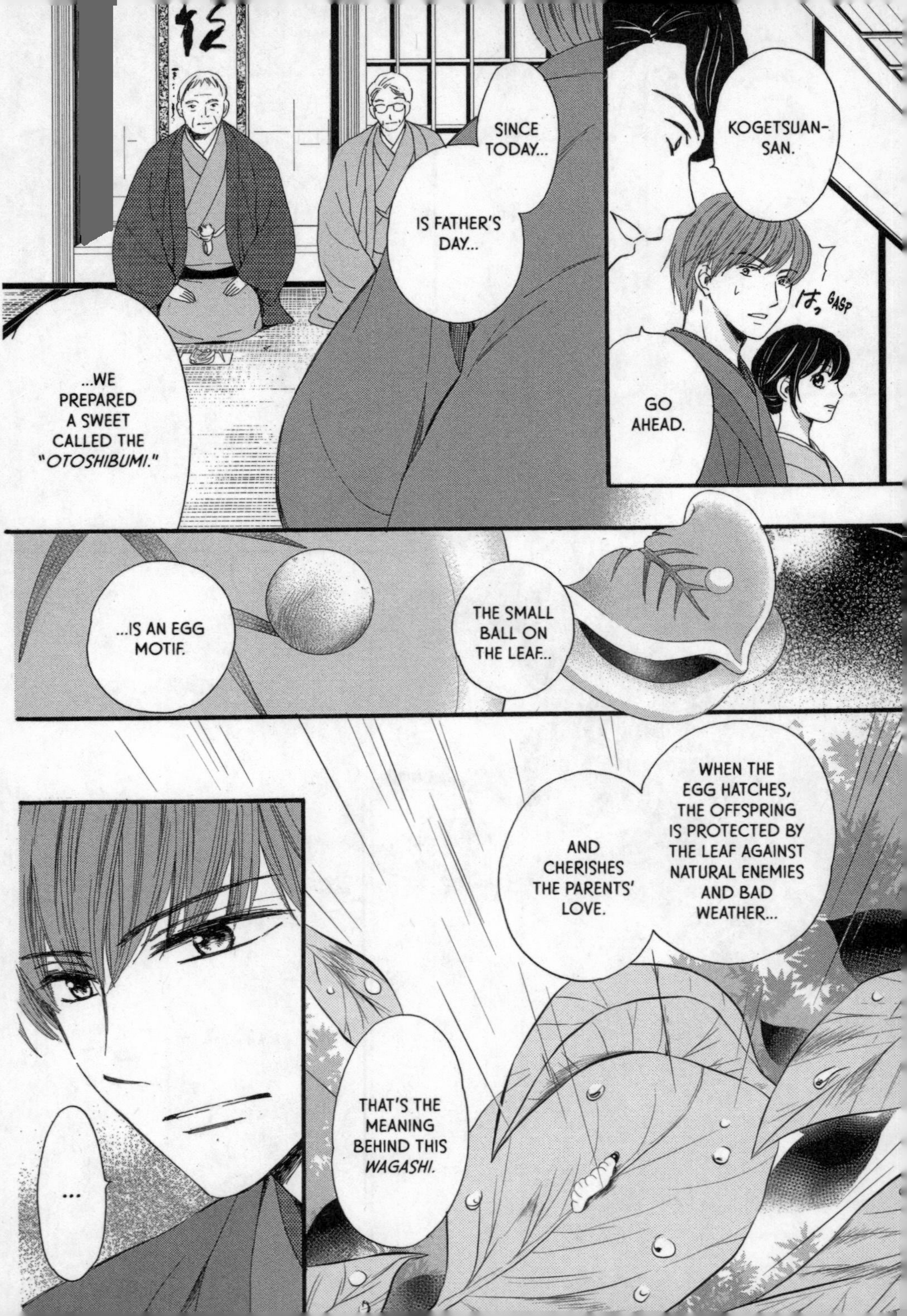
KOGETSUAN-SAN.
はっ GASP
GO AHEAD.
SINCE TODAY...
IS FATHER'S DAY...
...WE PREPARED A SWEET CALLED THE "*OTOSHIBUMI*."
THE SMALL BALL ON THE LEAF...
...IS AN EGG MOTIF.
WHEN THE EGG HATCHES, THE OFFSPRING IS PROTECTED BY THE LEAF AGAINST NATURAL ENEMIES AND BAD WEATHER...
AND CHERISHES THE PARENTS' LOVE.
THAT'S THE MEANING BEHIND THIS *WAGASHI*.
...

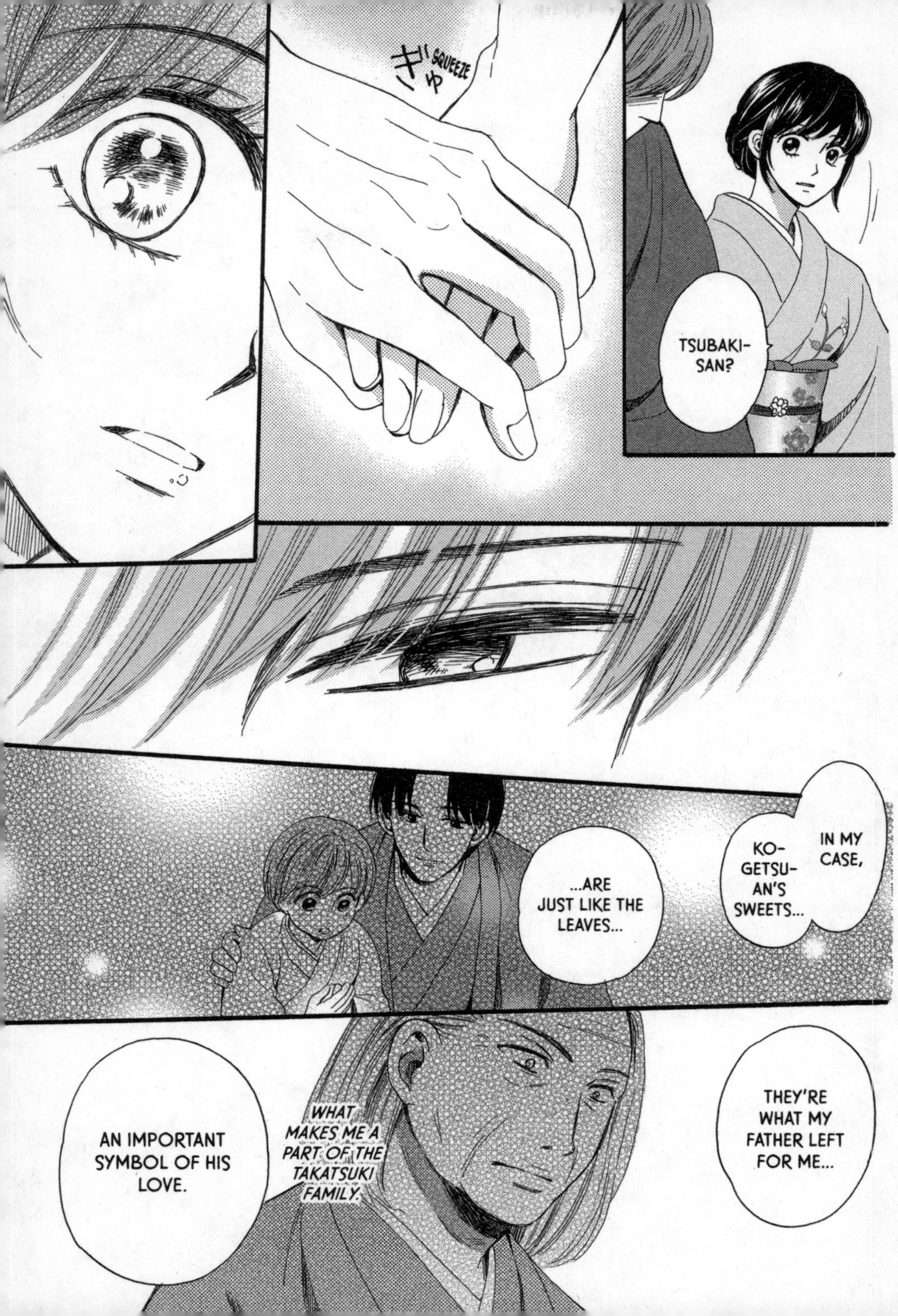
TSUBAKI-SAN?
ぎゅ SQUEEZE
IN MY CASE,
KO-GETSU-AN'S SWEETS...
...ARE JUST LIKE THE LEAVES...
THEY'RE WHAT MY FATHER LEFT FOR ME...
WHAT MAKES ME A PART OF THE TAKATSUKI FAMILY.
AN IMPORTANT SYMBOL OF HIS LOVE.

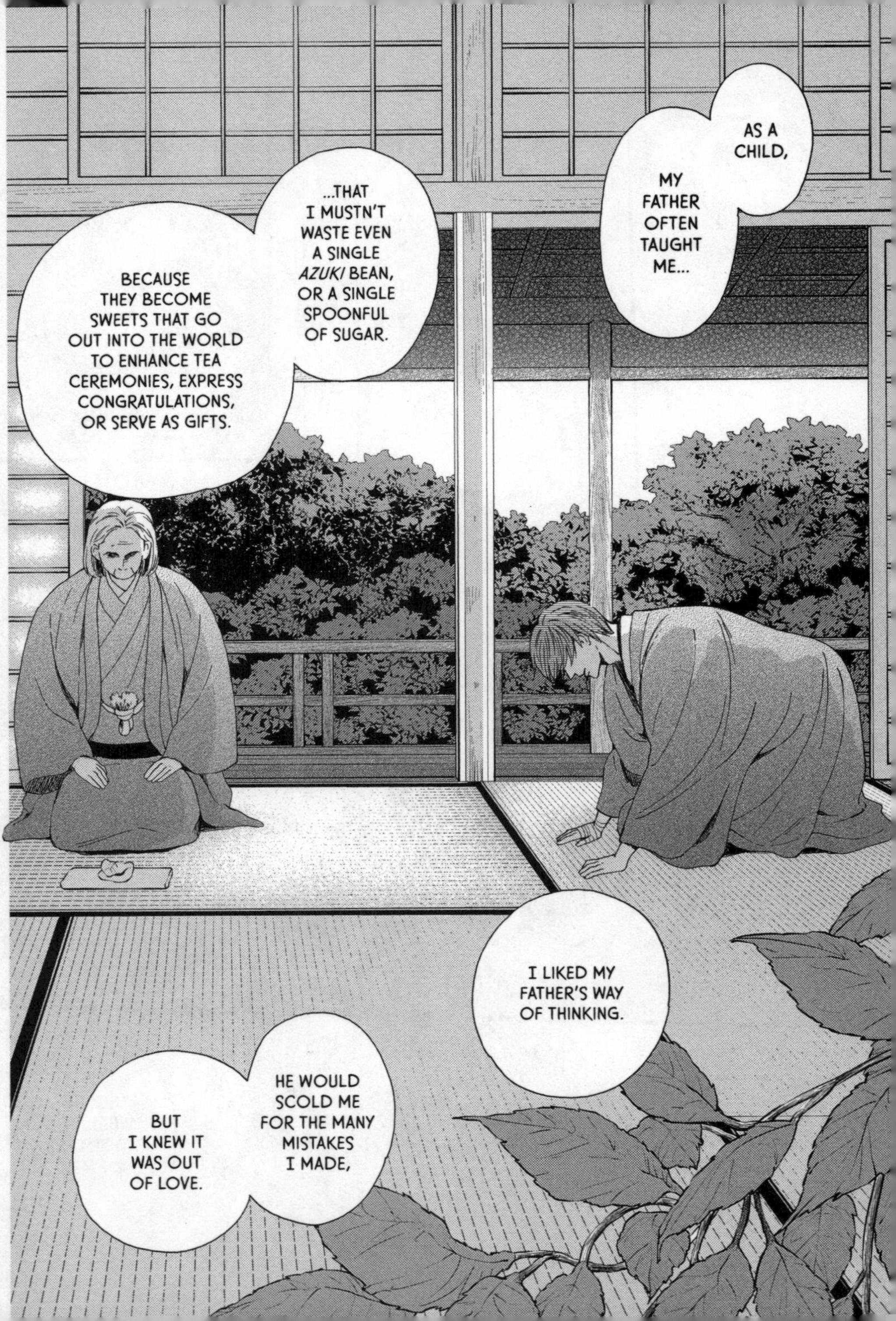
AS A CHILD, MY FATHER OFTEN TAUGHT ME...
...THAT I MUSTN'T WASTE EVEN A SINGLE *AZUKI* BEAN, OR A SINGLE SPOONFUL OF SUGAR.
BECAUSE THEY BECOME SWEETS THAT GO OUT INTO THE WORLD TO ENHANCE TEA CEREMONIES, EXPRESS CONGRATULATIONS, OR SERVE AS GIFTS.
I LIKED MY FATHER'S WAY OF THINKING.
HE WOULD SCOLD ME FOR THE MANY MISTAKES I MADE,
BUT I KNEW IT WAS OUT OF LOVE.

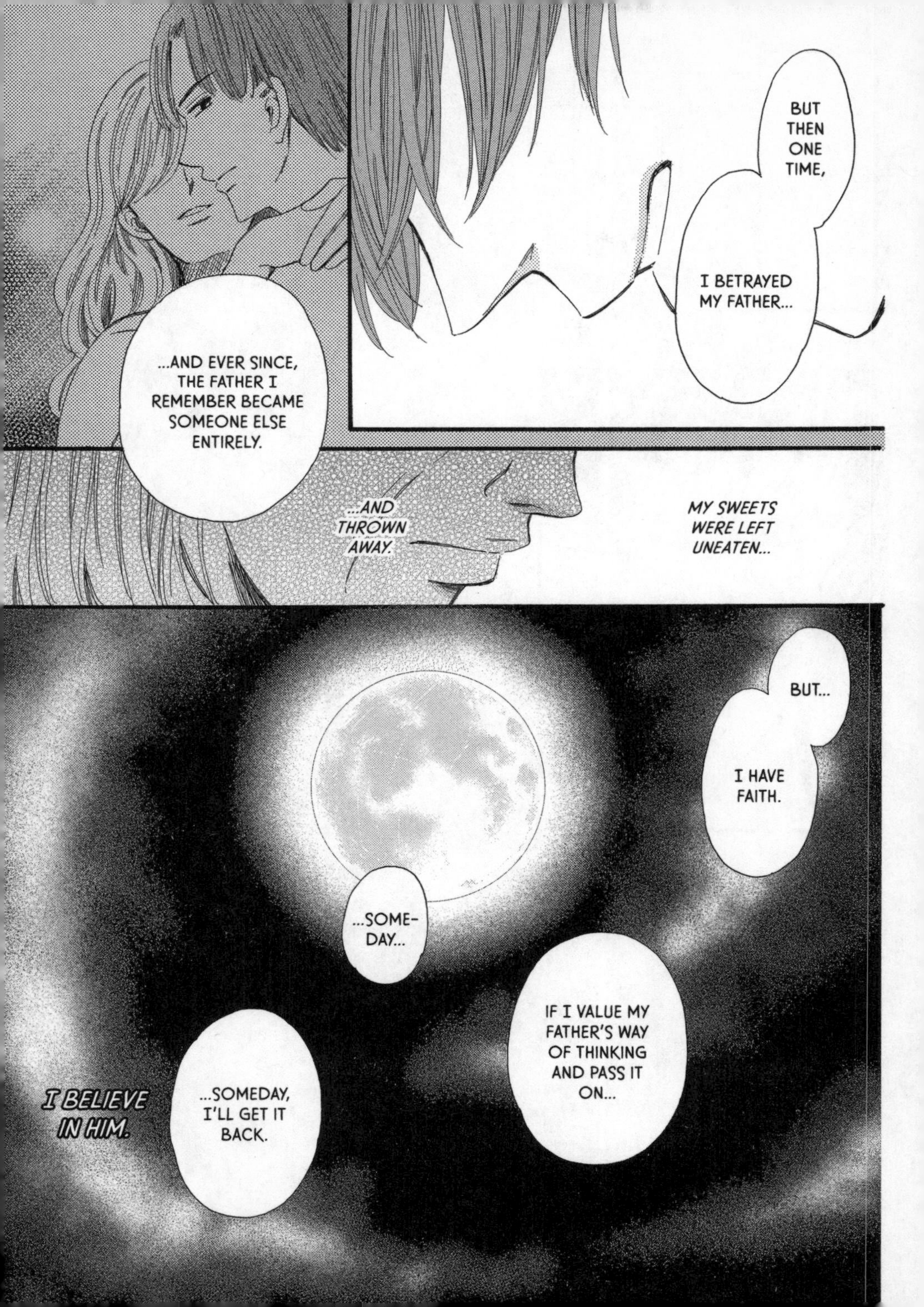
BUT THEN ONE TIME,
I BETRAYED MY FATHER...
MY SWEETS WERE LEFT UNEATEN...
...AND THROWN AWAY.
...AND EVER SINCE, THE FATHER I REMEMBER BECAME SOMEONE ELSE ENTIRELY.
BUT...
I HAVE FAITH.
...SOMEDAY...
IF I VALUE MY FATHER'S WAY OF THINKING AND PASS IT ON...
...SOMEDAY, I'LL GET IT BACK.
I BELIEVE IN HIM.

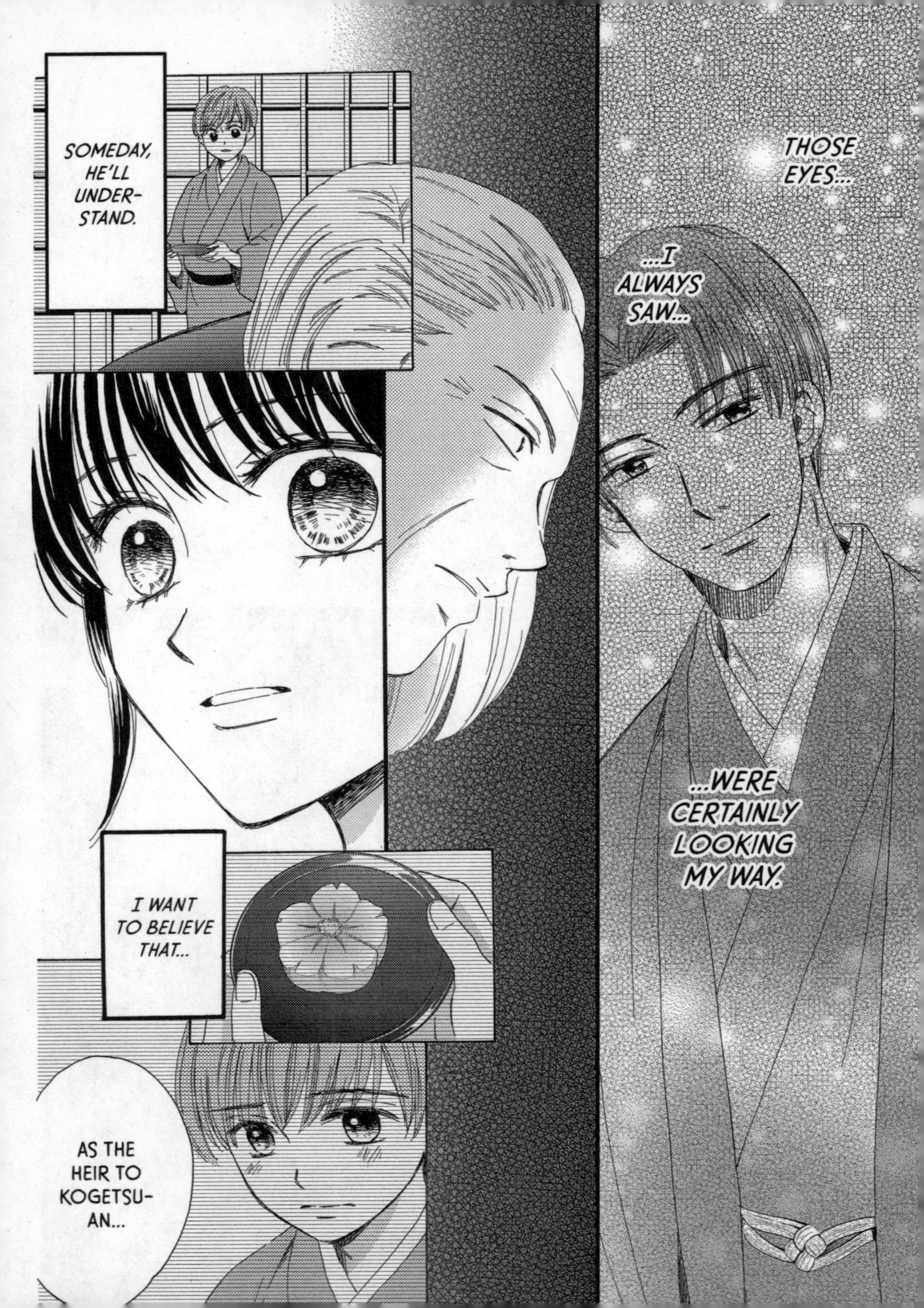
THOSE EYES...
...I ALWAYS SAW...
...WERE CERTAINLY LOOKING MY WAY.
SOMEDAY, HE'LL UNDER-STAND.
I WANT TO BELIEVE THAT...
AS THE HEIR TO KOGETSU-AN...

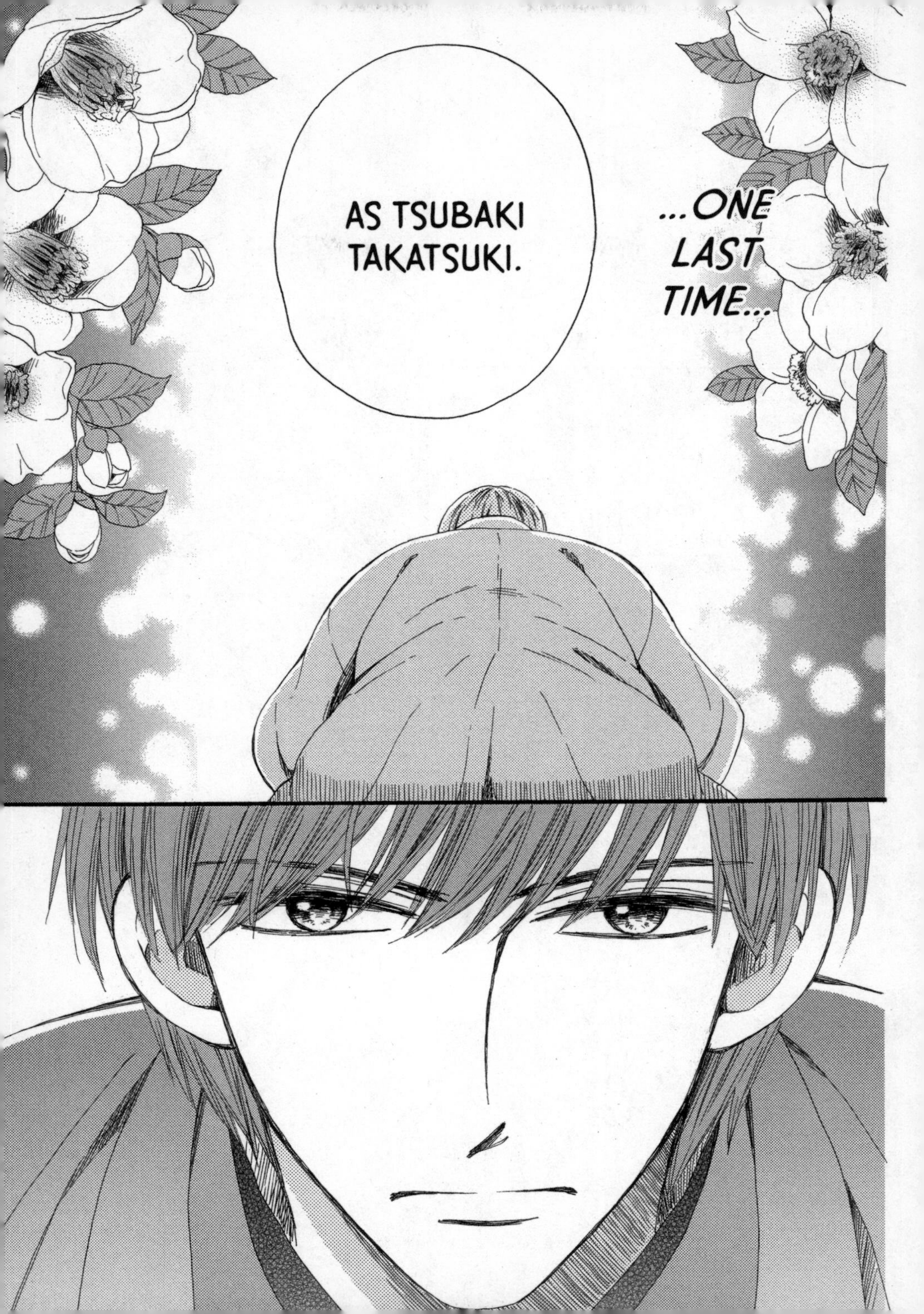
...ONE LAST TIME...
AS TSUBAKI TAKATSUKI.

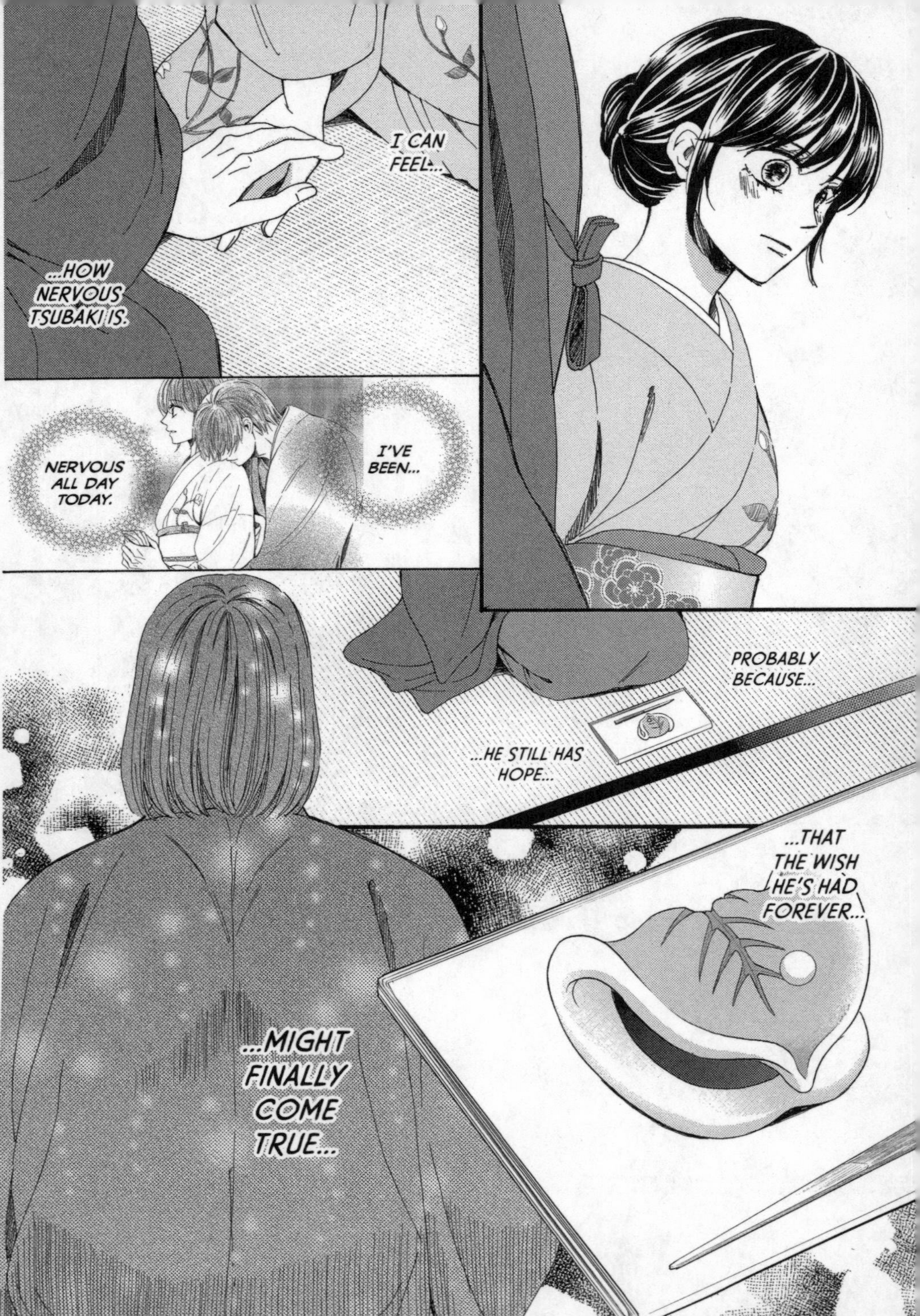
I CAN FEEL...
...HOW NERVOUS TSUBAKI IS.
I'VE BEEN...
NERVOUS ALL DAY TODAY.
PROBABLY BECAUSE...
...HE STILL HAS HOPE...
...THAT THE WISH HE'S HAD FOREVER...
...MIGHT FINALLY COME TRUE...

Something's
Wrong
With Us

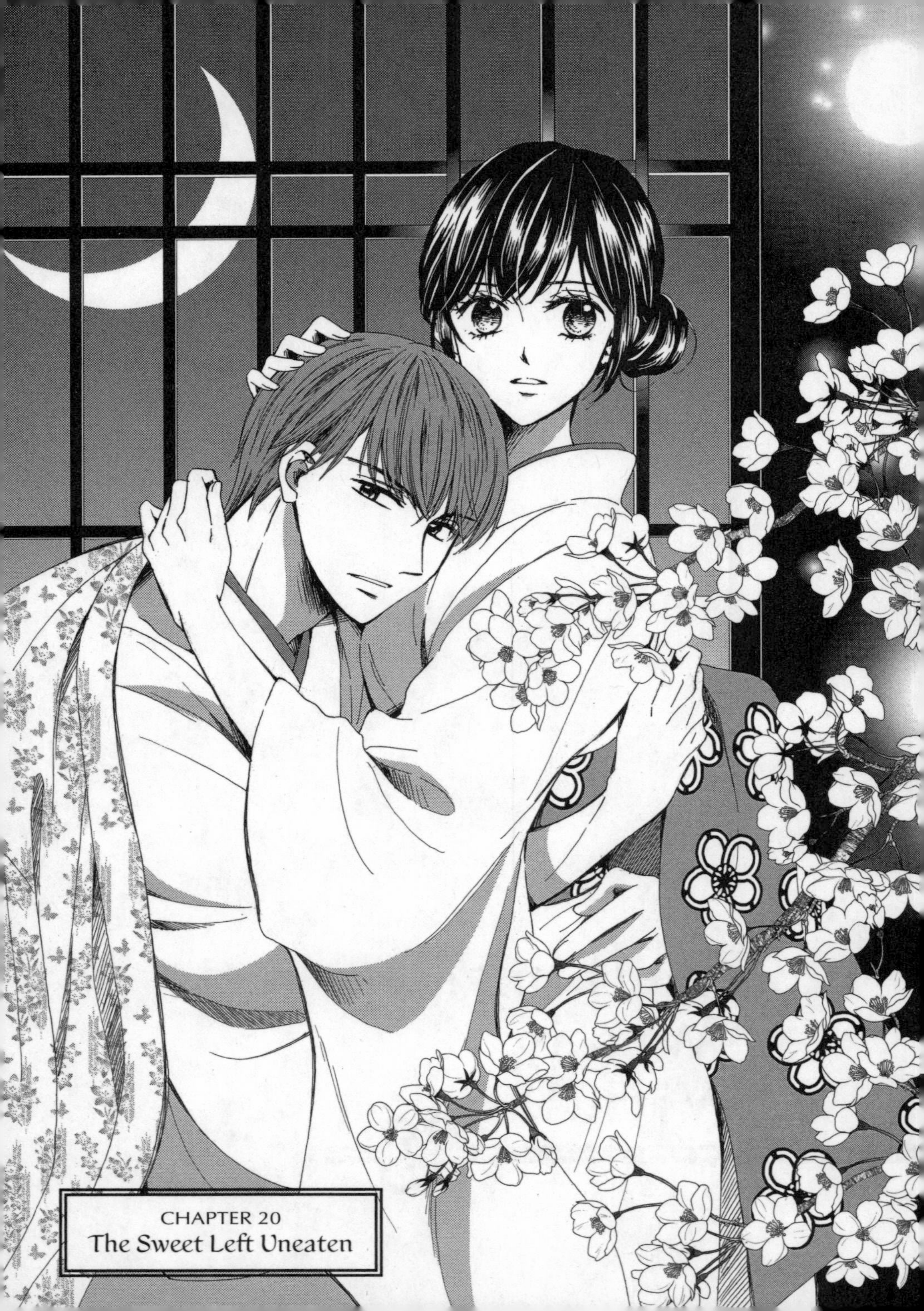

CHAPTER 20
The Sweet Left Uneaten

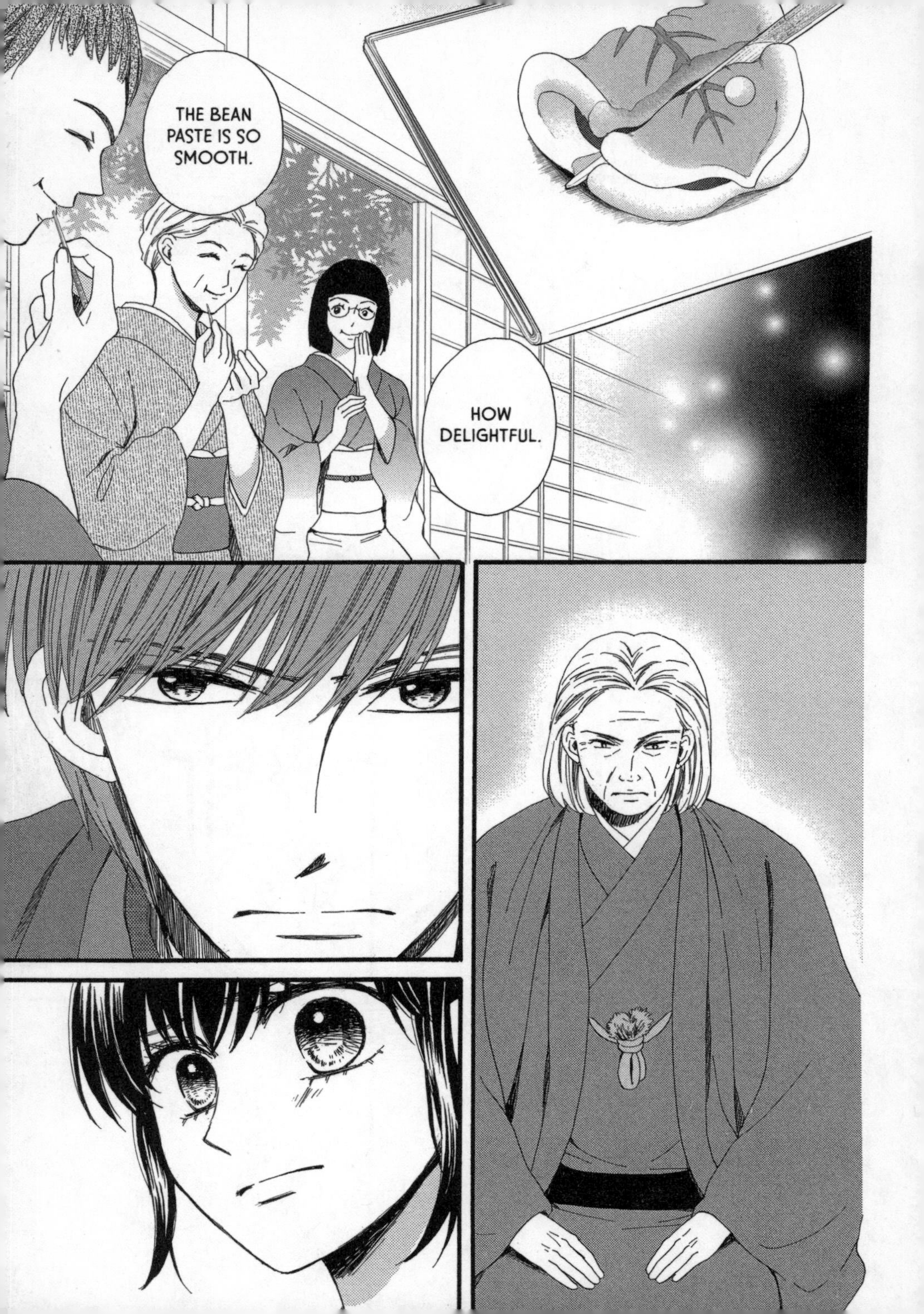
HOW DELIGHTFUL.
THE BEAN PASTE IS SO SMOOTH.

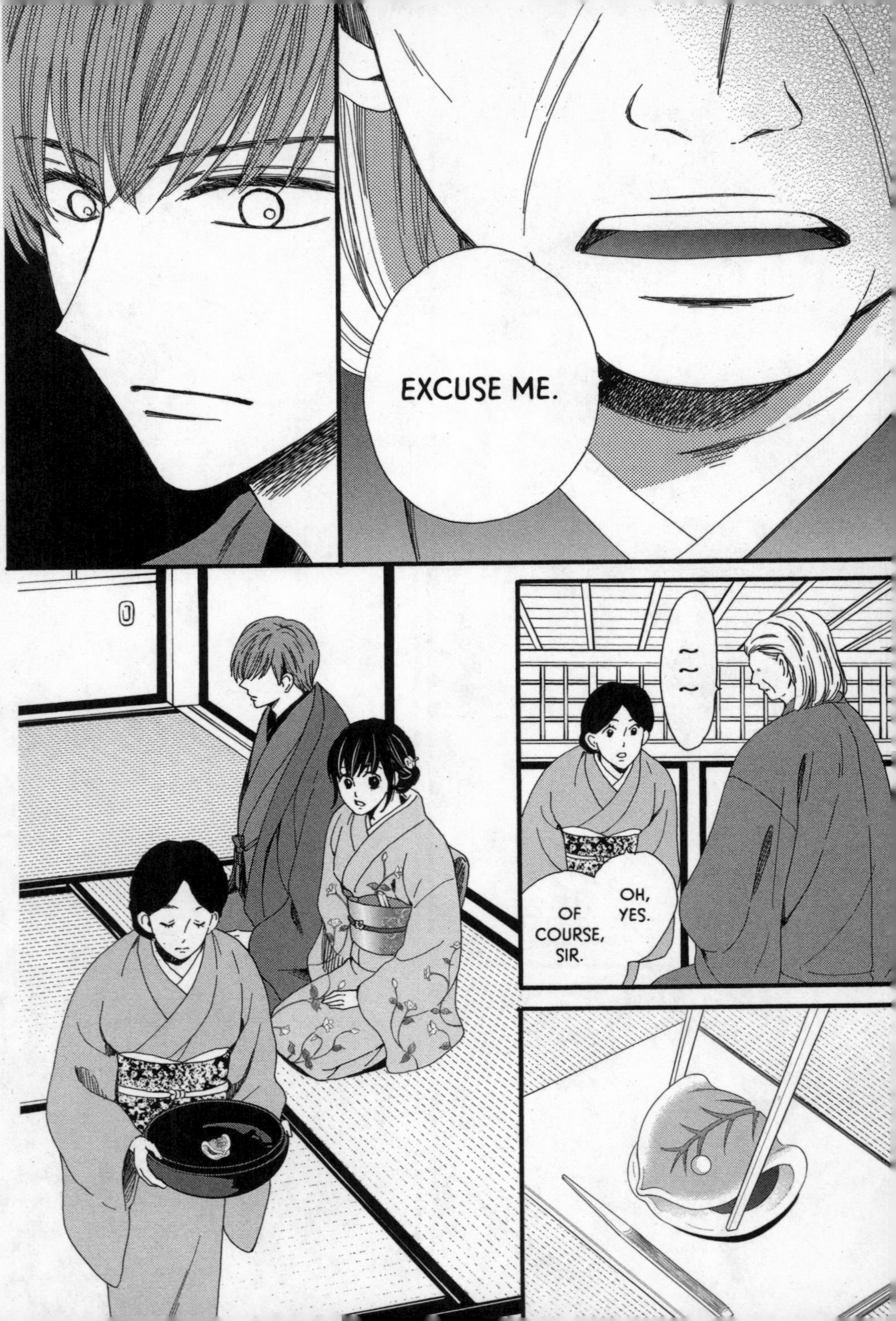
EXCUSE ME.
~~~
OH, YES.
OF COURSE, SIR.
~~~

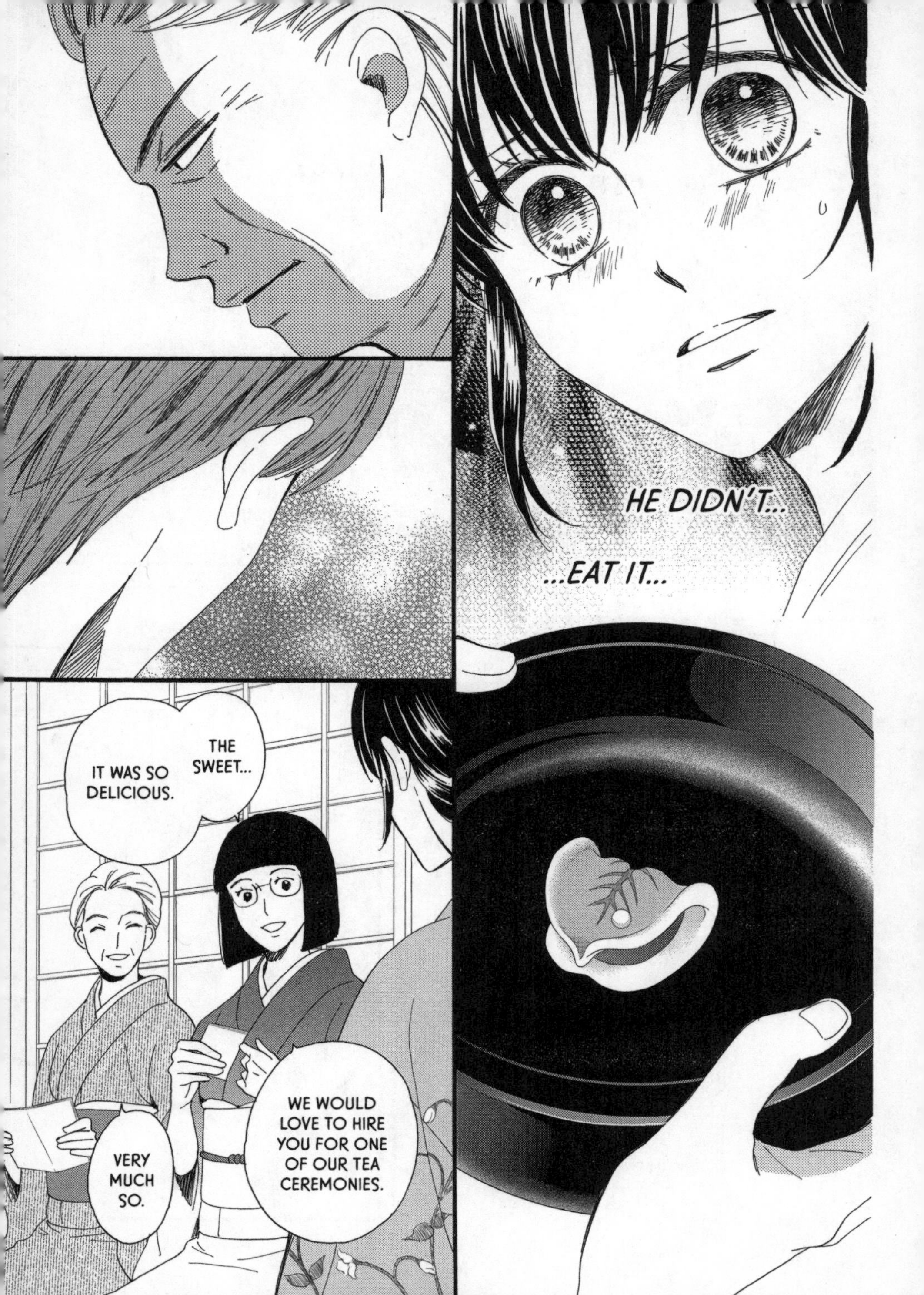
HE DIDN'T...
...EAT IT...
THE SWEET...
IT WAS SO DELICIOUS.
WE WOULD LOVE TO HIRE YOU FOR ONE OF OUR TEA CEREMONIES.
VERY MUCH SO.

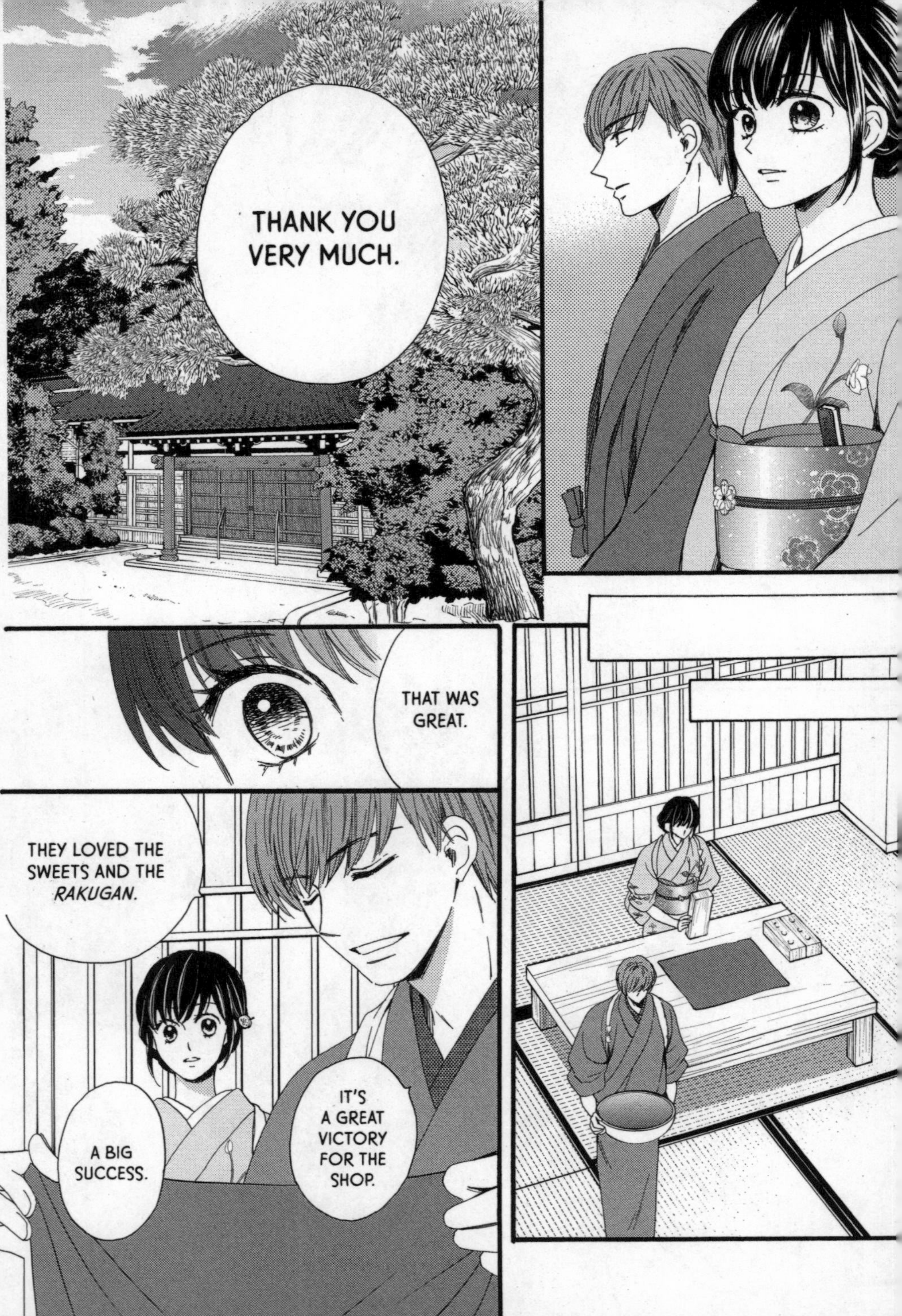
THANK YOU VERY MUCH.
THAT WAS GREAT.
THEY LOVED THE SWEETS AND THE *RAKUGAN*.
IT'S A GREAT VICTORY FOR THE SHOP.
A BIG SUCCESS.

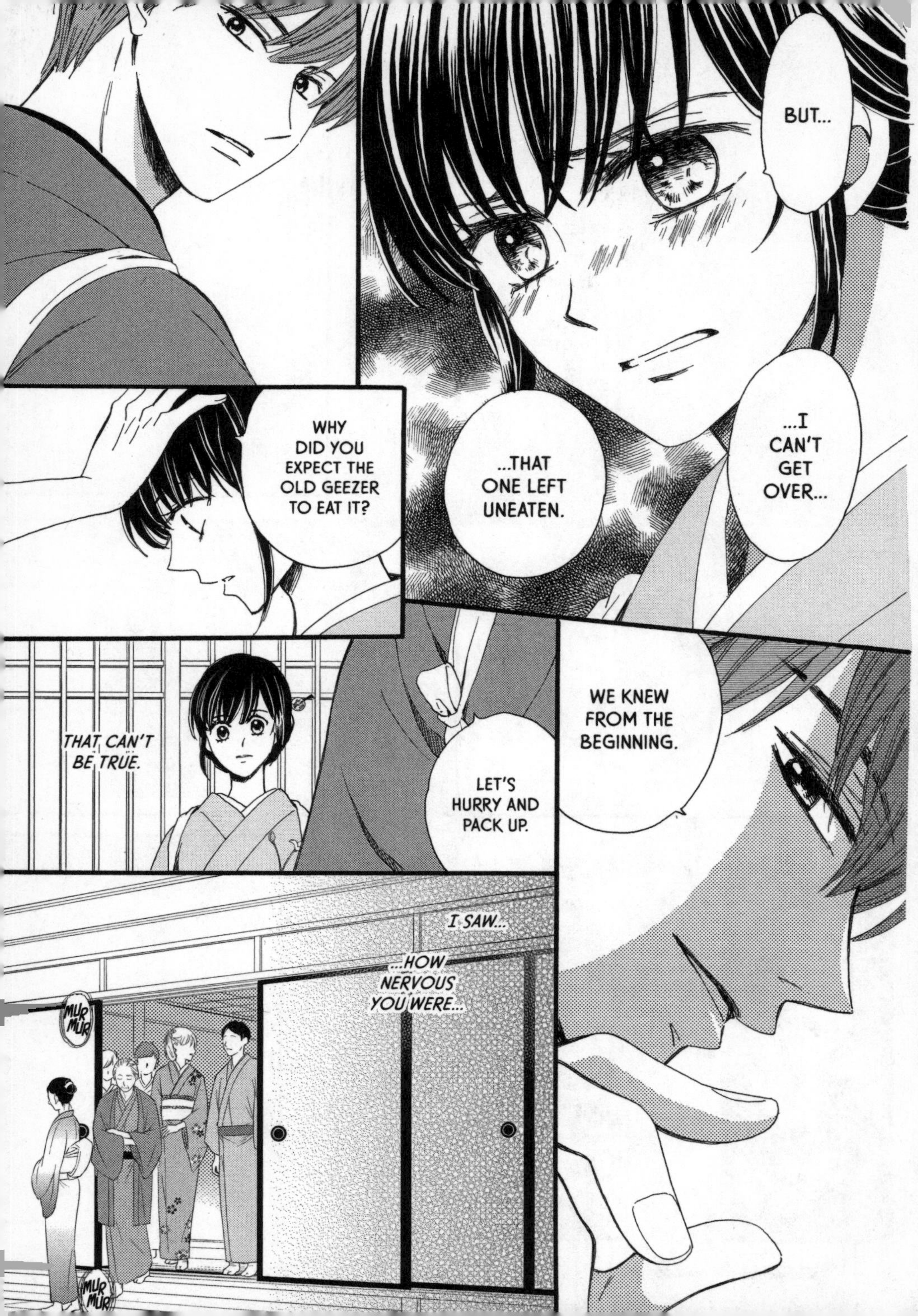
BUT...
...I CAN'T GET OVER...
...THAT ONE LEFT UNEATEN.
WHY DID YOU EXPECT THE OLD GEEZER TO EAT IT?
WE KNEW FROM THE BEGINNING.
LET'S HURRY AND PACK UP.
THAT CAN'T BE TRUE.
I SAW...
...HOW NERVOUS YOU WERE...
MUR MUR
MUR MUR

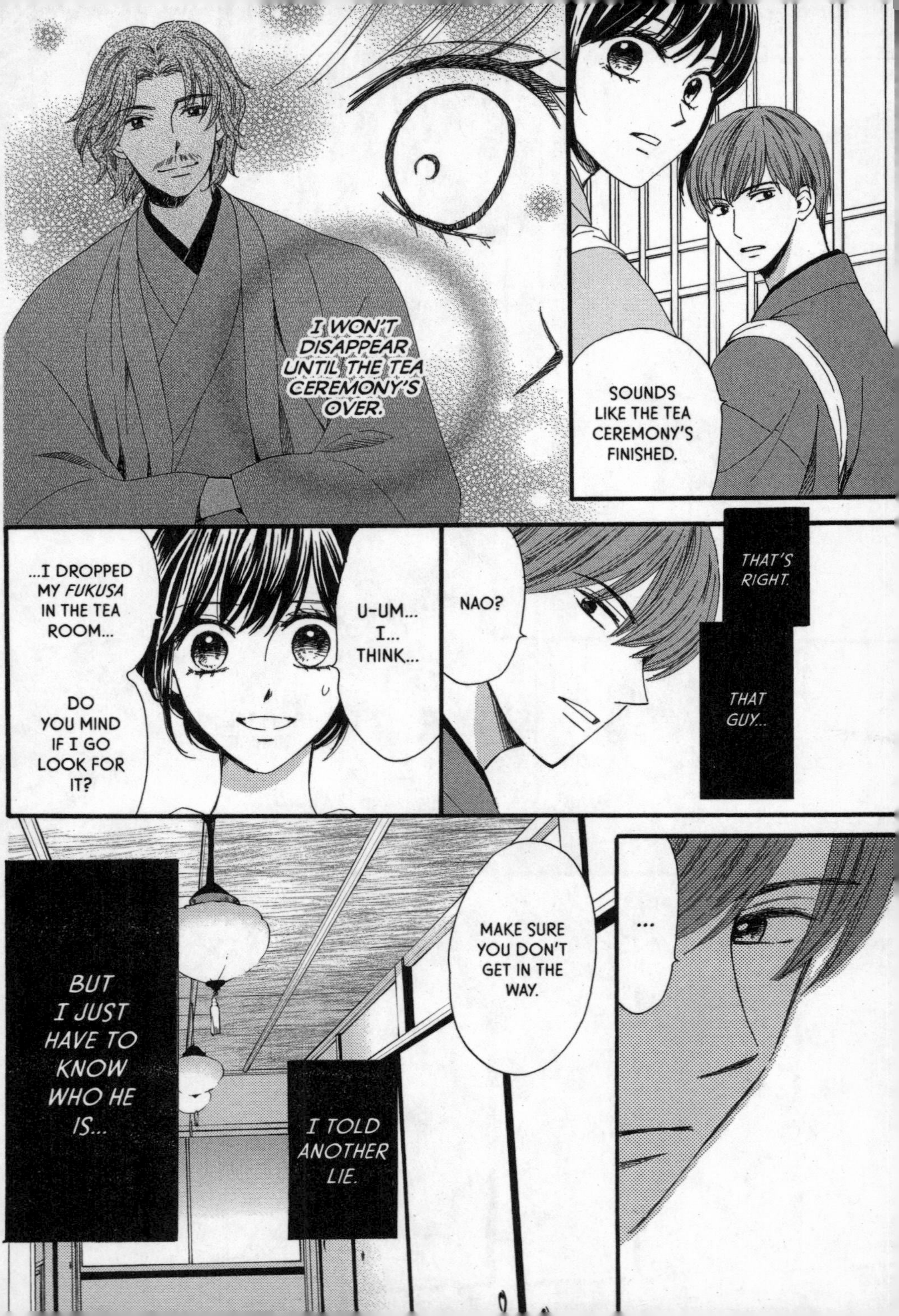
SOUNDS LIKE THE TEA CEREMONY'S FINISHED.
I WON'T DISAPPEAR UNTIL THE TEA CEREMONY'S OVER.
THAT'S RIGHT.
THAT GUY...
NAO?
U-UM... I... THINK...
...I DROPPED MY *FUKUSA* IN THE TEA ROOM...
DO YOU MIND IF I GO LOOK FOR IT?
...
MAKE SURE YOU DON'T GET IN THE WAY.
BUT I JUST HAVE TO KNOW WHO HE IS...
I TOLD ANOTHER LIE.

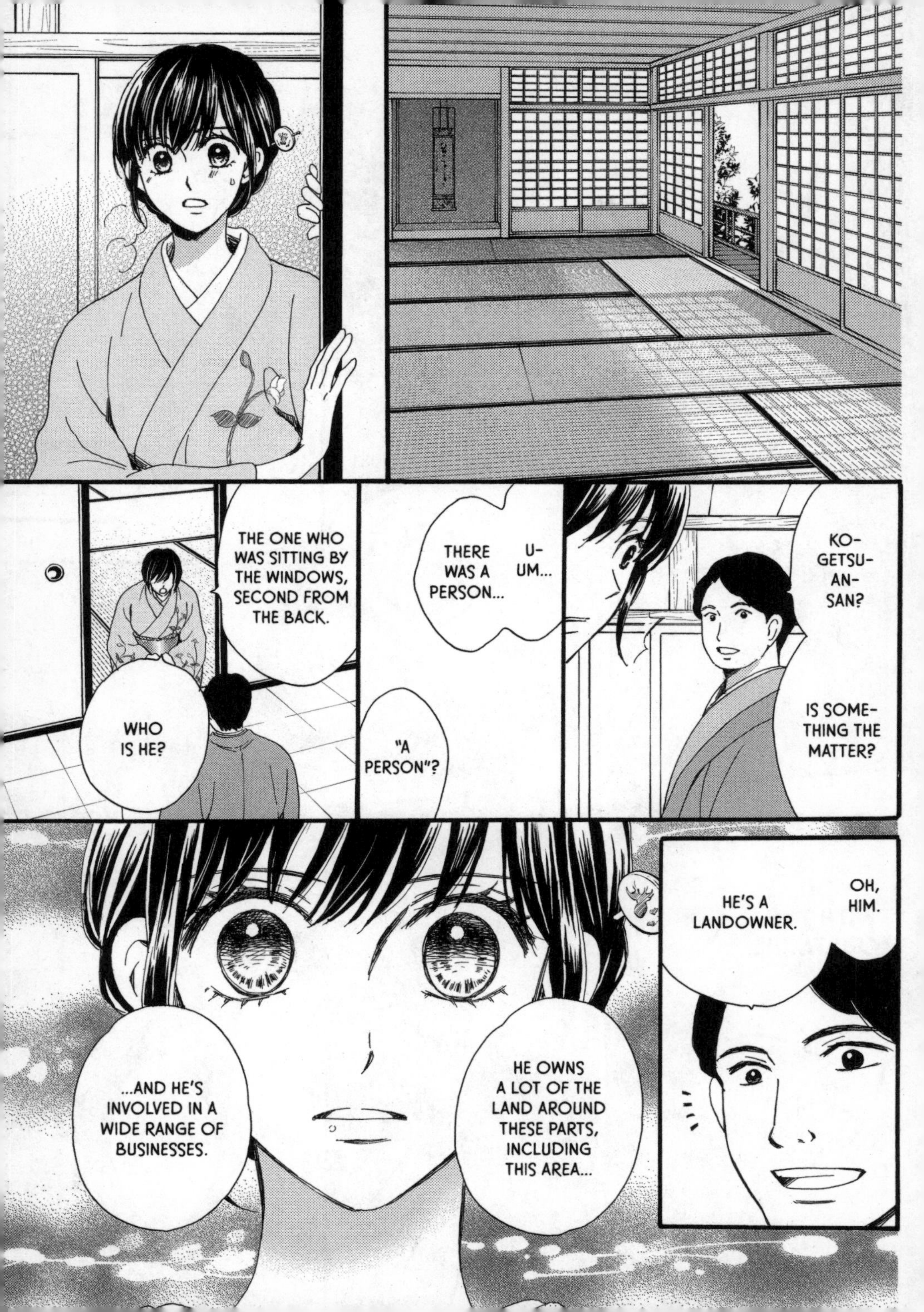
KO-GETSU-AN-SAN?
IS SOME-THING THE MATTER?
U-UM...
THERE WAS A PERSON...
"A PERSON"?
THE ONE WHO WAS SITTING BY THE WINDOWS, SECOND FROM THE BACK.
WHO IS HE?
OH, HIM.
HE'S A LANDOWNER.
HE OWNS A LOT OF THE LAND AROUND THESE PARTS, INCLUDING THIS AREA...
...AND HE'S INVOLVED IN A WIDE RANGE OF BUSINESSES.

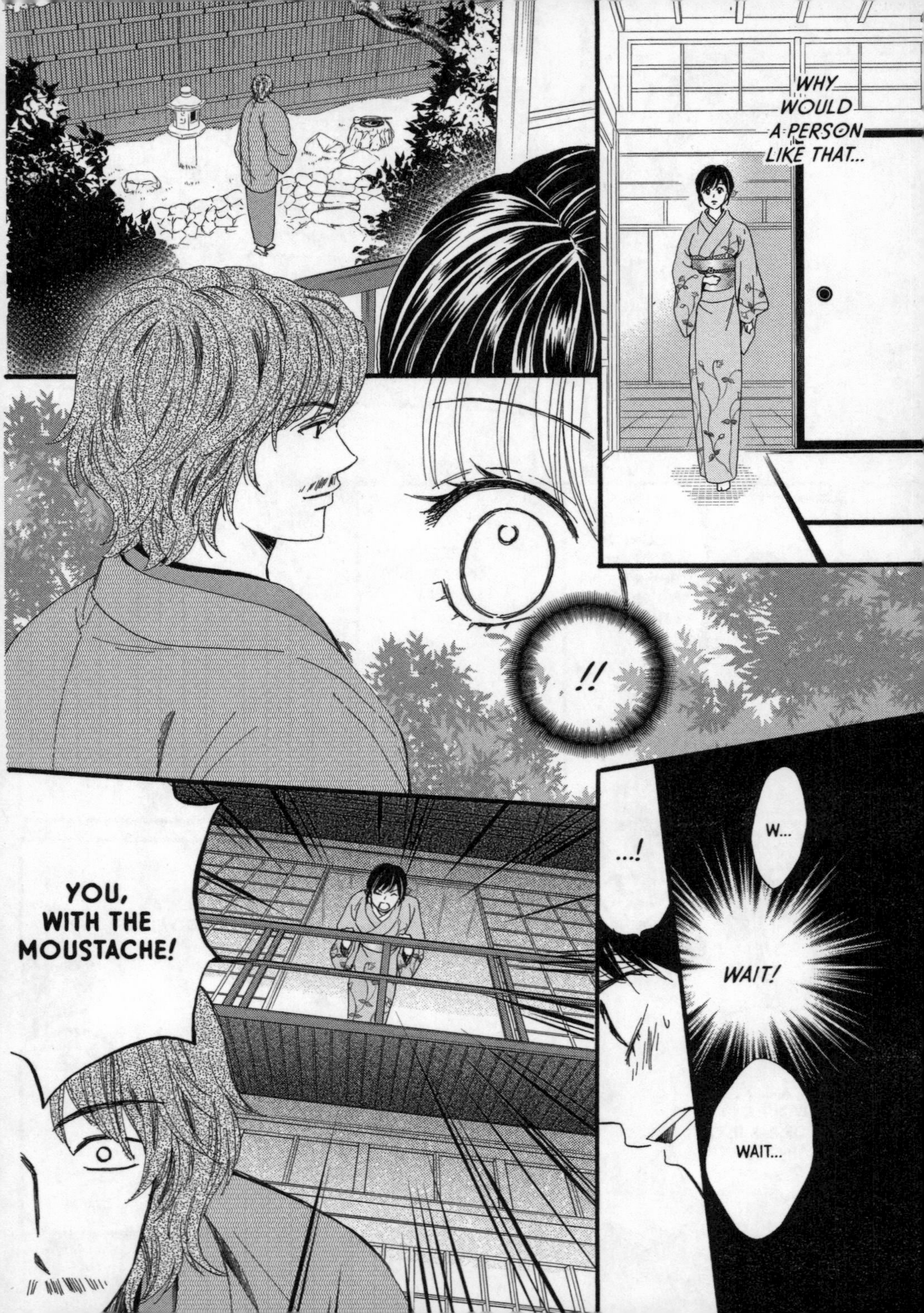
WHY WOULD A PERSON LIKE THAT...
!!
W...
...!
WAIT!
WAIT...
YOU, WITH THE MOUSTACHE!

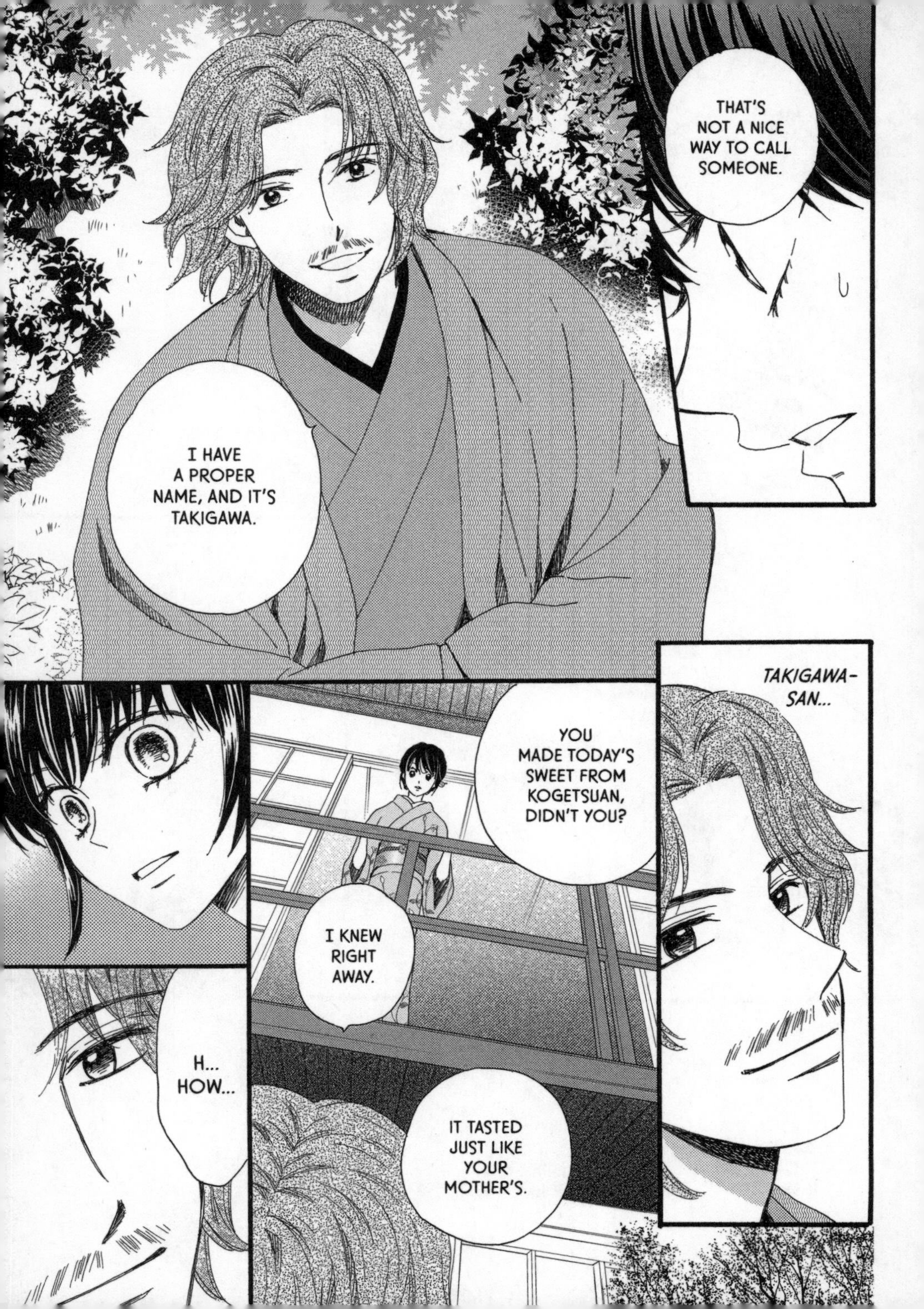
THAT'S NOT A NICE WAY TO CALL SOMEONE.
I HAVE A PROPER NAME, AND IT'S TAKIGAWA.
TAKIGAWA-SAN...
YOU MADE TODAY'S SWEET FROM KOGETSUAN, DIDN'T YOU?
I KNEW RIGHT AWAY.
H... HOW...
IT TASTED JUST LIKE YOUR MOTHER'S.

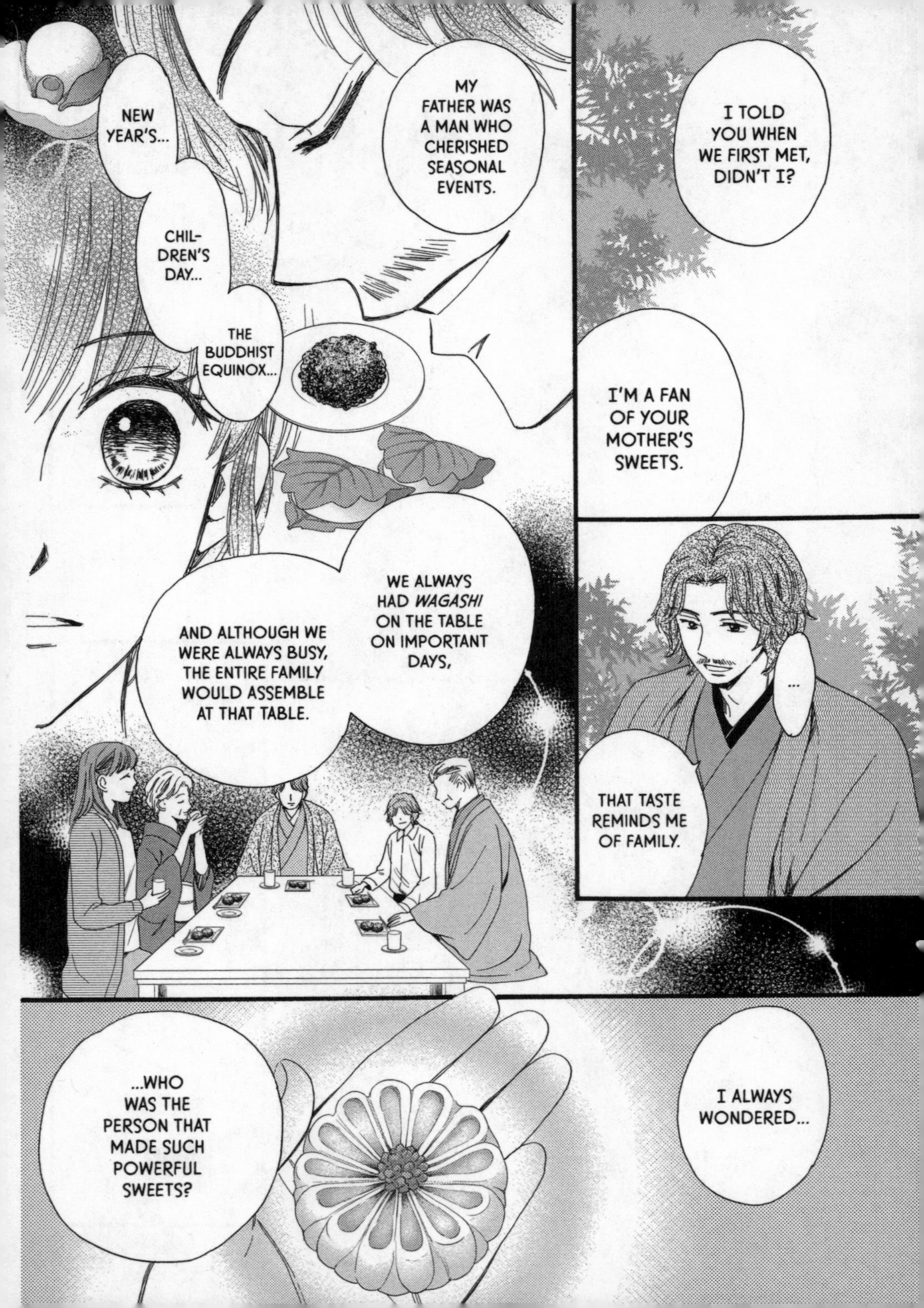
I TOLD YOU WHEN WE FIRST MET, DIDN'T I?
I'M A FAN OF YOUR MOTHER'S SWEETS.
...
THAT TASTE REMINDS ME OF FAMILY.
MY FATHER WAS A MAN WHO CHERISHED SEASONAL EVENTS.
NEW YEAR'S...
CHIL-DREN'S DAY...
THE BUDDHIST EQUINOX...
WE ALWAYS HAD *WAGASHI* ON THE TABLE ON IMPORTANT DAYS,
AND ALTHOUGH WE WERE ALWAYS BUSY, THE ENTIRE FAMILY WOULD ASSEMBLE AT THAT TABLE.
I ALWAYS WONDERED...
...WHO WAS THE PERSON THAT MADE SUCH POWERFUL SWEETS?

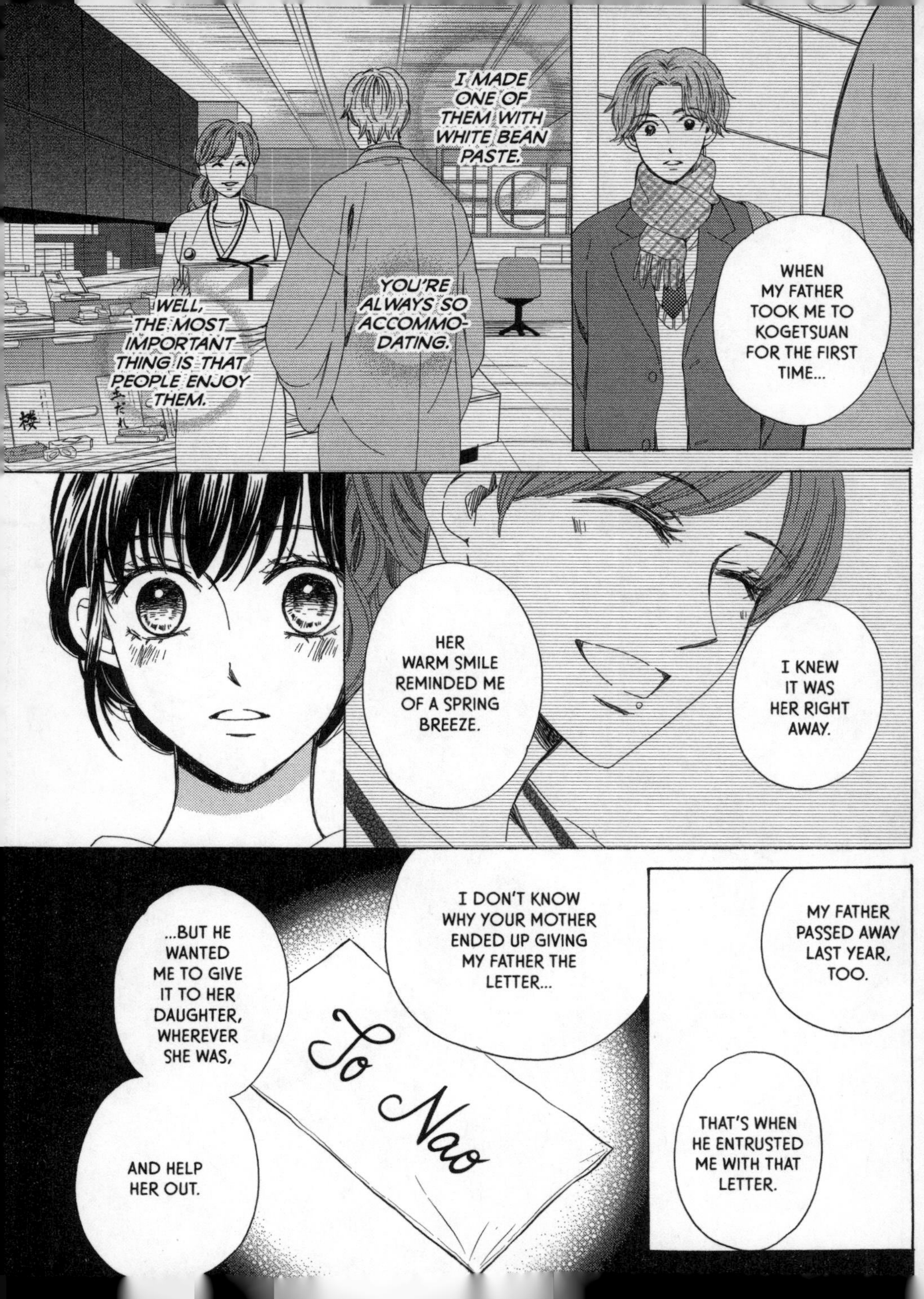
WHEN MY FATHER TOOK ME TO KOGETSUAN FOR THE FIRST TIME...
I MADE ONE OF THEM WITH WHITE BEAN PASTE.
YOU'RE ALWAYS SO ACCOMMO-DATING.
WELL, THE MOST IMPORTANT THING IS THAT PEOPLE ENJOY THEM.
I KNEW IT WAS HER RIGHT AWAY.
HER WARM SMILE REMINDED ME OF A SPRING BREEZE.
MY FATHER PASSED AWAY LAST YEAR, TOO.
THAT'S WHEN HE ENTRUSTED ME WITH THAT LETTER.
I DON'T KNOW WHY YOUR MOTHER ENDED UP GIVING MY FATHER THE LETTER...
...BUT HE WANTED ME TO GIVE IT TO HER DAUGHTER, WHEREVER SHE WAS,
To Nao
AND HELP HER OUT.

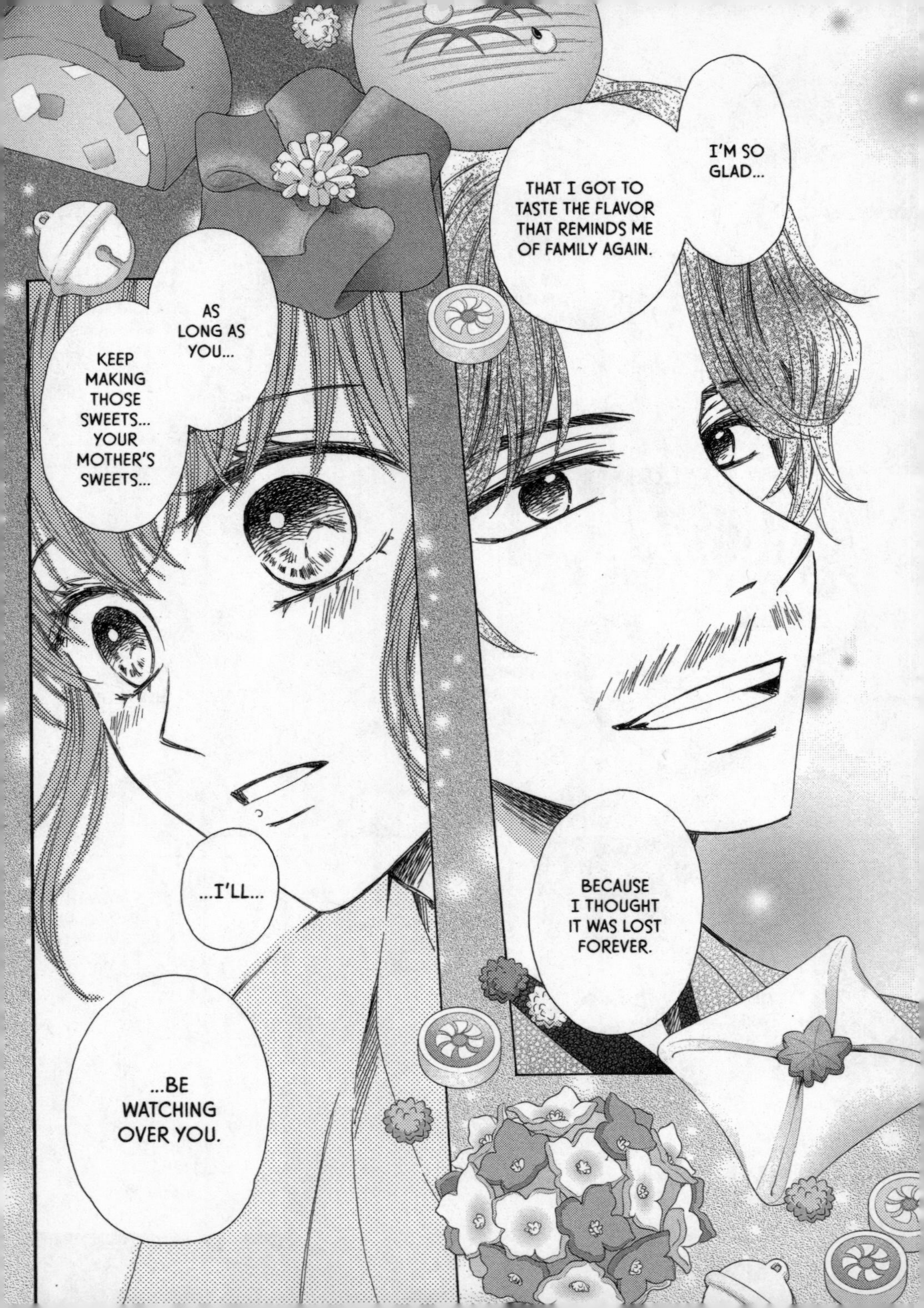
I'M SO GLAD...
THAT I GOT TO TASTE THE FLAVOR THAT REMINDS ME OF FAMILY AGAIN.
BECAUSE I THOUGHT IT WAS LOST FOREVER.
AS LONG AS YOU...
KEEP MAKING THOSE SWEETS... YOUR MOTHER'S SWEETS...
...I'LL...
...BE WATCHING OVER YOU.

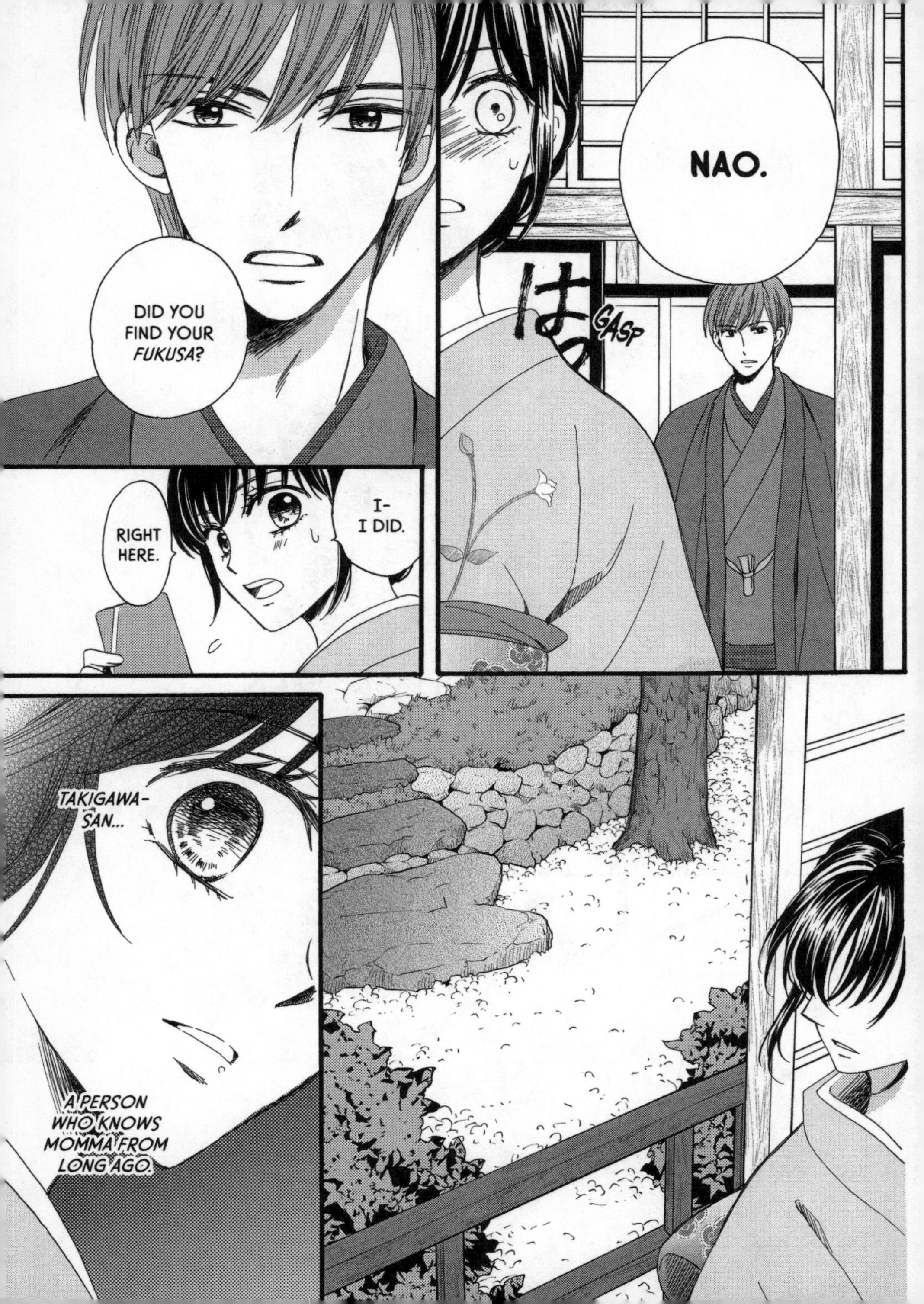
NAO.
はっ
GASP
DID YOU FIND YOUR *FUKUSA*?
I- I DID.
RIGHT HERE.
TAKIGAWA-SAN...
A PERSON WHO KNOWS MOMMA FROM LONG AGO.

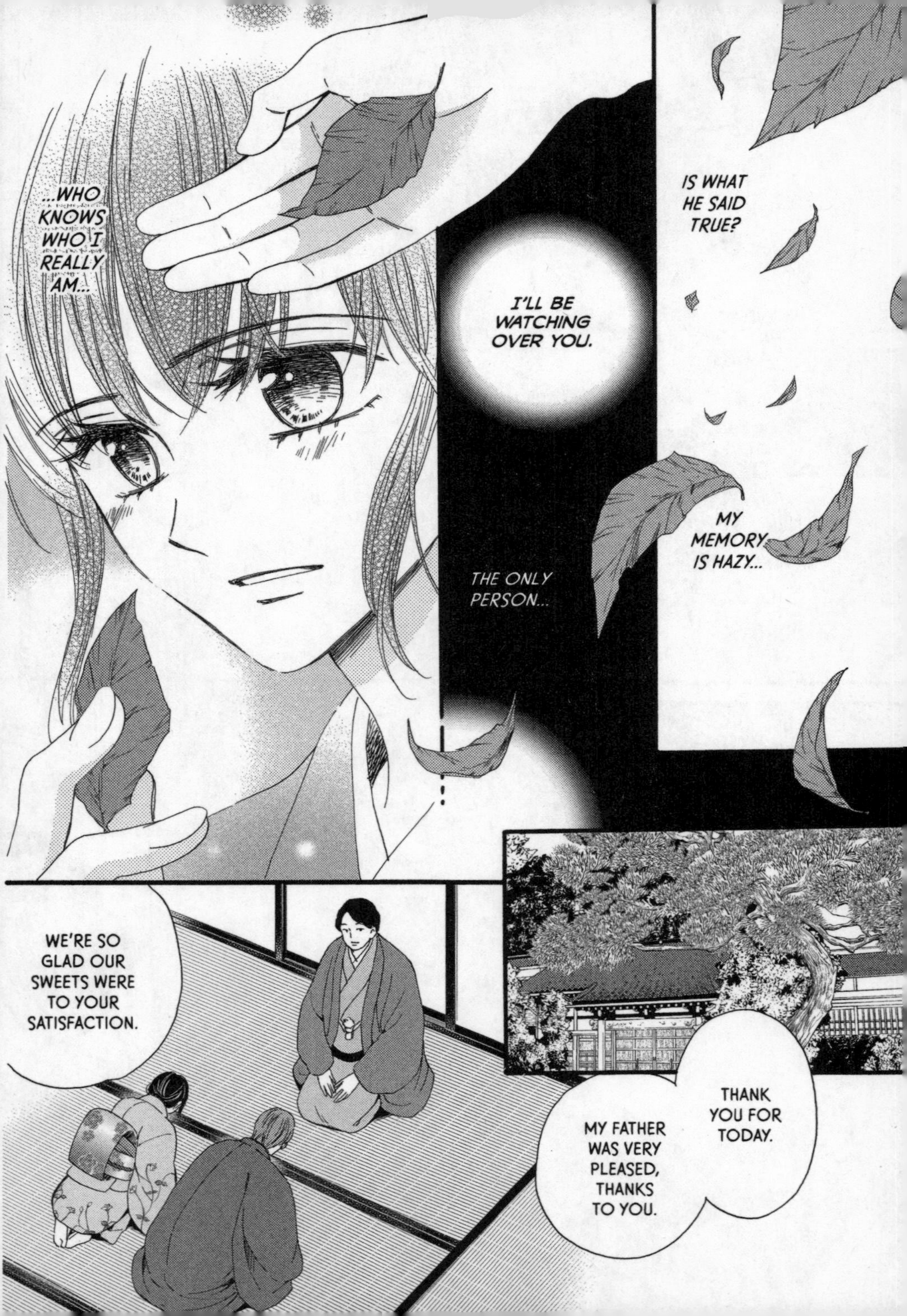
IS WHAT HE SAID TRUE?
MY MEMORY IS HAZY...
I'LL BE WATCHING OVER YOU.
THE ONLY PERSON...
...WHO KNOWS WHO I REALLY AM...
THANK YOU FOR TODAY.
MY FATHER WAS VERY PLEASED, THANKS TO YOU.
WE'RE SO GLAD OUR SWEETS WERE TO YOUR SATISFACTION.

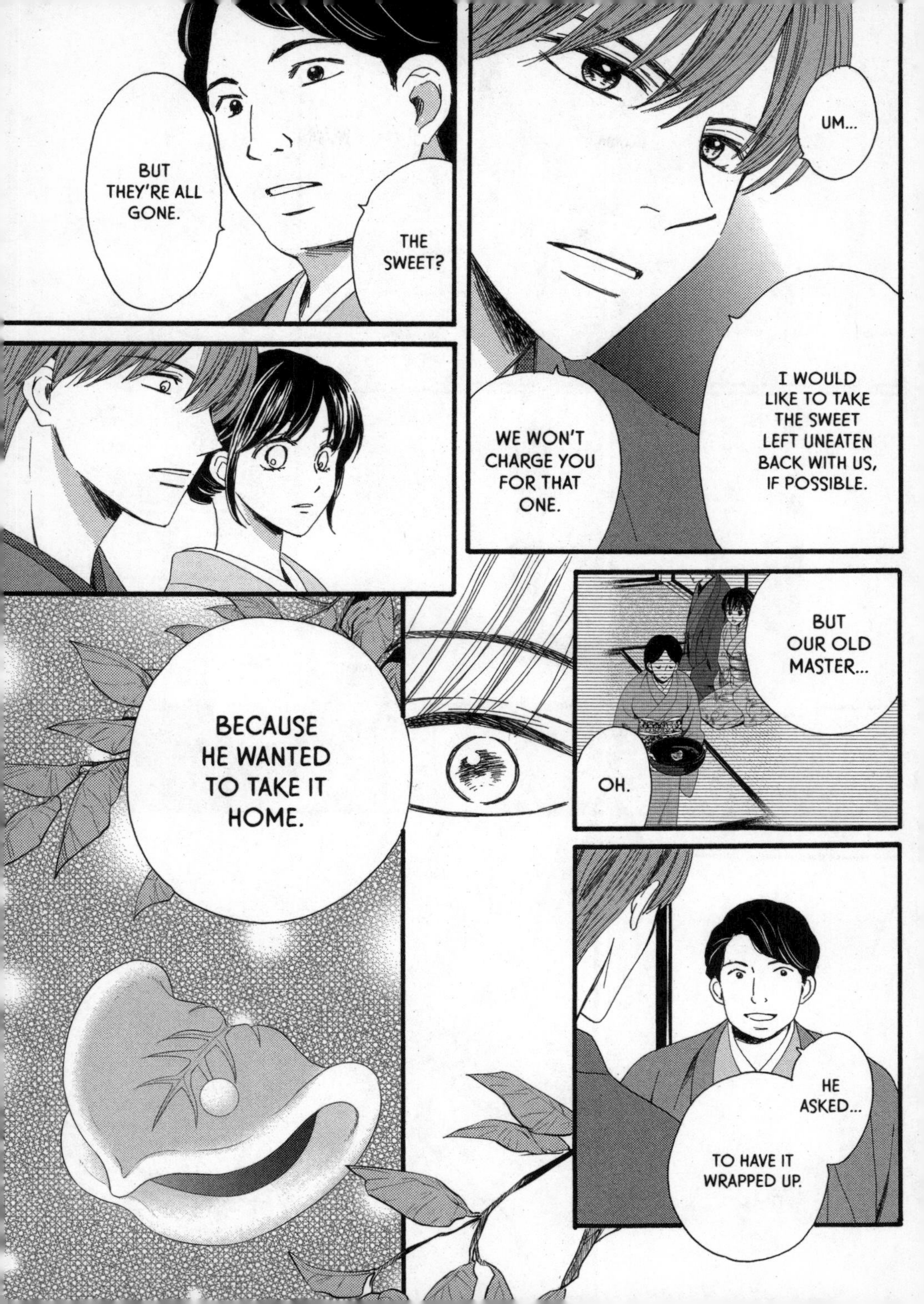
UM...
I WOULD LIKE TO TAKE THE SWEET LEFT UNEATEN BACK WITH US, IF POSSIBLE.
WE WON'T CHARGE YOU FOR THAT ONE.
THE SWEET?
BUT THEY'RE ALL GONE.
BUT OUR OLD MASTER...
OH.
HE ASKED...
TO HAVE IT WRAPPED UP.
BECAUSE HE WANTED TO TAKE IT HOME.

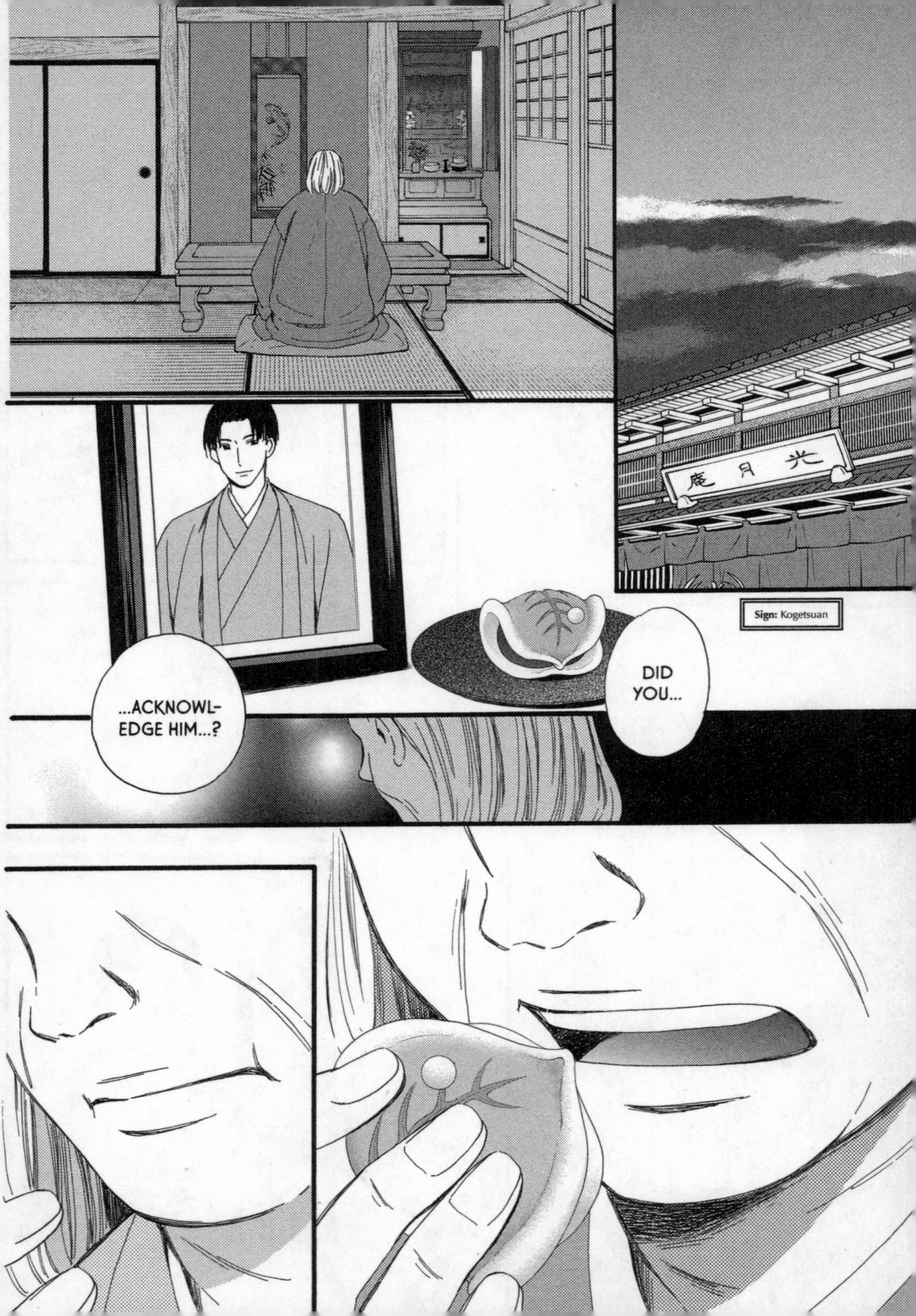
光月庵
Sign: Kogetsuan
DID YOU...
...ACKNOWL-EDGE HIM...?

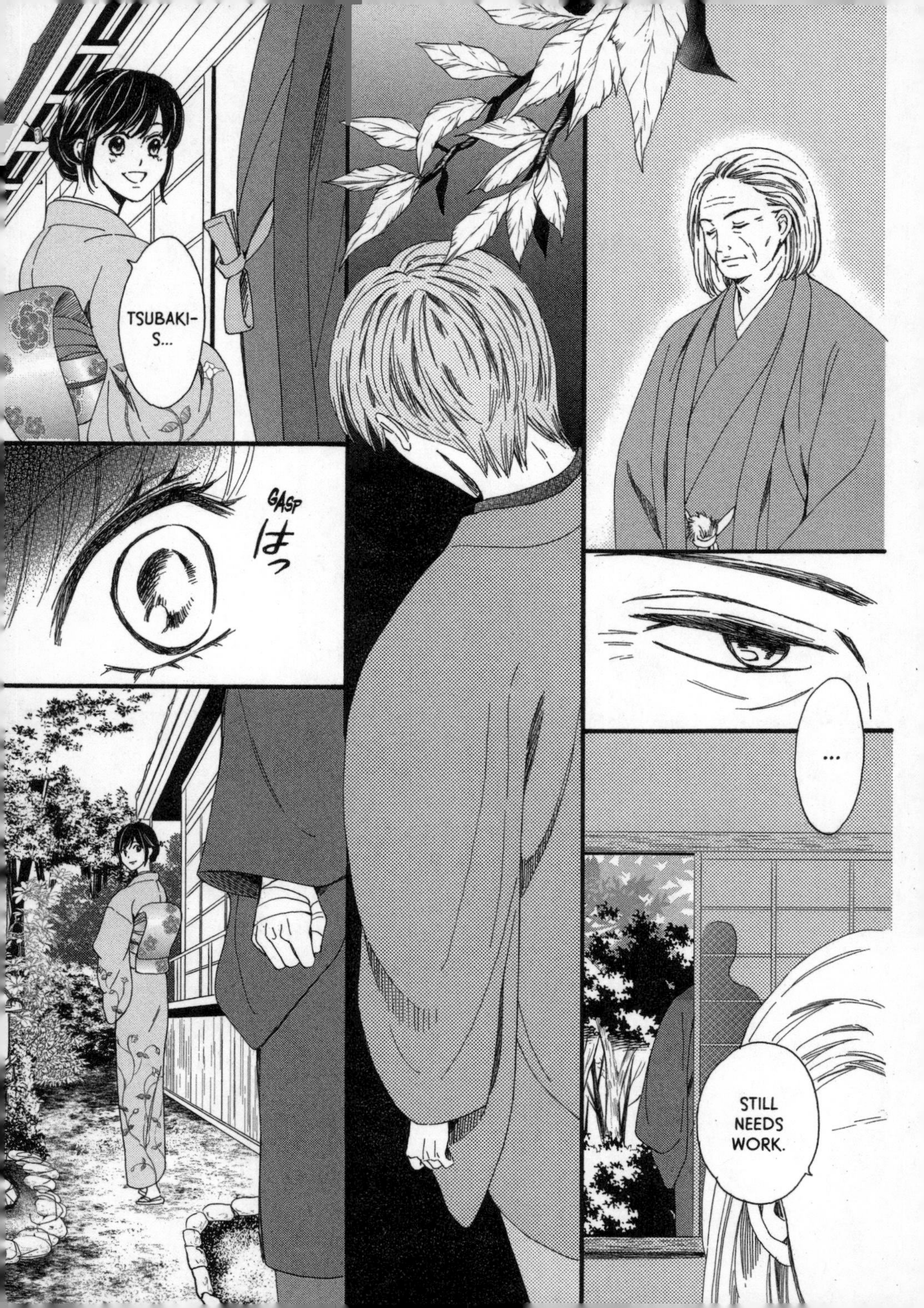
TSUBAKI-S...
...
GASP
はっ
STILL NEEDS WORK.

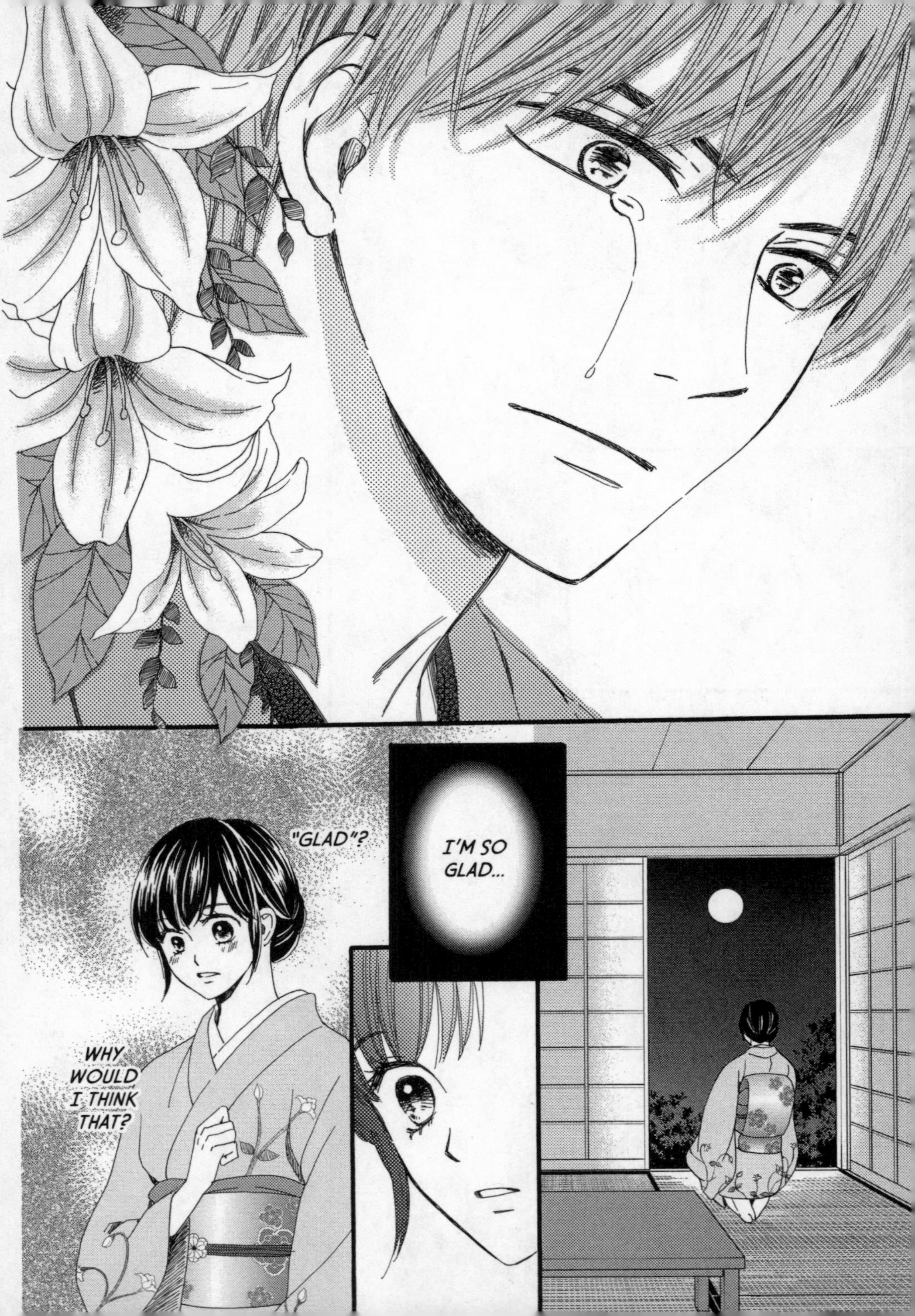
I'M SO GLAD...
"GLAD"?
WHY WOULD I THINK THAT?

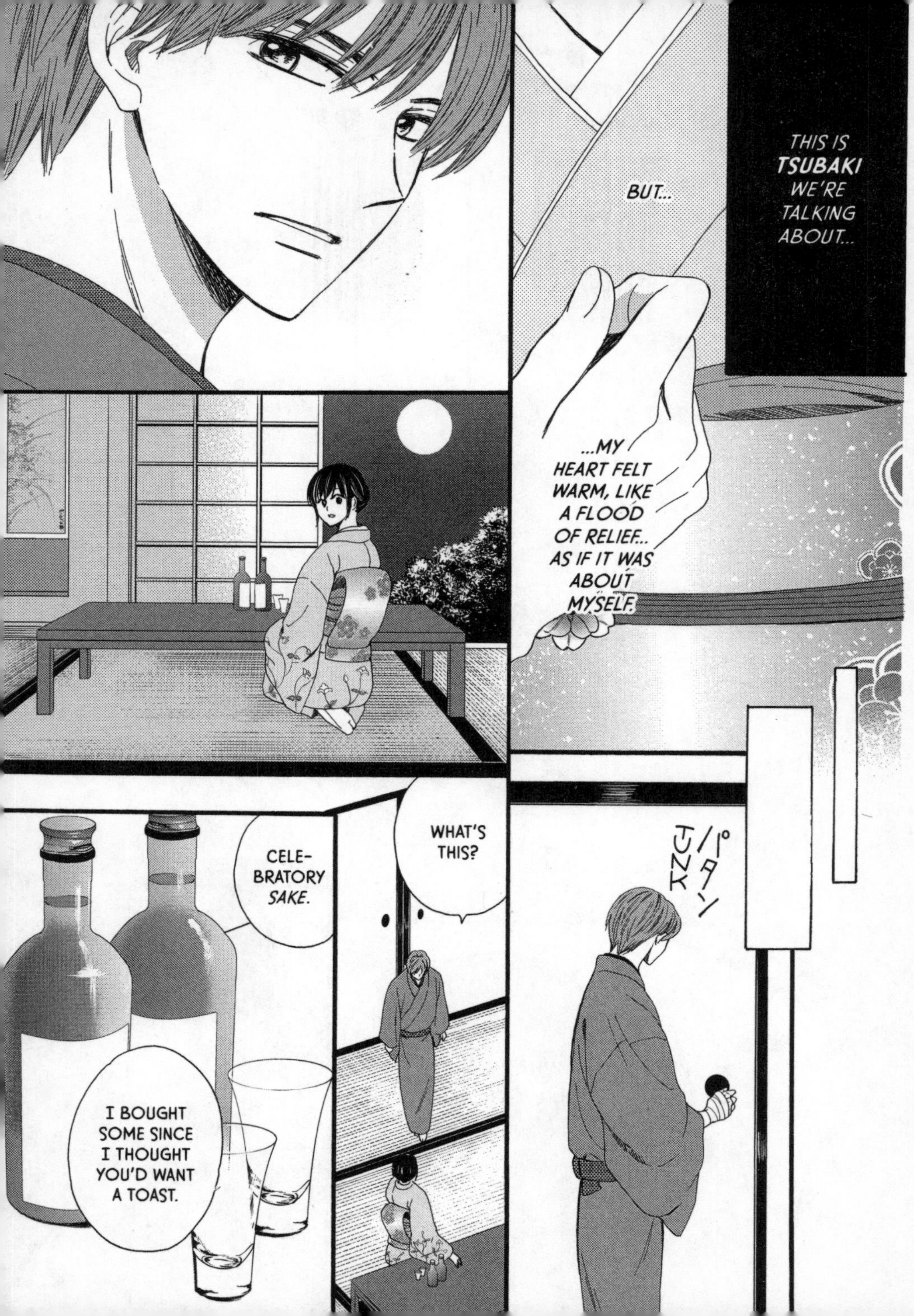
THIS IS **TSUBAKI** WE'RE TALKING ABOUT...
BUT...
...MY HEART FELT WARM, LIKE A FLOOD OF RELIEF... AS IF IT WAS ABOUT MYSELF.
パタン
TUNK
WHAT'S THIS?
CELE-BRATORY *SAKE*.
I BOUGHT SOME SINCE I THOUGHT YOU'D WANT A TOAST.

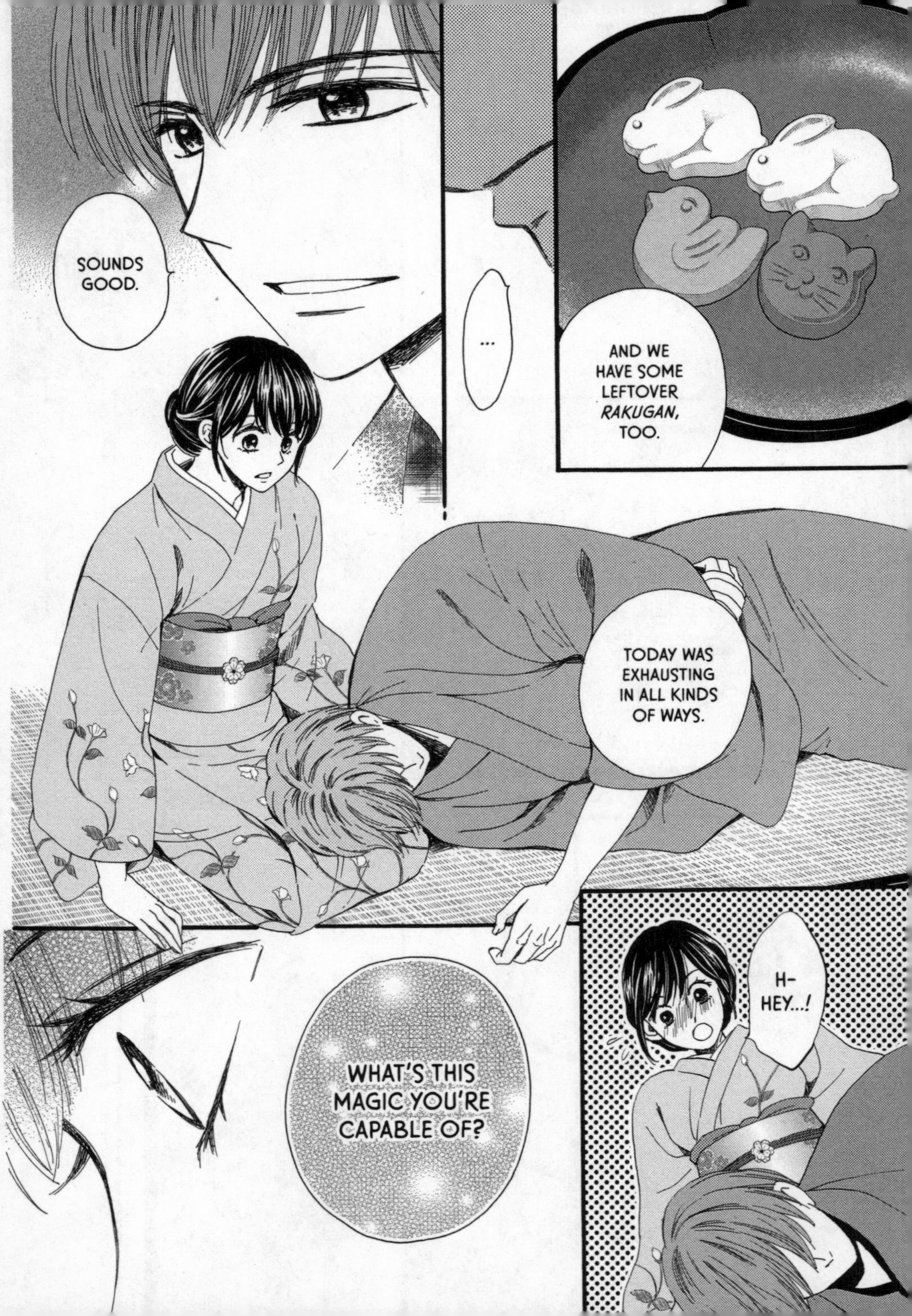
AND WE HAVE SOME LEFTOVER *RAKUGAN*, TOO.
...
SOUNDS GOOD.
TODAY WAS EXHAUSTING IN ALL KINDS OF WAYS.
H-HEY...!
WHAT'S THIS MAGIC YOU'RE CAPABLE OF?

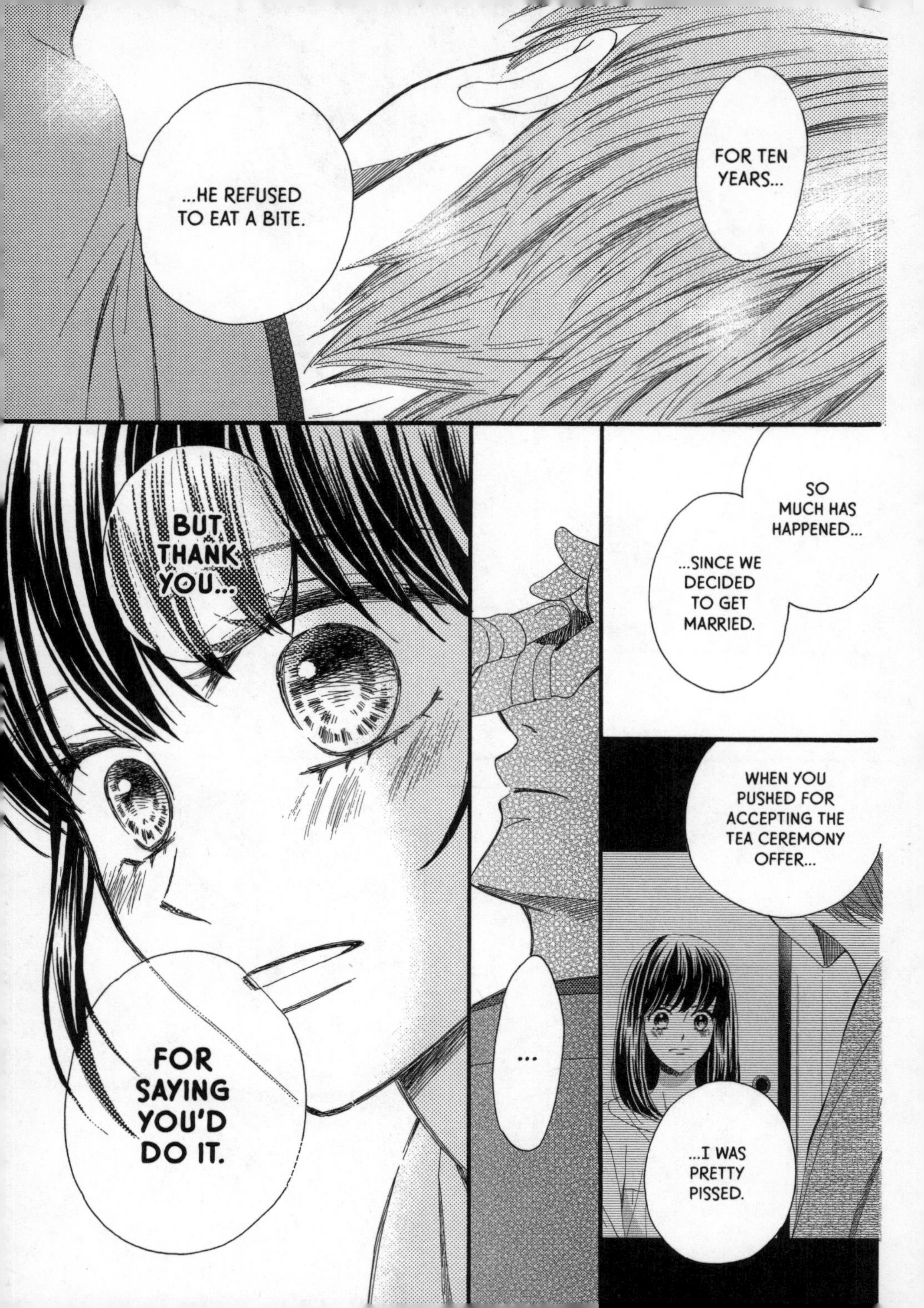
FOR TEN YEARS...
...HE REFUSED TO EAT A BITE.
SO MUCH HAS HAPPENED...
...SINCE WE DECIDED TO GET MARRIED.
WHEN YOU PUSHED FOR ACCEPTING THE TEA CEREMONY OFFER...
...I WAS PRETTY PISSED.
...
BUT THANK YOU...
FOR SAYING YOU'D DO IT.

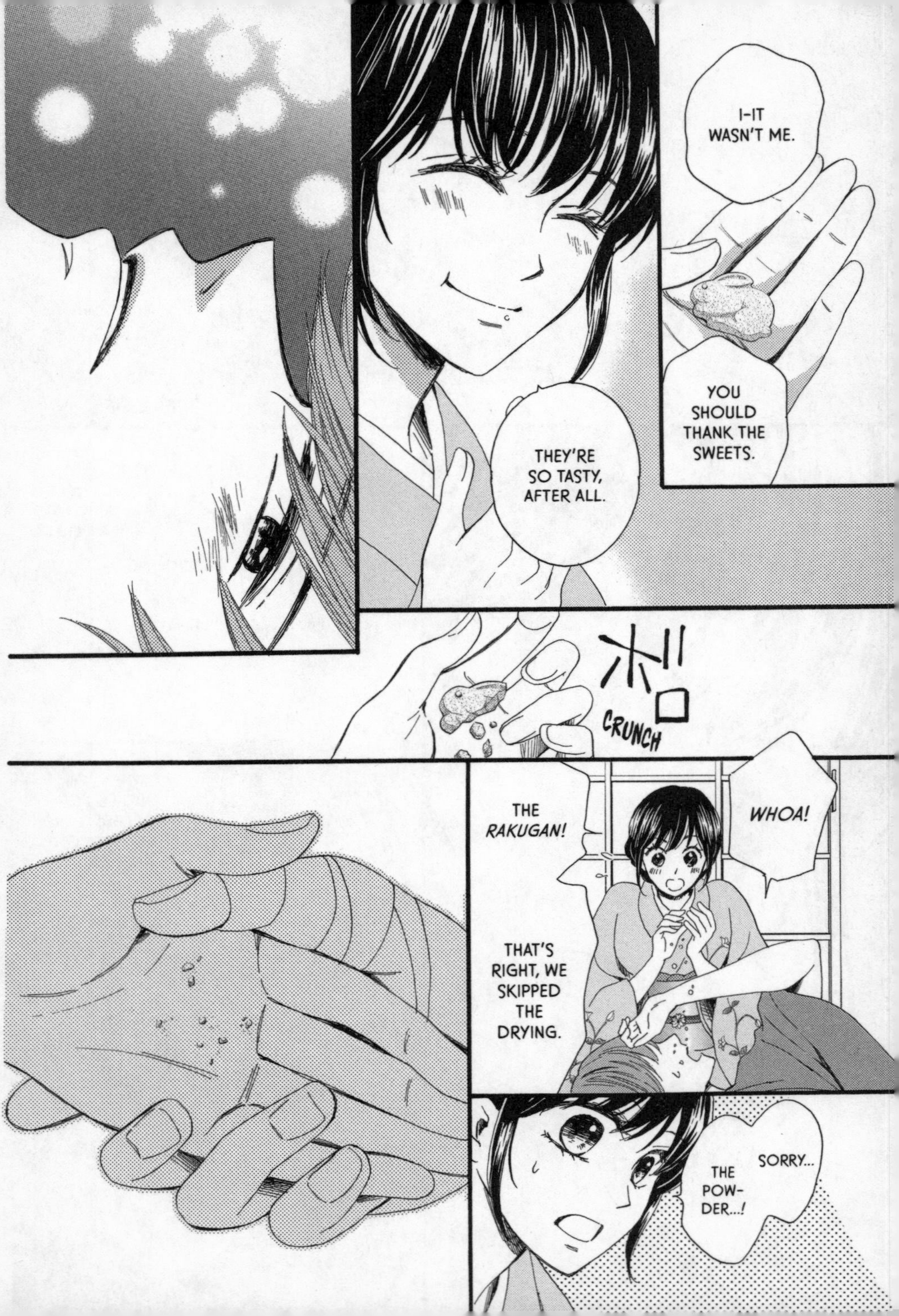
I-IT WASN'T ME.
YOU SHOULD THANK THE SWEETS.
THEY'RE SO TASTY, AFTER ALL.
CRUNCH
WHOA!
THE *RAKUGAN!*
THAT'S RIGHT, WE SKIPPED THE DRYING.
SORRY...
THE POW-DER...!

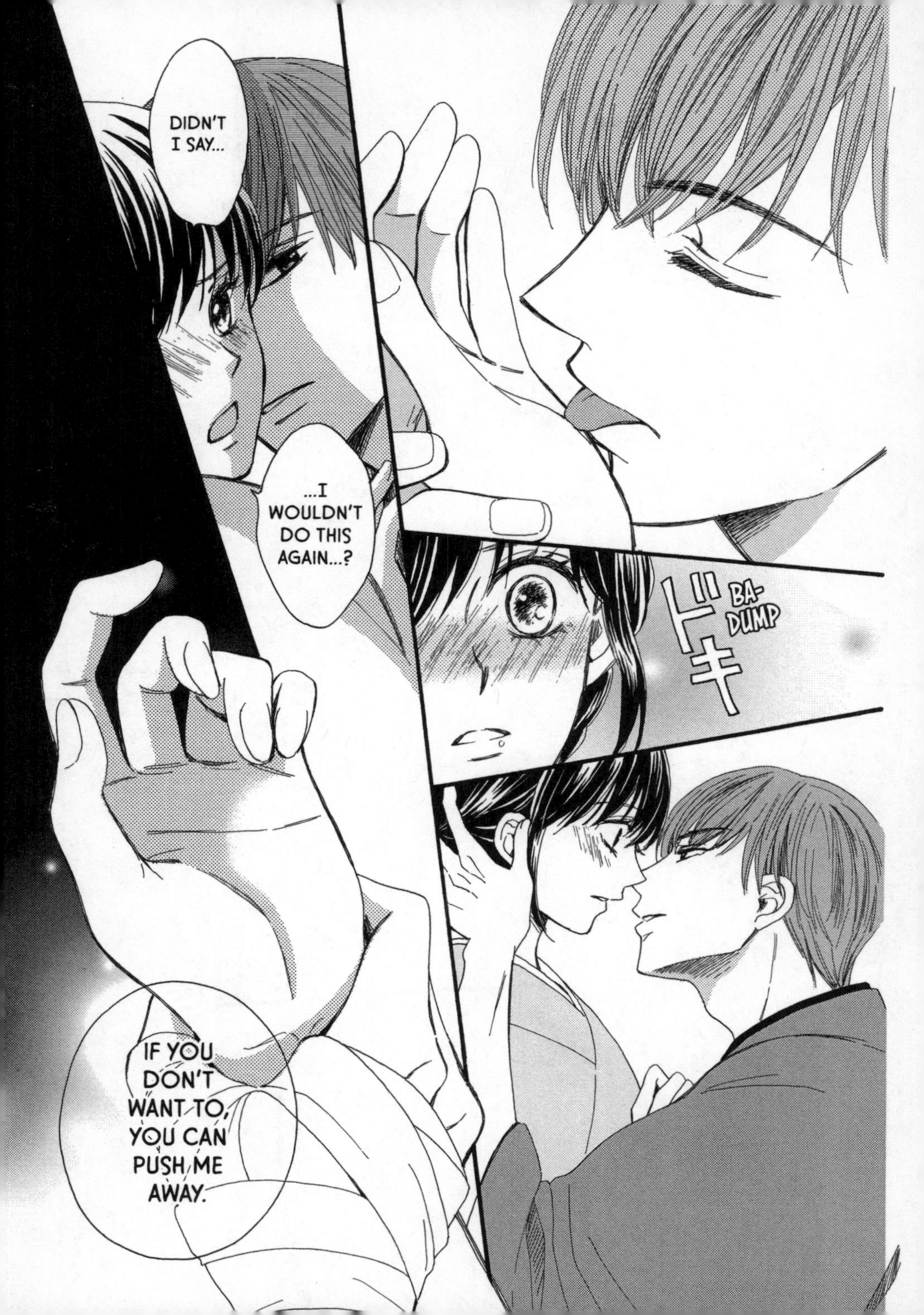
ドキ
BA-DUMP
DIDN'T I SAY...
...I WOULDN'T DO THIS AGAIN...?
IF YOU DON'T WANT TO, YOU CAN PUSH ME AWAY.

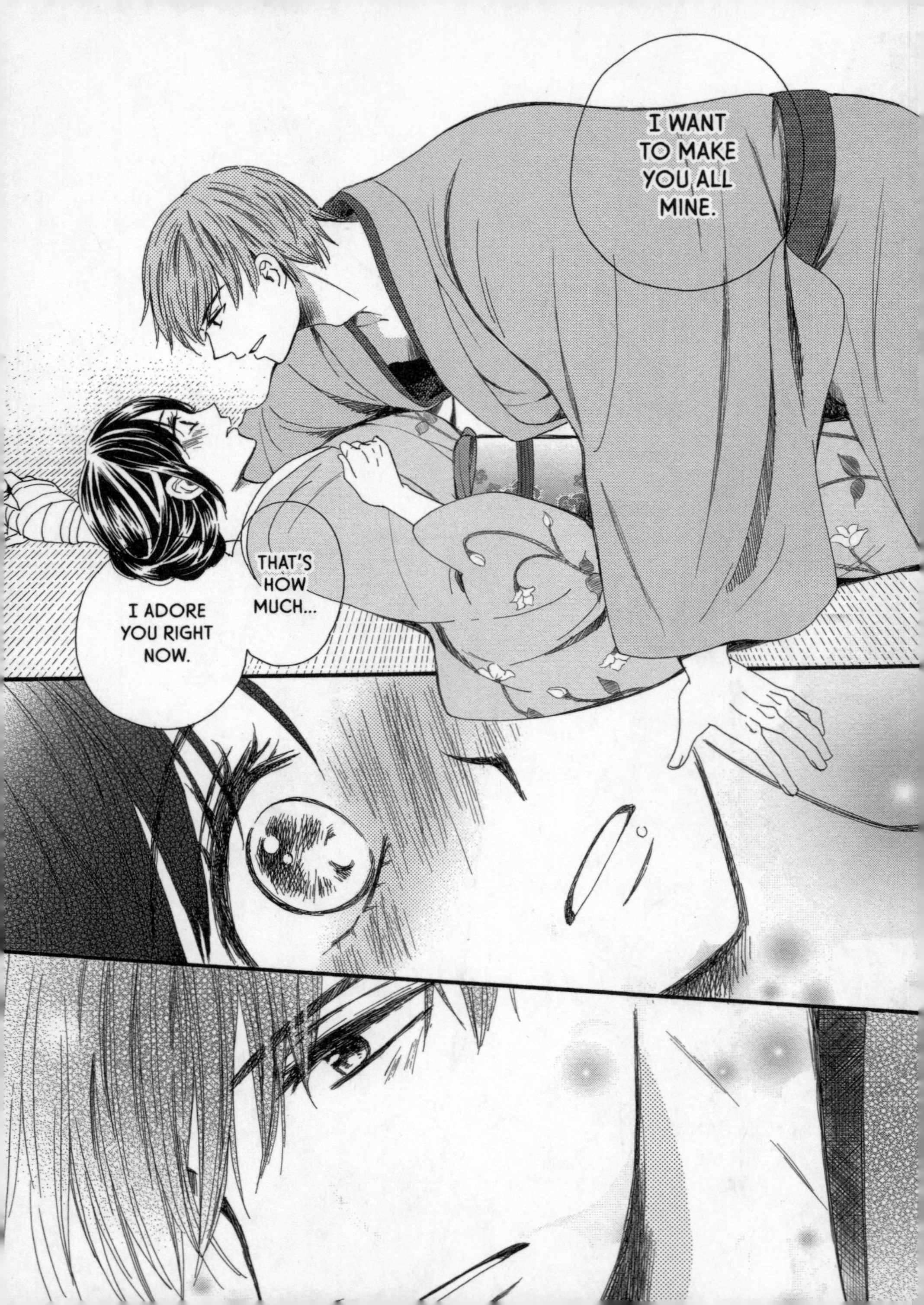
I WANT TO MAKE YOU ALL MINE.
THAT'S HOW MUCH...
I ADORE YOU RIGHT NOW.

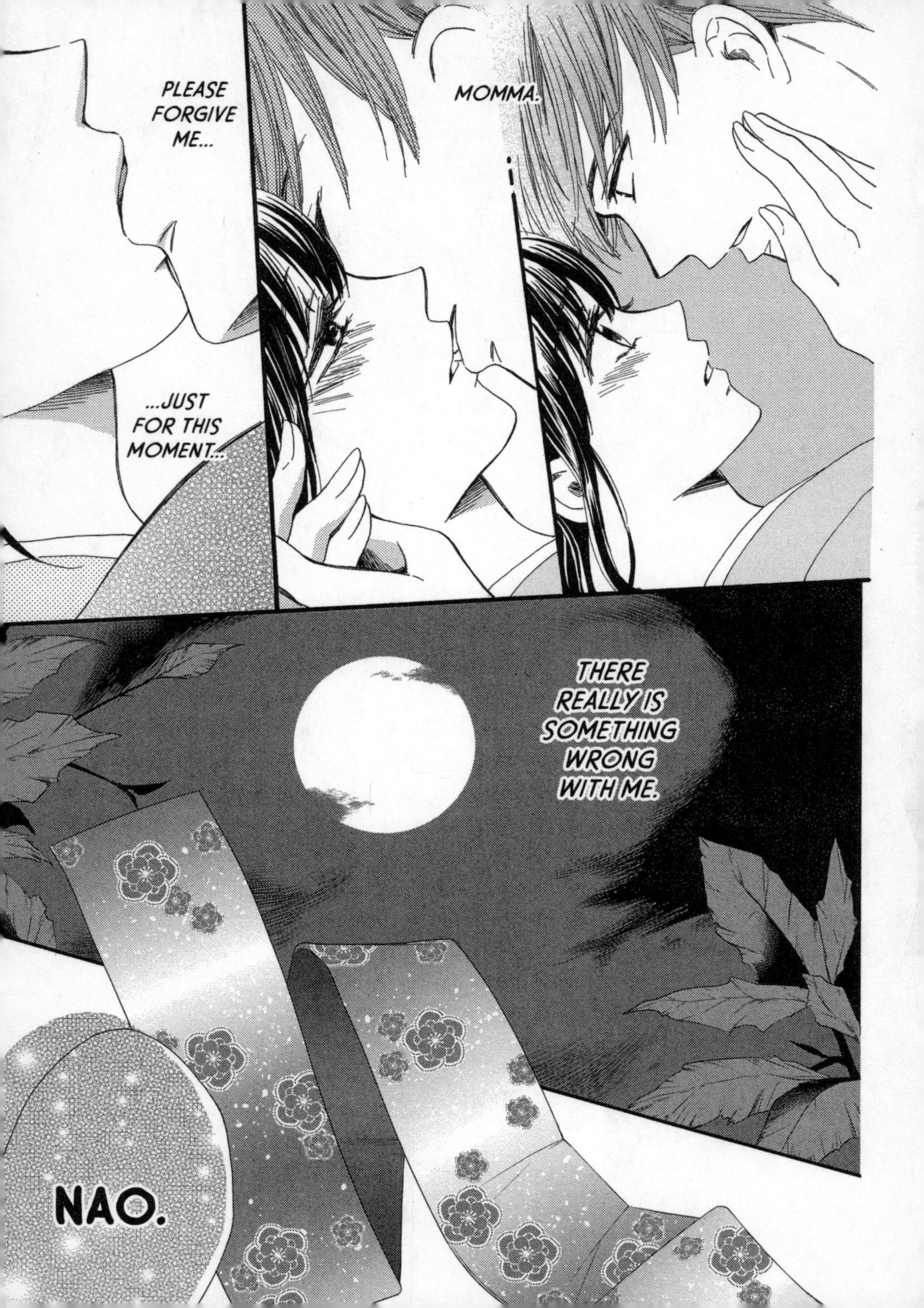
MOMMA.
PLEASE FORGIVE ME...
...JUST FOR THIS MOMENT...
THERE REALLY IS SOMETHING WRONG WITH ME.
NAO.

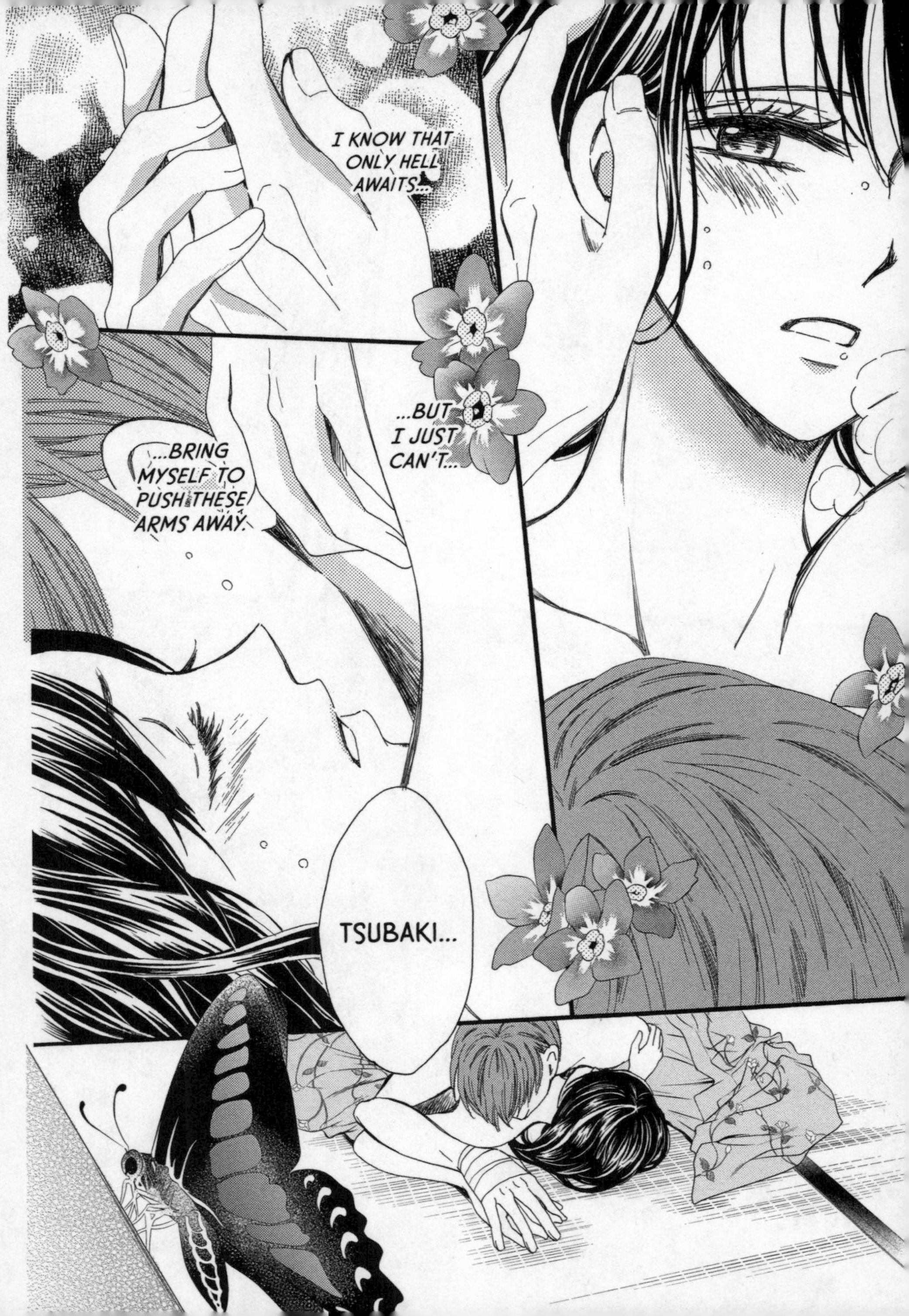
I KNOW THAT ONLY HELL AWAITS...
...BUT I JUST CAN'T...
...BRING MYSELF TO PUSH THESE ARMS AWAY.
TSUBAKI...

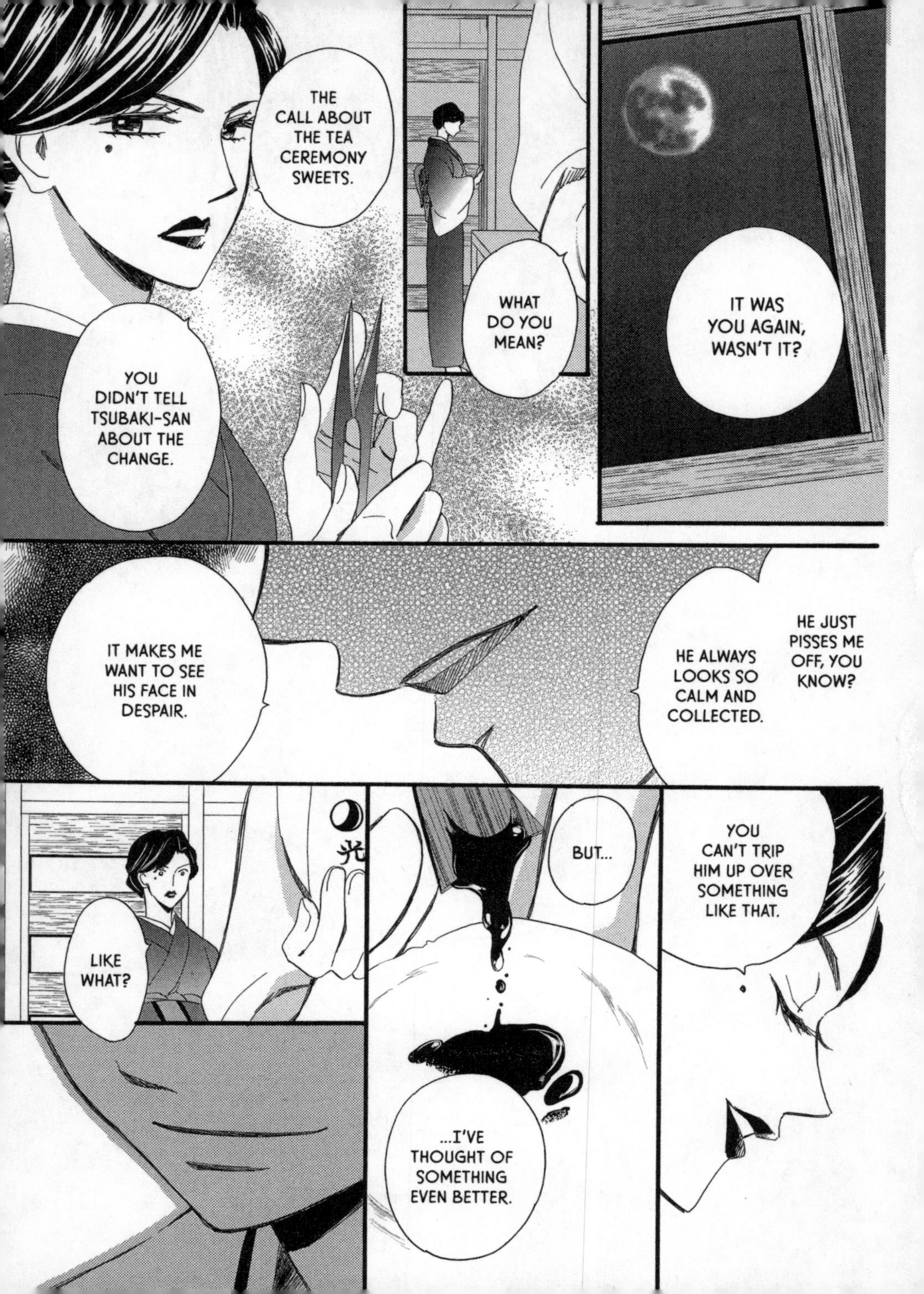
IT WAS YOU AGAIN, WASN'T IT?
WHAT DO YOU MEAN?
THE CALL ABOUT THE TEA CEREMONY SWEETS.
YOU DIDN'T TELL TSUBAKI-SAN ABOUT THE CHANGE.
HE JUST PISSES ME OFF, YOU KNOW?
HE ALWAYS LOOKS SO CALM AND COLLECTED.
IT MAKES ME WANT TO SEE HIS FACE IN DESPAIR.
YOU CAN'T TRIP HIM UP OVER SOMETHING LIKE THAT.
BUT...
...I'VE THOUGHT OF SOMETHING EVEN BETTER.
LIKE WHAT?

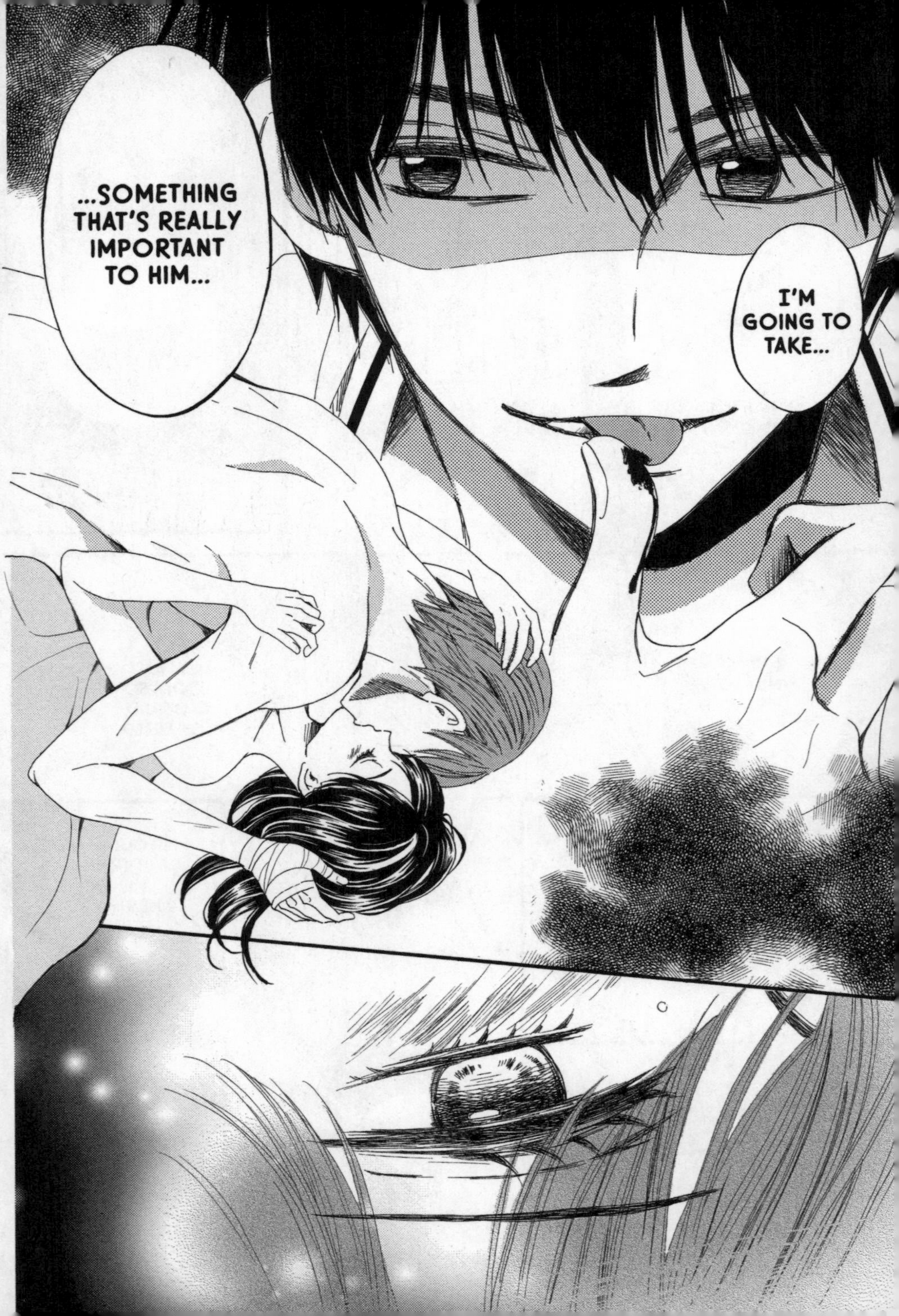
I'M GOING TO TAKE...
...SOMETHING THAT'S REALLY IMPORTANT TO HIM...

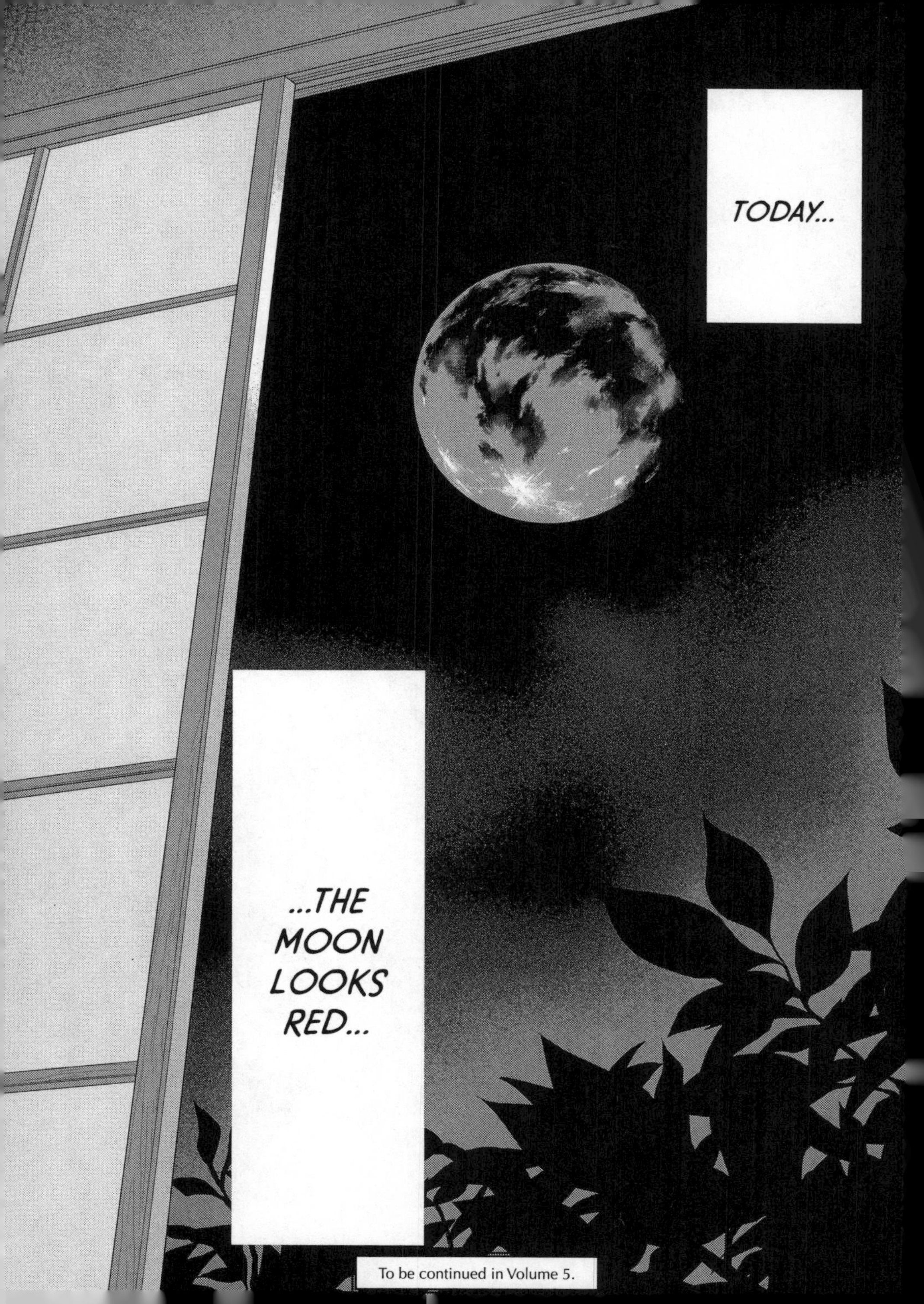
TODAY...
...THE MOON LOOKS RED...
To be continued in Volume 5.

THANK YOU SO MUCH,
UMESAKURA-SAMA
MIYAJI-SAMA
MY EDITOR
DOI-SAMA
MORIZANE-SAMA
CHIKADA-SAMA
NAGANAWA-SAMA

I NOW HAVE A TWITTER ACCOUNT:
HTTPS://TWITTER.COM/NATUMIANDO

I SOMETIMES TWEET ABOUT BEHIND-THE-SCENES STUFF FROM THE SERIES, SO PLEASE COME AND TAKE A PEEK ♥

HOPE TO SEE YOU AGAIN IN VOLUME 5...!

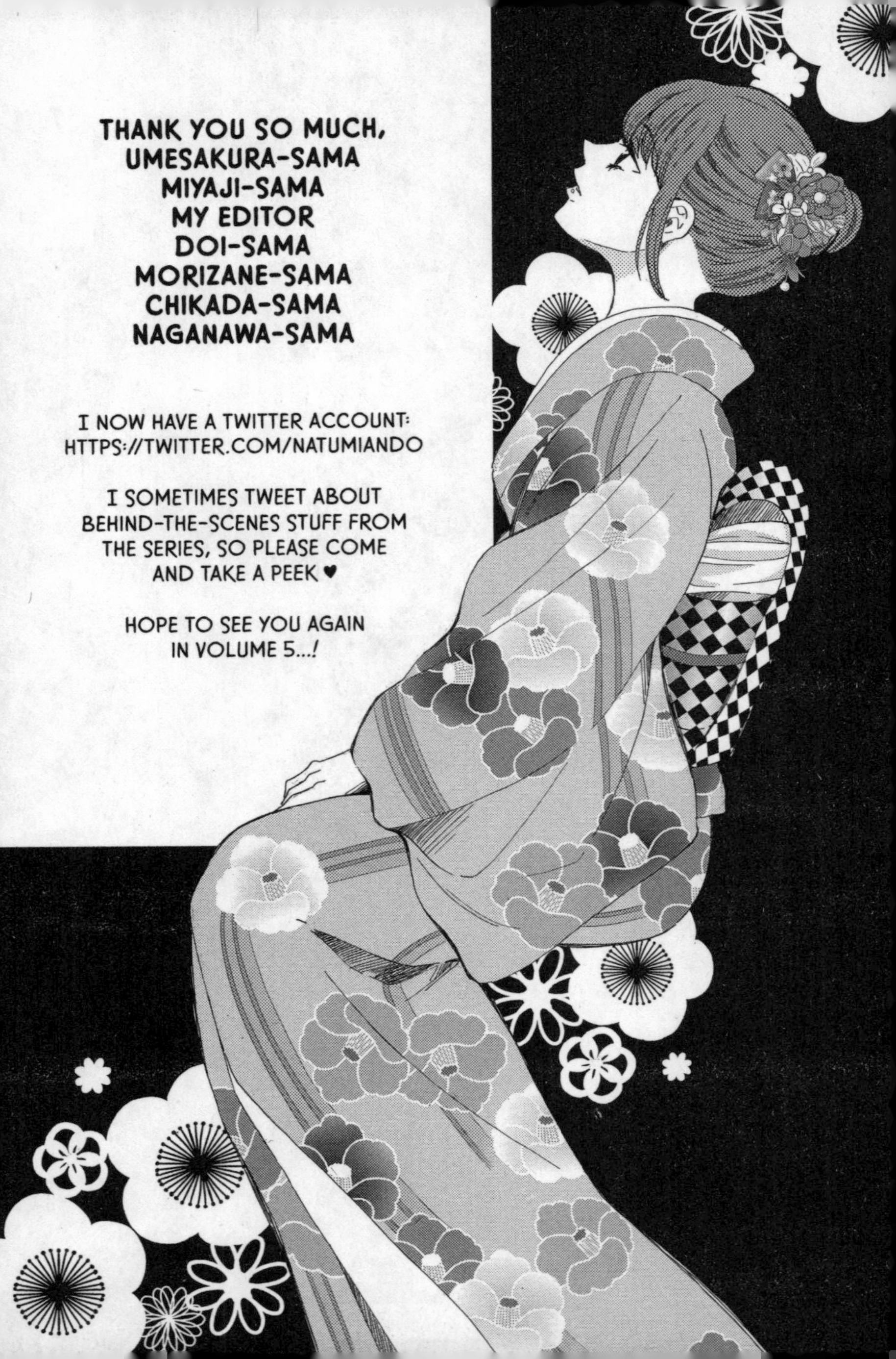

Translation Notes

otoshibumi, page 15
Otoshibumi (literally: dropped letter) originally refers to the old practice of rolling up secret letters (often romantic in nature) and dropping them for the recipient to pick up. The weevil *otoshibumi* takes that name because the "cradle" it makes by curling up a leaf looks like a rolled up letter. For more details, see volume three.

Encase bean paste, page 18
One of the fundamental techniques in *wagashi* making, involves encasing a small ball of bean paste in an even outer layer of different-colored bean paste.

kaiseki, page 29
Fine, traditional Japanese cuisine that is served in multiple courses. Using seasonal ingredients, *kaiseki* is beautiful to look at and requires many years of training to make.

Kenrokuen Garden, page 34
A traditional Japanese garden iconic to Kanazawa that is considered one of the three most beautiful landscaped gardens in Japan.

omogashi, page 92
Fresh sweets served before thick green tea in a tea ceremony to prepare the palate for the tea's bitter taste.

kanbaiko, page 101
One of the finest grades of rice flour made by grilling thin sheets of *mochi*, grinding them into a powder, then sifting it into even finer powder.

Ichigo ichie, page 103
A tea ceremony concept that means, "every moment is unique, and will never come again." Something Tsubaki mentioned in volume three.

Kogetsuan-san, page 119
Tsubaki's last name isn't Kogetsuan, but when people run a business (especially in retail) they can be addressed by the store's name with the "-san" honorific attached.

fukusa, page 134
A traditional piece of silk cloth used for gift giving and in tea ceremonies. Here, Nao has a *fukusa* in the form of a cloth envelope, usually used to wrap money.

Children's Day, page 138
May 5th. Also known as *Tango no Sekku*, this day marks the beginning of the summer and celebrates the happiness of all children.

A Kodansha Comics Trade Paperback Original
Something's Wrong With Us 4 copyright © 2017 Natsumi Ando
English translation copyright © 2020 Natsumi Ando

All rights reserved.

Published in the United States by Kodansha Comics, an imprint of Kodansha USA Publishing, LLC, New York.

Publication rights for this English edition arranged through Kodansha Ltd., Tokyo.

First published in Japan in 2017 by Kodansha Ltd., Tokyo as *Watashitachi wa doukashiteiru*, volume 4.

ISBN 978-1-64651-067-2

Printed in the United States of America.

www.kodanshacomics.com

9 8 7 6 5 4 3 2 1
Translation: Sawa Matsueda Savage
Lettering: Sara Linsley
Editing: Haruko Hashimoto
Kodansha Comics edition cover design by Matthew Akuginow

Publisher: Kiichiro Sugawara

Director of publishing services: Ben Applegate
Associate director of operations: Stephen Pakula
Publishing services managing editor: Noelle Webster
Assistant production manager: Emi Lotto, Angela Zurlo
Logo and character art ©Kodansha USA Publishing, LLC